A New Muslim Order

A New Muslim Order

The Shia and the
Middle East Sectarian Crisis

By Nicolas Pelham

I.B. TAURIS

LONDON · NEW YORK

Published in 2008 by I.B.Tauris & Co Ltd
6 Salem Road, London W2 4BU
175 Fifth Avenue, New York NY 10010
www.ibtauris.com

In the United States of America and Canada distributed by
Palgrave Macmillan, a division of St. Martin's Press, 175 Fifth Avenue,
New York NY 10010

ISBN: 978 1 84511 139 7

A full CIP record for this book is available from the British Library
A full CIP record is available from the Library of Congress

Library of Congress Catalog Card Number: available

Designed and Typeset by 4word Ltd, Bristol, UK
Printed and bound in the USA

Contents

Introduction and Acknowledgements

If anyone personified the trinity of Iraq's fallen nation, it was my landlady, Um Taysir. She was Shia, her late husband was Sunni, and unusually for an Arab she graduated from the University of Irbil, the capital of Iraqi Kurdistan, and spoke Kurdish. Her hair was died with a red tinge to hide her years and attract a string of paramours she called her uncles. Together with her two children, she lived in a modest house in the plush district of Jadarriya, one of the favoured quarters of Baghdad's pre-war literati and upper crust.

I knocked on her door soon after the American invasion inquiring about somewhere to live. The fall of Saddam had released Iraqi and foreigner alike from the world of *mamnoua*, or forbidden, including the ban on consorting with foreigners. Um Taysir delighted in the promise of a new liberal order, and welcomed me warmly. But within a year she had turned from a vivacious tactile woman into an indecisive tearful recluse, who lived on the internet with the curtains drawn. She spent her days rearranging her glass menagerie, which rattled musically with each of Baghdad's explosions, and passed fitful nights disturbed by the dogs that howled at the gunmen as they moved through the palm groves at the back of the house firing mortars at the American headquarters over the river.

More remarkable was her religious transformation. When we first met, her spiritual world was limited to cooking fudge cakes and burning incense sticks on the birthdays of such secondary prophets as Zachariah. When a gecko scuttled up the walls, she would shriek in horror at this harbinger of impotency, known in Arabic as Abu Brais, or father of leprosy. Like many secular Shia integrated into Saddam's nomenklatura, she held typically Sunni prejudices. 'Mad mullahs', she would scoff at the flood of Shia turbans that surfaced on Baghdad's streets following the US invasion.

After the invasion, however, she began pinning red and green Shia bunting from her rooftop. When Sunni neighbours responded by gossiping about her supposed sexual proclivities, she turned to a relative in a Shia militia for protection. She joined the Shia Dawa party – a pre-war anathema – to regain her post at the university, and donned a scarf to get past the guards at the gate. Within barely a year, Um Taysir had forsaken her cross-confessional world.

The Balkanisation of Iraq – the merciless pitting of Iraqi Shia against Sunni – was neither inevitable, nor precedented. For decades before the war, Iraq's Sunnis and Shia had intermarried, and shared the same neighbourhoods, tribes, wars and five pillars of faith.[1] While they continued to pray in separate places of worship and bury their dead in separate graveyards, for most middle-class Iraqis the only outward display of difference was that Shias, if they prayed, did so with arms at their sides not folded in front of them, and shunned the eating of catfish – one of which, legend has it, once spat in the face of their Imam, Ali.

It took many months to reconcile myself to writing a sectarian account of Iraq's past. Like many students of the region, I hankered after Iraq's communal cocktail of faiths and ethnicities. Any explanation of Iraq's turmoil on confessional grounds, I feared, would only deepen the schisms. But five years after the invasion, the sectarian scars are not healing and the fires of irredentism burn ever more fiercely. As elsewhere in the Middle East, a pluralistic Iraq is history. What follows is an attempt to understand why.

Much of the book highlights the US role in stoking religious tensions – indeed its working title was 'Playing God in Iraq' – and traces its antecedents in European policies of divide-and-rule. But the Sunni–Shia conflict did not begin with western colonialism. In times of crisis, these sects as others in the Middle East have repeatedly found security amongst their own, drawing on and deepening rival historical narratives, which are at once antagonistic and intertwined. Battles some 1,400 years ago are re-enacted in pageants and massacres mourned as if they were yesterday's tragedies. Contemporary events are viewed through the prism of past tensions. And despite intermittent attempts to paper over the differences, the ancient heroes of one sect remain the villains of the other.

The mythological conflict began as a family dispute. Iraq, then as now, was the crucible. In 656 near the Basra flats, the Prophet Mohammed's dearest wife, Aisha, led a rebellion against her (step) son-in-law, Ali, who as the Prophet's nearest surviving male relative had been nominated Caliph of the Muslim community. After a series of clashes, Ali was assassinated in Kufa in 661. His partisans – or Shia – turned the Euphrates valley into both a base to continue the struggle for Muslim leadership and a refuge from the disciples of a rival tradition, Sunnis, determined to hunt them down. Of Ali's 11 successors, or Imams, eight died in Iraq, for the most part poisoned, beheaded or buried alive.

In 873 Ali's twelfth heir and descendant, Mohammed the Mahdi, disappeared, leaving the struggle for control of Iraq and Islam in animated suspense pending his messianic return. Caliph Mutawakkil ploughed over the shrines of Imams Ali in Najaf and Hussein in Karbala in 850, and ordered a clown to ridicule Ali's memory at voluptuous banquets. He did not have the last laugh. A century later, Shia Persian Buyid dynasties came from Iran to capture Iraq, reducing its then Sunni Caliph to a rubber-stamp monarch, while another offshoot of Shiism, the Fatimids, swept west from North Africa. By the turn of the eleventh century Sunni emirates were mere islands in a Shia world stretching from the western Mediterranean to the Caspian Sea.

In contemporary Sunni-dominated Arabist ideology, the period is one of ignominy, better sidestepped in history books. Philip Hitti, author of the authoritative *History of the Arabs*, condemns the epoch as the region's 'deepest humiliation' from which the Arab world was only salvaged with the coming of Saladin in 1171.[2] In fact, the two centuries of Shia dominance mark the high-water mark of Classical Islam. From their new city of Cairo, founded in 969, the Fatimids established the great mosque of al-Azhar, and its accompanying university – the world's first. A gate through its magnificent walls still bears the inscription 'And Ali is the deity of Allah'. In Baghdad, the Buyids adopted the title *shahnashil* – king of kings, and married into the Sunni Caliphate. The Buyid leader Adud al-Dawla constructed Baghdad's most advanced hospital, al-Bimaristan al-Adudi, at a cost of 100,000 dinars, ordained the staging of Shia festivals in the streets of Baghdad and in 977 built Ali's Najaf shrine. The leading literati of the day attended his court, and the greatest medieval poet Ahmad ibn-Hussein Mutanabbi sang his praises. A generation later another poet, Abu al-Ala al-Maarri – a comrade in the secret society of neo-platonians, Ikhwan al-Safa, or Brethren of Sincerity – shunned the city's worldly delights after no one paid for his panegyrics. 'We mortals are composed of two great schools, enlightened knaves and religious fools,' he huffed.

The two centuries of Shia rule also shine as amongst the Middle East's most pluralistic and enlightened. In both Baghdad and Cairo, Muslims, Christians and Jews lived side-by-side (there was a street of winemakers, but no ghetto), and Shia rulers appointed Christian and Jewish to high office. Adud al-Dawla's vizier in Baghdad was the Christian Nasr ibn-Haroun, a patron of monasteries and churches. In Cairo, the second Fatimid Caliph, Nizar al-Aziz, made a Christian, Isa ibn Nastur, his vizier and a Jew, Yaqub ibn-Killis, his treasurer. Another Jew was his physician.[3] A host of 'free-thinking' societies proliferated in the region. Perhaps the most prominent were the Qarmatians, who spilled out of their clandestine base near Najaf in 890 to wrest control of the west coast of the Gulf and much of Syria with a manifesto of equality between races, castes and, incredibly, creeds.

Modern Sunni writers with the tide of history on their side are less laudatory. Hitti calls the Qarmatians 'a most malignant growth in the body politic of Islam', and damns them as revolutionary Bolsheviks for their practice of sharing property, wealth and reputedly wives.[4] Only with the Sunni counter-attack does he sound triumphant. He cheers the Seljuks – nomadic Turks from Central Asia – who in the early eleventh century toppled 110 years of Buyid rule in Baghdad, and the puritanical Berbers who burst out of the Sahara to oust the Fatimids from the Maghreb. But he reserves his warmest words for Saladin al-Ayyubbi, a turncoat Kurd hired by the Fatimids to defend their receding empire. After deposing his masters in 1169 and restoring Cairo for Sunni Islam, Saladin banned Shiism and threw open the doors of the Fatimids' forbidden city, al-Qahira, to looters. The city's library and 2,400-carat rubies were sold to pay for the troops. The victors celebrated by burning Shia manuals from Cordoba to Karbala. The Fatimid's advanced bureaucracy was replaced with a feudal system, which parcelled out the Nile delta to army officers for tax-farming. Hitti calls it 'a new and more benevolent tutelage'.

Memories die hard. While Sunni leaders from Nasser to Saddam hail Saladin as their saviour, Shias in southern Lebanon curse him as the Jazzar, or butcher, and still abandon the ruins of his castle, Tabnin, to the weeds. After Saladin, Shiism never recovered its glory. In the West, Sunni Berber revivalists hounded Shia remnants to a few disparate mountain outposts in Algeria. In the Fertile Crescent, Shia clerics were chased from the cities, retreating to such safer havens as Najaf, where Abu Jafar Muhammad al-Tusi founded a Shia scholastic retreat, the Hauza.

To consolidate their religious victory, the Sunni Sultans converted existing universities from Shiism to Sunni orthodoxy and funded the mass construction of *madrassas*, or law schools, to teach the new orthodoxy. Colleges replaced studies in *ijtihad*, or independent and innovative legal reasoning, with curricula based on the rote-learning of rigid, uniform almost totalitarian codes. In Baghdad, the Seljuk vizier, Nizam al-Mulk, established his great eponymous law school, the Nidhamiya, which published a single Sharia code in 1210. In Cairo and Damascus, Saladin and his successors built scores of Sunni schools, but restricted the curriculum to divinity, banning philosophy and *ijtihad*. Al-Azhar, the font of Shia Islam, was converted to Sunnism, and overshadowed on the hills above by a new citadel, the largest fortress in the Middle East, as a testament to the new martial age into which Egypt was plunged. 'Merchants lost their prestige to soldiers,' wrote Max Rodenbeck in his delightful history of Cairo. 'Tolerance and a cosmopolitan outlook had given way to narrow-mindedness...and intellectual life withered.'[5] The final humiliation came in the fourteenth century. The Fatimid Caliphs were disentombed, flung on a dung dump, and their graves ploughed into foundations for the city's main shopping parade, Khan al-Khalili. Non-Muslim communities remained in the city, but increasingly as subordinates.

Attempts at reclaiming the Shia past grew increasingly melodramatic and desperate. In 1092, a member of the Shia dissident sect of Assassins[6] stabbed Nizam al-Mulk to death. Other Shia movements sought alliances with non-Muslims such as Christian crusaders – almost always with disastrous results. Only the Mongols brought meaningful deliverance. In 1258, Genghis Khan's grandson, Hulegu Khan, sacked Baghdad and ended 600 years of the Sunni Caliphate by killing the Sunni Caliph, his Seljuk viziers and 800,000 of the city's inhabitants. The chief advisor to the Mongols was a Shia cleric and philosopher–astronomer, Nasir al-Din al-Tusi.

Where Sunnis weep of desecration and decimation, Shia historians portray the Mongol invasion as a renaissance. Sunnis remember Hulegu for sacking Baghdad's law schools and emptying its great libraries into the Tigris. Shias recall that he constructed another at his home in Maragha near Lake Urmya, alongside a great observatory, and made Tusi its first director. Flush with new endowments and freed from the clutches of Sunni control, the Hausa flourished. While Sunni clerics taught increasingly fossilised law codes, Shiism debated new and extraneous ideas. The gate of *ijtihad*, declared its clerics, would remain open, and *aql*, or rational intellect, serve as a legitimate a source for deriving God's will as the Qur'an.[7] Shias even returned to the streets of Baghdad to resume public mourning for the martyrdom of Imam Hussein; 'proclivities', puffs Hitti, 'which were deeply resented in Sunnite Baghdad'.[8]

Faced with the combination of Mongol ravages and a Shia revival, Sunni clerics codified their laws and shut fast the gate of *ijtihad* in a defensive attempt to preserve 700 years of intellectual tradition. By 1286, the Sunni scholar Abdullah al-Baidawi could proclaim: 'in our age no *mujtahid* exists'. The onslaught also spurred Sunni clerics to new heights of anti-Shia malice. In the thirteenth century Taqi al-Din ibn Taymiya, a fiery troubled cleric from Damascus, argued that the only fitting response to the Mongol occupation was to kill their Shia collaborators. Though enraged by the turpitude which greeted his call to Jihad, his detractors correctly argued that patience is often a virtue. Within four decades of decapitating the Caliph, the Mongols had succumbed to the lure of Sunni Islam. In 1295, Hulagu's sixth successor, Ghazan Mahmud, declared Sunni Islam the state religion and converted his court. Harried from Iraq, Shia Islam shifted east. In the sixteenth century the Safavid Persian leader, Shah Ismail, equipped with a force of 300 Sufi Shiites, forcibly converted Iran's Sunnis to Shiism. In the East–West confrontation, Iraq again formed the frontline between the two main Muslim sects.

At least as late as the eighteenth century, Iraq under Ottoman rule was still majority Sunni. But, from its base in Iran, Shiism continued to seep into Iraq, particularly after 1722, when Sunni Afghans conquered Isfahan, and precipitated the flight of Persian merchants and Shia clerics to Iraq. Endowed with material as well as spiritual wealth, the Persian Ayatollahs rapidly attracted nomadic tribes to the southern shrine cities. Over the course of the next 200 years, tribe after rebellious southern tribe switched allegiance from Ottoman suzerain to clerical Ayatollah in a semi-feudal relationship. Lured by the commercial advantages of a booming pilgrimage trade in the mid-nineteenth century, prominent Sunni clans, such as the Chalabis, converted en masse to Shiism. By the turn of the century, southern Iraq was a largely Shia preserve.

The replacement of the Ottomans by the British during the First World War did nothing to alter the sectarian balance of power. The British conscripted Sunni officers from the ex-Ottoman army into their administration, and anointed a Sunni king. A largely Shia revolt against the British order, launched by the Ayatollahs in Najaf in 1920, killed hundreds of occupation troops and wounded over 10,000, and was only suppressed by aerial bombardment. Defeated militarily, the Ayatollahs opted for civil disobedience, issuing a fatwa in 1922 forbidding their followers from supporting the British or their Sunni Hashemite vassal. British officials considered they were still seeking to regain the power that the Seljuks had robbed from them 900 years earlier. 'Alone of all Arab countries', wrote Freya Stark, a British traveller and one-time journalist on the *Baghdad Times*, 'one may still see at work here [in Iraq] that Persian influence which had so profound a power twelve centuries ago'.[9]

The sectarian struggle also coloured Iraq's regime-change in 1958. The Sunni monarchy quickly collapsed in a republican coup led by the son of a Fayli, or Shia, Kurd, Abdel Karim Qassem. A succession of Baath Party putsches finally restored Sunni supremacy in Iraq, but simultaneously propelled the Alawites, an offshoot of Twelver Shiism, to power in Syria.[10] In 1978, Hafez al-Assad, Syria's Alawite overlord, ordained the death penalty for all members of the main Sunni party, the Muslim Brotherhood. Saddam followed suit a year later, banning Shia religious parties, and imposing the death penalty for membership. As talk of fraternal Baathist unity disintegrated into murderous enmity, Saddam and Assad backed the other's sectarian opposition. In the wake of his invasion of Shia Iran, Saddam armed and trained Muslim Brotherhood fighters to target Syria. Jordan's ruling Sunnis rallied to his cause, and together helped succour the Muslim Brotherhood. The Assads only survived after flattening the Brotherhood's stronghold, the city of Hama. Saddam required even more brutal methods to repress his ever-growing Shia population. By the end of his reign, Iraq's Sunni Arab core had shrunk to some 20 per cent of the population, and required ever heavier weights to maintain its supremacy until they became no longer tenable. Ultimately, Saddam's suppression of Shia engendered his downfall. Nine hundred years after Saladin, Iraq is again tipping the regional balance of power the way of the Shia.

ACKNOWLEDGEMENTS

I have strung up too many debts during my travels through Iraq and the region; I can list but a tiny proportion. In a cold Tehran winter in 2001, Hala Anvari, an Iranian journalist, first alerted me to the impending Shia resurgence in the Arab world – predicting with typical Persian snobbery that the Arab world lags 25 years behind Iran, and that a Shia revolution was on its way. She was wrong by a year. Dr Norman Calder, my Islamic studies lecturer at university, introduced me to *ijtihad* and its preservation by Shia Ayatollahs, and his lessons still ring in my ears 15 years after his premature death. Xan Smiley, my avuncular editor at *The Economist,* nudged me to close my Iraq chapter with a book. So too did Toby Dodge of St Mary's College, London. Together with Joost Hiltermann, the Middle East director of International Crisis Group, he properly punctured my more optimistic flights of fancy that Iraq might somehow pull through. Dr Khalid Shammari, who chaperoned me in both Amman and Baghdad, was ready with a glass of arak whenever my spirits began to flag. My inspiring agent, Michael Sissons, offered a similar service in London. And Iradj Bagherzade, Hanako Birks and Abigail Fielding-Smith at I.B.Tauris offered the encouragement and the forbearance to make it all happen.

Almost all of the names that appear in this book, with the exception of those in Washington, were the subject of interviews, many on repeated occasions. I am grateful for their patience.

The fate of a peripatetic journalist, particularly in a war-zone, is to beg and borrow, and I have done so more than most. Many gave me hospitality at considerable inconvenience and often greater risk to themselves. In addition to Um Taysir, Charles Clover and James Drummond – *Financial Times* correspondents both with exceptional panache – and Ammar Shahbandar, of the International War and Peace Reporting Institute in Baghdad, let me long outstay my welcome. So too for shorter periods did Peter Bouckaert of Human Rights Watch in Baghdad, Ali Shaalan of the Iraqi aid agency MRS, Kais Nazzal al-Ani in Falluja, and Sufi master Thahir al-Sheikh Qummer al-Rifai in Baghdad. I still regret that I did not accept his offer to swap my air-conditioned world of west Baghdad for the spiritually richer garret above his Sufi lodge. On more than one occasion, my driver, Samir, turfed his children out of their room to accommodate me when he felt kidnappers were getting too close. We were virtually wedded for over a year, bickering perpetually not least over the propensity of his car to break down in such awkward moments as the Kirkuk souq after curfew. His long-suffering temperament and parental nature made it impossible to part with him, even after I discovered he was recording my movements for his Baathist superiors. I treasure every moment.

Above all, I remain indentured to my wife, Lipika, and children, Rishi and Sara, who have selflessly traipsed after me across the region, and almost came to Iraq. May the day not be long coming when we will go to Baghdad together.

Nicolas Pelham

SECTION 1

BEFORE THE FALL

CHAPTER 1

From Trilby to Turbans

Saddam Hussein was nothing if not a good Mesopotamian. He followed loyally in the footsteps of Sargon the Akkadian, Nebuchadnezzar and the Assyrian tyrant who, in the words of a 3,200-year-old stele which until the US invasion sat on a plinth in the Baghdad museum, 'trod on necks with my feet, as if they were footstools'. For 35 years, he trampled over Iraq's composite identities, making footstools of the country's kaleidoscope of cultures. He had a name to match. Derived from the Arabic trilateral root s-d'-m – to go crashing – Saddam is perhaps best translated as Bruiser. And over the course of a generation of cultural brutalism, he decked the country in Bruiser monuments. There were Bruiser schools, Bruiser hospitals and Bruiser cities. And Bruiser's likeness hung from every lamp-post, school wall, bridge, home and railway carriage.

Even in those final months, when Iraqis knew that the end was nigh, Saddam still decreed like a deity. In October 2002, as Washington quickened its drum-roll to war, he ordained a pledge of allegiance to defy the West's call for regime-change. State television – there was none other – hailed the referendum as a wedding between the people and their potentate, framed in digital hearts. Pop-stars sung love-songs to the betrothed. Presenters gushed through the groom's album, displaying Hussein in his various guises of tribal leader, champion swimmer, poet, father and – his favourite – country gent in a trilby stoically firing a rifle into the air.

As befitted a wedding, there no rival candidates, lest rival suitors tempt Iraqis into committing adultery. And to dispel even adulterous thoughts, there was no secret ballot, no voting booth, and no box for No votes.

Dancing girls and trumpeters pranced on makeshift stages to celebrate the happy union, and the ballot boxes for Yes votes were festooned with plastic tulips. Wizened elders marked the nuptials by banging their walking sticks, war veterans with amputated arms rhythmically rotated their stumps and voluminous mamas kissed their ballot papers. Boys pricked their fingers with needles to show their self-sacrifice and signed their ballots in blood. That evening the television news declared that Saddam had received a 100 per cent Yes vote on a 100 per cent turnout. There was not a single Iraqi adulterer.

But the marriage was forced. Even in Bruiser's birthplace – the province of Tikrit, 110 miles north of Baghdad – the personality cult flagged whenever television cameras stopped filming. A generation of wars on Kurds, Iranians, Kuwaitis and Iraqi Shia, and a dozen years of sanctions, had up-ended the Arab world's most developed, secular and pluralist state. In the 1950s, it launched its first computer (before Israel), and exported its own wheat. Flush with oil wealth by the 1970s, its per capita GNP exceeded Australia's. Thirty years on, the best-endowed Arab state was reduced to its poorest – despite possessing the world's second largest oil reserves and the region's richest farmland. In Saddam's effort to convert Iraq's civil society into a military machine, harvests shrunk to barely a quarter of their earlier levels.

Iraq's patchwork of cultures was rendered as barren as its pastures (60 per cent of which fell out of cultivation). Increasingly chauvinist and greedy regimes expelled their non-Arab minorities, confiscating their wealth. First went some 120,000 Jews in 1950, then, 20 years later, 100,000 Shia of allegedly 'Persian' origin, and from the 1970s onwards under the banner of Arabisation, the eviction of Kurds, Turkomen and Assyrian Christians, culminating in a campaign dubbed the Anfal, or booty, after the Qur'anic chapter meaning spoils of war.

The buildings reflected their master. Honeycomb after honeycomb of Ottoman alleyways fell to eight-lane flyovers and municipal megaliths. Statues of Iraq's bygone heroes gave way to Saddam colossi. And the entire conurbation was shrouded in the martial camouflage of desert dust. The wooden latticed balconies the Ottomans called *shahnashil*, or kings' seats, had once cast patterned shadows on the walkways. Now they flopped to the ground like the wringed necks of chickens. Beams ingrained with mother of pearl were removed for firewood. Iraq's millennial marshlands were slashed and burnt, and their waters redirected. The reputed Garden of Eden, sited near Basra, was entombed in concrete slabs. And a half-finished dam threatened to sink the ziggurats of Ashur, the ancient Assyrian Empire. War interrupted Saddam's plans for the Flood.

The country – like its buildings – was drafted into serving its master. Armies of secret police surveyed each other. People in cafes feared spilling their coffee over the morning newspaper lest they face charges of defacing the photo of the leader that invariably graced the front page. Orwellian road-signs exhorted drivers to keep their eye on traitors, textbooks taught children how to count with images of long-range missiles and how to monitor their parents, and couples shied from pillow-talk fearful of what their spouse might divulge in a divorce suit. Cut off by sanctions, exit visa requirements and book bans, the children of a generation who had studied abroad had scant exposure abroad. Art students, deployed in propaganda departments, painted and sculptured Saddam, and in their spare time resorted to the realm of the abstract, dominated by the stricken colours of black and red. Portrait artists left out mouths since loose tongues cost lives. In a reign of terror, only silence – or death – was safe.

The death toll was mere conjecture. After the invasion, even pathologists confessed they were surprised by the scale of mass graves. In its later years, the regime had transferred responsibility for registering the dead from the mortuaries to the secret police, who earned a living selling the cadavers back to the families. The only independent measure doctors had for the death toll was the eyes. 'By law, the eyes belonged to hospitals for research,' said Rikab Alousi, a pathologist at Baghdad's Yarmouk hospital. 'We knew it had been a bloody month by the high cornea count.'

Bellies of those who survived wilted as fast as their brains. After the imposition of sanctions, the annual GDP collapsed from $3,900 per capita to a pittance approaching Chad's. A teacher's monthly salary of $6 bought three kilos of meat. Chronic malnutrition amongst children reached Sahel African levels. Modern industrial plants built by Germans, Japanese and Koreans rusted in scorching winds. 'We are in the process of destroying an entire society. It is as simple and terrifying as that,' said the Humanitarian Coordinator in Iraq, Denis Halliday.[11] But sanctions were only partly to blame. Long before western armies took over Saddam's palaces, Iraqis joked that Europe lay on the far side of the palace walls. Even in Tikrit, children in rags ran barefoot beneath the parapets. And while his people depended on rations, Saddam ordered 128 daily feasts at each of his 128 palaces to disguise his whereabouts.

Despairing of earthly salvation, Iraqis looked to the spiritual, but Saddam followed them there. In the wake of the Gulf War, he declared a *hamla imaniya*, or faith struggle, forsaking the party's secular tenets and ravaging non-sectarian public space. He closed down the clubs and watering holes of the nomenklatura along Abu Nawas Street – named after a poet from the golden age of Islam famed for his erotic and bacchanalian verse. Atop the racecourse, hitherto the prized retreat of Baghdad's passionate gamblers, Saddam constructed the Mother of all Battles mosque. Walls in ministry buildings sported posters reminding women that Saddam Hussein – not God – would like to see them abide by standards of Islamic decency.

As war neared, he assumed the mantle of defender of the faith holding back western armies at the gates of Islam. In his televised appearances, Saddam forsook his western trilby for more traditional garb, and bombast for sanctimony. Televised homilies gushed with religious idiom. In his speech to mark his post-referendum investiture, the all-powerful leader appealed to God to ensure that if he could not win in this world Iraq would triumph in the next. He had prepared his 'army of Jihad' for battle, he said, 'with hearts filled with faith in God and the spirit of martyrdom to win a place in paradise'.In recognition of the odds against Iraqi success in a conventional battle, he gave notice of a guerrilla war that would continue for years. In an uncharacteristic tone of introspection and piety, he recalled the Prophet Mohammed's own flight from Mecca and the subsequent launch of a Jihad to recapture the city eight years later.

Loyal wags compared the coming war to the Prophet's battles against pagan forces. 'It's proper for us Iraqis to remember the flight of our Prophet as a symbol of Jihad,' wrote Lieutenant-General Wajih Hunayfsh in the state paper *al-Qaddissiyah*, a Saddam mouthpiece. 'The people will remain steadfast and patient in the face of this evil, burning with the spirit of battle inspired by the flight of the Prophet.' The director of a Baathist think-tank, Mahdi Saleh Hussein al-Mashadani, published a book praising Saddam Hussein, alone amongst Arab leaders, for 'resisting Western attempts to eradicate the meaning of Jihad from the Arab mind'. Saddam was learning, said Saad Jawad, a politics professor at Baghdad University, from Iran. 'The regime realizes that if Iran could use Islam, so could Iraq. I think Saddam is imitating Khomeini. His state is speaking in a religious tone to ride the tide and get the newly religious on side. Every Friday, it's Jihad and aggression.'

Few were convinced. In these dying months of the regime, many Iraqis took enormous risks to convince visiting journalists that they were desperate for change, despite the prohibition on fraternising with foreigners. In the open gardens of writers' clubs, where the tables were strategically spaced too far apart to allow eavesdropping, Iraqis spoke earnestly of their desire for a regime-change *à la* Abdel Karim al-Qassim, who toppled the monarchy. With eyes trained on the road, a taxi-driver spoke in a deadpan expression of his brother whose ear the authorities had severed. A barber pulled down the shutters on his tiny shop in the Baghdad suburb of Arassat to confess his alarm that mounting anti-war protests in the West might deter US intervention. 'We just want deliverance,' said a second-hand book seller (there were few new bookshops in sanctioned Iraq). 'Whether by a Hashemite king, or the Americans, or even Sharon, we don't care as long as they free us.'

Even former regime stalwarts lined up to declare their distance. 'The government is out of touch with the spirit of the age. We need a constitutional democratic government,' said a septuagenarian communist, Mukarram Talibani, who for eight years in the 1970s had been one of Saddam's ministers.[12] 'We already have a multi-party state in Iraq, though the government denies it. We have the Baath, but we also have the Kurdish parties, the KDP and the PUK, the Communists, the Nationalists, and the banned Shia organizations. We need a system which conforms to reality.' Wamidh Nadhmi, an avuncular politics professor with the unkempt appearance assumed by Sunni patricians (in more than one interview he appeared in his pyjamas), damned Saddam with a quote a British Health Minister, Aneurin Bevan, had used of Prime Minister Winston Churchill: 'When I was a minister during the war, I respected his resolution and efficiency. Then I noticed that he was enjoying the war.' Iraq, said this former graduate of London University, should follow Britain's peacetime example. 'We need a Labour government who can build hospitals not palaces, and houses not armies and fantastic mosques.'[13]

In the repressed clamour for salvation, few paused to consider that foreign invasion was a blunt bloody tool for instilling change, or that the West after the Second World War had deployed less traumatic methods for toppling tyrants. (Constructive external engagement in tandem with internal pressure had turned Portugal, Spain, Greece, Turkey, South Africa and much of Eastern Europe from military dictatorships into fledgling democracies.) Since the regime ruled by force, few thought that anything but force could save them, and their own attempts in the past had fallen foul of Saddam's helicopter gunships. Nadhmi was one of the few in pre-war Iraq who argued passionately for regime-change within not without, and doubted Washington's declared intentions of waging war for democracy. If London and Washington cared so passionately about Iraqis, he asked, why had they not tied the lifting of UN sanctions to political reform as well as disarmament? 'For thirteen years, the UN sent us thousands of weapons inspectors, and not one human rights monitor,' he said.

Was there scope for internal change? In the regime's last weeks, Iraqis were treated to unprecedented glasnost. University refectories buzzed with students voicing their plans to avoid the draft into the Saddam Fedayeen militias, and mocking the walls with ears. From the cubby-holes lining Baghdad's courtyard cafes, artists burbled, swapping photocopied collections of *samizdat* poems or paintings of dungeons yet to escape the censor. The minders escorting foreign journalists abandoned their charges. And when Shias in the city slums openly celebrated their saint-days, the security forces refrained from enforcing a 25-year-long ban. Loulouwa Rashid, a researcher for the advocacy group International Crisis Group and a graduate from Mosul University, found to her astonishment that Iraqis were openly championing regime-change.[14]

A gaggle of mothers pushed the limits even further, protesting at the gates of Baghdad's *mukhabarat*, or intelligence, headquarters for the return of their disappeared. When the *mukhabarat* forced them back, they had the effrontery to resurface two hours later outside the information ministry, where the international press was ensconced reporting on a general amnesty. 'Give us our sons,' they chanted. When the guards in leather jackets again tried to disperse them, the women protected themselves by chanting paeans of praise to the leader and demanding he complete his amnesty. Not only did the women challenge the state and survive, but officials at the information ministry undertook to investigate.

But rather than seek to salvage his regime with multi-party reforms and a parliament, not a president who was sovereign, Saddam continued with a theatre in which he hogged centre stage. He offered to open his country to the CIA, pulverised his longest-range missiles on the eve of war, and, most histrionic of all, two days after his investiture ordered his dungeons emptied of all 100,000 inmates, bar Zionist and US spies. It was insufficient to rally the masses. While the world's sole superpower amassed its divisions on Iraq's frontiers, programmed its satellite-guided missiles, and directed its drones over its skies, Saddam staged parades, whose pathos was surreal for such a militarised state. In the holy city of Karbala, a

4,000-strong ragbag of schoolchildren, students and pensioners, brandishing an arsenal of Kalashnikovs, farm prongs and walking sticks, vowed to battle America. As soon as the Dad's Army completed their brief march-past, Karbala's governor, General Latif Mahal Humoud, and a gaggle of clergymen hurried off. Iraq was preparing to fight a twenty-first-century superpower with the implements of the First World War, and the morale of Macbeth's Dunsinane.

On paper Iraq could muster a 350,000-man standing army. Saddam also boasted a praetorian guard comprised of 80,000 Republican and Special Republican Guard troops, and 15,000 Special Security Force Organization presidential bodyguards. But despite the imminence of the attack, he stopped short of a call to mobilisation. Conscripts on military service went home at four in the afternoon. 'To call up reservists, Iraq has to feed and house them, and for that the regime lacks the means,' said one of the few remaining European ambassadors in Baghdad, rightly predicting an American walkover. 'In the end winning a war is just a question of money.'[15] Few Iraqis expected the war to last more than a few days. The Iraqi army was less than half its strength during the Kuwait war, and then it had crumpled in a 100-hour ground attack.

Almost the only visible sign of fortifications were regiments of shovel-wielding gardeners and conscripts criss-crossing the capital. Tanks were buried up to their turrets on the approach roads to Baghdad (though providing scant artillery rounds for fear they might be turned on the regime) and a trench dug ringing Baghdad. Sandbagged positions three bags high sprouted alongside the Tigris bridges, at road junctions and further south amid the web of dykes and canals. Bridges were wired with explosives – although the advancing Americans were later surprised at how many failed to detonate. So lax did preparations appear that few remaining nervous diplomats speculated that activity at a long-delayed renovation of Baghdad's Zahra zoo was a cover for the storage of weapons of mass destruction.

For the regime, the people were less an asset than a threat to be contained. Weeks before the first bombing, Baath apparatchiks armed with machine guns patrolled the streets at night in dress-rehearsals of the curfew they ordained would ensue as soon as the invasion began. Local Baath-party cells staged impromptu gatherings at major crossroads, particularly on Fridays after communal prayers. 'If you cooperate with us, we'll cooperate with you,' the party faithful shouted through megaphones at passers-by.

And as a sign of his diminishing circle of loyalists, Saddam appointed his youngest son, Qusay, aged 37, on the eve of war to lead the defence of Baghdad and Tikrit. At best the population was viewed as cover. To maintain an urban shield even in the event of a power and water outage, the state swamped the market with electricity generators and water pumps. And the UN distributed a double supply of food rations.

The state did, however, seek to court three key constituencies in the build-up to war. The first were the criminals. Two days after his 2002 investiture, Saddam decreed a general amnesty for his entire 100,000-strong prison population, an act of forgiveness his loyal Christian deputy, Tariq Aziz, likened to Jesus. The lifting of the portcullis of Saddam's gulag had all the prisoners emerging from their underground cells into the daylight. As the main gates opened, guards retreated behind one gate after another as waiting relatives stormed in. Guards, who tried to beat back the crowds with army-issue belts, were pelted with stones. Within hours of the broadcast of amnesty, Saddam's most infamous prison, Abu Ghraib, became a fairground. In the dusty wasteland that human rights groups had hitherto dubbed 'a death camp… littered with shallow graves', children banged tin trays, wives hugged and mothers ululated. From somewhere a minibus appeared with loudspeakers strung onto its roof, blaring Iraqi pop. In the shadows of cells where human rights workers reported inmates were forced to eat their own severed genitals, hawkers peddled cola and sweet-cakes. Beggars appeared from nowhere. Saddam Hussein's portraits and aphorisms adorning the prison's windowless walls looked down scowling at their absent audience. 'I had three death sentences pending for murder,' said a baffled burly convict, elbowing his way to freedom. 'We released even murderers,' smirked Hussein in a televised interview. Many Iraqis were less thankful. 'Fine, release the army deserters and the political prisoners, but did they have to let the paedophiles loose as well?' asked a restaurateur in Baghdad's well-to-do neighbourhood of Mansour. As anticipated in the chaos after the US invasion, the criminal class rapidly emerged as the foot-soldiers of the rebellion, first as looters and later as hired assassins.

In addition to his new army of jailbirds, Saddam rallied the tribes that over the previous decade he had reconstructed to favour party cadres. Vast tracts of land were redistributed on the eve of war to mainly Sunni chieftains, in an attempt to enjoin their support. Win the support of one chieftain, argued Hassib Odeibi, a presidential advisor on foreign affairs, and 20,000 Iraqis would follow.[16] In a dramatic boost to their authority, chieftains were given responsibility for law and order. Colourful drapes denoting tribal arbitrations, or *fasl*, appeared on the roadsides of even the most cosmopolitan districts of Baghdad, and the capital's once developed civil society was required to rediscover its tribal roots.

The third and most powerful support-group Saddam wooed was Arab Sunni. With latent sectarianism, the regime had long regarded Sunni Arabs as its bedrock. A mere 20 per cent of the population, they dominated in positions of brute power. And in the 1991 uprising, Iraq's three Sunni Arab provinces alone outside the capital had remained loyal to the regime. With the onset of his *hamla imaniya*, or faith struggle, he appointed Sunni preachers to senior faculty positions at Iraq's best universities. But while promoting normally apolitical religious groups, such as Sufis, or loyal ones, such as the Muslim Brotherhood, he continued to fight shy of Jihadis. Unlike other Gulf and North African leaders, he shunned sponsorship of the Afghan Jihad, and during his Kuwait invasion he and Usama bin Laden had stood on opposing sides – Bin Laden even reportedly offered his services in place of western infidels to expel the godless Baath from Kuwait. The tensions continued late into the 1990s, when Saddam crushed a rebellion sparked by the infusion of Saudi-financed anti-Shia Puritanism – Salafiya – amongst the Sunni tribes of the Euphrates valley north of Baghdad.

Twelve years on, the Jihadis were actively courted. In the two years before his downfall, Saddam's vice-president and cousin, Ezzat al-Douri, who handled the regime's religious portfolio, commissioned the construction of Salafi mosques from Mosul in the north to the Shia shrine city of Najaf – a hitherto Sunni-free zone – in the south. Sunni prayer leaders rushed to fill them. In the rising tide of sectarian rivalry, the Papal Nuncio in Baghdad complained of growing attacks on Christian communities, particularly in Mosul,[17] and preachers routinely denounced Shias as a fifth column over megaphones strung from minarets. In a sermon of almost operatic delivery at Baghdad's al-Adab al-Islamiya mosque on the west bank of the Tigris, Imam Hisham alternated crescendos of yelps against the encroaching fifth column of Shia with pianissimo sobs for the offended Sunnis. 'The warriors are again coming from Iran,' the Imam wept at Baghdad's Islamic Arts mosque. 'Shia traitors say they will search all identity papers for righteous names, and kill Iraqis named Omar [an exclusively Sunni name].[18] We are all martyrs. In this land of Prophets and Saints, go to Jihad.' The faithful overflowing down the steps of the mosque snuffled an Amen.

Subsequently, Iraqis would apologise that Jihadi death cults were not the Iraqi way. But on the eve of the war officials did little to disguise the engagement – if not the marriage – of convenience between Baathists, tribesmen, Jihadis and criminals. The regime laid on rallies of 'martyrdom-seekers' garbed in funereal white tunics and explosive belts, who paraded on successive mornings through the Baghdad rush-hour. And officials issued a clarion call to party bureaux across the Arab world to recruit an expendable volunteer corps of suicide bombers. At Salman Pak, a base on the southern rim of Baghdad, reports surfaced of paramilitaries offering training courses for would-be suicide bombers not just from Iraq, but also Yemen, Syria and Palestine. 'We are preparing for all probabilities. We are preparing for war,' said Lieutenant-General Hussein Mohammed Amin, the head of the Iraqi arms-monitoring team accompanying the UN, when asked about the reports. In their fixation on advanced but ephemeral missile systems, Washington blithely ignored Iraq's most potent weapon of mass destruction – religion.

CHAPTER 2

Stirring in the Shia Slums

If Sunni preachers rallied to Saddam's battle cry, their Shia counterparts were a study in silence. The traditional clerical establishment responded to Saddam's religious outreach with *taqiya*, the centuries-old Shia practice of dissimulation permitted in the event of danger. Shia preachers – unlike their Sunni counterparts – had long abandoned the practice of Friday communal prayers, revelling in their ambiguity.

The few elderly Ayatollahs cajoled into television studios gave little away, dutifully intoning a message to defend the homeland without once mentioning a call to Jihad. Hussein Sadr, Ayatollah of Baghdad, ambiguously called on the faithful 'not to follow those who lead you to evil'.[19] For more precise instructions I went in search of his three-storey mansion, only to be rebuffed by his Persian-speaking guards.

His deputy had less sacerdotal surroundings. I found the stout Hojetalislam Ali Mudamarragh on a pavement beneath a black umbrella and wooden board marked 'Islamic law expert'. Bedecked in a black turban and tattered cape, he sat on a stool opposite Baghdad's Personal Status court, selling religious stamps of approval for the judgments of Saddam's secular courts. He charged 500 dinars, or 20 cents, per petitioner, a fee clientele often sweetened with bon-bons. I duly paid. Word had spread through Shia communities that Jihad was proscribed during Moharram, the first Muslim month of the year, which by coincidence was when Anglo-American forces planned to invade, and I asked his opinion. 'Politics,' he replied with a dismissive wag of his finger.

Others unversed in the tactics of the Sadducees openly flouted the state's sanction against displays of Shia religiosity. Bus drivers in Shia neighbourhoods played sectarian chants on their stereos mindless of the mandatory five-year prison terms. Haider, a taxi-driver with a clipped Lenin goatee, rhythmically thumped his chest to the beat of Shia lamentations, oblivious to the surrounding traffic as he crawled through Saddam City, Baghdad's largest shantytown, which even from the vantage point of my 22-storey hotel stretched beyond the horizon.

Saddam City dated back to 1958, when tens of thousands of rural migrants streamed to the capital from southern Iraq after the overthrow of the monarchy. First named al-Thoura, or Revolution, by the 1990s it had mushroomed into the largest Shia conurbation in the Arab world. Its 2 million residents eked out a living in uniform hovels. By night, the squalor acquired Dickensian proportions. In the shell of the market stalls, a gypsy woman boiled sweet syrupy tea on a brazier, serving vagabond clientele. Human waste spilled out of the open drains into soggy alleyways or, worse, the ground floors of tenement blocks. Tuberculosis was rife. To soak up the sludge, Haider had covered his mud-floors with reed matting. Three toddlers who slept there were blotched red with skin disease.

When I visited in November 2002, Haider's family wore the white Shia tunics of bereavement. His younger brother had died in a prison cell, and the family had had to pay 5 million dinars, or $2,500, to recover the corpse, as well as agree to bury the body before dawn. From a slit cut into the sleeve of a family album, his mother eased a blotched black-and-white photo. It bore the image of a cleric with beady eyes, a black turban, well-nourished jowls, and a moustache extending not quite symmetrically into two S's gave him the whimsical appearance of a court jester. The image was soon to proliferate across Iraq, but in Saddam's Iraq was banned, and carried a sentence of death. Twenty years after his execution, Mohammed Baqir al-Sadr remained Saddam's most powerful opponent.

Sadr was Iraq's Ayatollah Ruhollah Khomeini. The Shia party he founded – Dawa, or Religious Call – had been passed from generation to generation, despite the brutal attempts of the regime to extirpate it. Unbowed by a presidential decree condemning Dawa members to death, tens of thousands, like Haider's brother, had followed their leader into the torture chamber, and echoed his refusal to recant their membership. 'If my little finger was Baathist, I'd chop it off,' Sadr taunted the guards who tortured him to death in April 1980 in the crackdown that followed Iran's Islamic Revolution.[20] Saddam suppressed the Shia riots that followed his death by declaring martial law across southern Iraq, but failed to extinguish his influence. His martyrdom was embellished with the detail familiar from the Passions of Shia Islam's founding fathers, ensuring him an enduring place in their pantheon before driving nails into his skull. Dubbed 'the First Martyr', Sadr posthumously inspired at least four revolts, and 25 years on Saddam City remained his Soweto.

Sadr's movement owed much to Liberation theology – that heady mix of religion and anti-colonialism – which percolated into the crusty theological seminaries of Iraq's Shia in the second half of the twentieth century. A recognised scholar by his early twenties, Sadr broke with clerical tradition by acquiring a secular as well as religious education, and sought to coin a new creed for Iraq's newly urbanised Shias, who were falling sway to the twin secular ideologies of communism and Baathism. In his writings, he propounded a thesis of *wilayat al-umma* – whereby God handed temporal authority from the prophets to the people – in contrast to Khomeini's authoritarian *wilayat al-faqih*, which invested authority in the hands of a supreme scholar. Where Iran's revolution was ecclesiastical, Iraq's he envisaged would be popular. Together with a circle of like-minded seminarians who had gravitated to Najaf's colleges, including Khomeini and Mohammed Fadlallah of Lebanon, he laid the foundations of Revolutionary Islam. Pilgrims swarming to shrines on saints-days chanted 'No Government but Ali'.

The ideology challenged not just secularism, but Iraq's pyramid power structure, which bar brief interludes of foreign invasion had been dominated by Sunnis since the birth of Islam. Having seized control of the Baath party (then 75 per cent Shiite[21]) in a 1968 coup, Sunni tribesmen from Tikrit quickly moved to curb clerical authority. They ended the exemption of military service for trainee clerics, channelled the plentiful flow of Shia alms-giving to the state treasury, and expelled hundreds of thousands of Shias from the shrine cities on the grounds of their Persian origin. In the name of Arabisation, Saddam subsidised Arab men to divorce their Persian Shia wives and expel them abroad.[22] To further clip the clerics' financial as well as spiritual clout, civil servants were banned from making the pilgrimage to Shia shrines, and Iranian pilgrimage reduced to a trickle. Shia rites of collective mourning – such as self-flagellation, immolation with swords and even chest-beating, or *lutm* – were banned. Armed guards erected checkpoints on the highways to shrine cities and sporadically sprayed gunfire into the palm-groves to prevent pilgrims taking back routes. In 1977, on the holiest day in the Shia calendar, Ashoura –

commemorating the slaughter of the Prophet's grandson, Hussein, and his 72 followers at Karbala – 25 barefoot Shia were shot dead.

The Iran–Iraq war forced the Baath leadership to make some concessions to maintain Shia loyalty. Following his assumption of the presidency in 1979, Saddam Hussein declared Imam Ali's birthday a national holiday and paid homage at Shia shrines. But power remained ever more firmly in Sunni hands. Shias were all but barred from the Republican Guard, the senior ranks of intelligence, and the military academy. Officers were Sunni, their foot-soldiers Shiite. Meanwhile, the state promulgated ever more acts to cut the ties between lay Shia and their sources of emulation, the Ayatollahs. In a move tantamount to Henry VIII's dissolution of the monasteries, clerical colleges outside Najaf were closed down, sometimes by bulldozer, and scores of clerics jailed. Many Iraqi clerics are missing a forefinger, the amputation of which was a favourite method of torture.

It took Saddam Hussein 13 days of butchery to quell the Shia revolt that erupted in the wake of Iraq's 1991 retreat from Kuwait. Much of the ancient city of Kabala was razed by tanks inscribed with the slogan 'After today, no more Shiites'. Libraries housing sacred tomes were converted to barracks, and manuscripts burned to boil tea. 'Our holy books were treated like us,' a son of Grand Ayatollah Syed Hakim told me amid the wreckage of his family library. 'Some they executed, some they locked in their libraries, and the rest they put under house arrest. It was a *Kulturkampf* – they thought that by eliminating our books they could eliminate us.'

For years, timid reformers in the nomenklatura had called on the regime to relax its ban on Shia religiosity in the interests of national reconciliation. 'What's your problem if the Shia beat themselves up?' pleaded a former minister, Mukarram Talabani, an octogenarian who continued to act as a presidential interlocutor with the opposition. But younger counsellors claimed the regime was the necessary antidote to Ayatollahs whose zeal was akin to the Khmer Rouge. 'We're civilising the zealots,' said a presidential advisor, Hassib Obeidi. 'Is it not enough that we let them picnic in the courtyards of holy shrines?'[23]

Rooted in a popular theology of suffering, Dawa was the only opposition group to retain a popular base inside Saddam's Iraq. Eight years after the 1991 uprising, Shia activists again rebelled, this time in protest at the assassination of Sadr's distant cousin, Ayatollah Mohammed Sadiq al-Sadr, who promptly acquired the sobriquet 'the Second Martyr'. Again the revolt was put down by indiscriminate gun-fire, which still scars the main thoroughfares of Saddam City.[24] Thereafter, the movement abandoned direct action, withdrawing from mainstream society to prepare in secret for the day after regime-change. 'Prophet Mohammed formed his own secret society in Mecca; we must follow his example,' said Haider, the taxi-driver, who later confided he had spent four years with Ahmed Chalabi's Iraqi National Congress in Kurdistan and who introduced me to two law students who had dropped out of university to help prepare for the new order. In their mindset, they had embarked on a mission to overturn 1,400 years of illegitimate Sunni rule, and restore Muslim leadership to the lawful successors of Imam Ali, the son-in-law and rightful heir of the Prophet Mohammed.

Washington's jargon of regime-change dovetailed well with their own. For them, 'liberation' was shorthand for a Shia awakening, and democracy for Shia majority rule. Regime-change evoked the millennial Shia promise that the oppressed would inherit the earth. But if the semantics were similar, the inherent meanings were fundamentally different. And while Haider looked to America as God's agent of change, he did so with no more love than a biblical prophet regarded Nebuchadnezzar. America and its British lapdog were remembered more as betrayers than saviours of Shias. Twelve years earlier, the two powers had abandoned Shia rebels after dropping flyers across southern Iraq calling for revolt. Their troops had barred Shia rebels access to arms depots and blocked the escape routes to Kuwait when Saddam had counter-attacked with his helicopter gunships. And for 12 years thereafter, they had championed the world's harshest sanctions, which impoverished Iraq's citizens while enhancing Saddam's totalitarian control with a rations regime. For proof of the duplicitous alliance, Haider looked no further than a glass box in the Triumph Leader Museum in central Baghdad. It contained a pair of gold-plated riding spurs, a plaque marked 'a Gift from President Ronald Reagan to Saddam Hussein', and a photo of the gift-bearer, one Donald Rumsfeld, dated December 1983, shortly before Saddam began using US satellite imagery to bomb Iranian troops with chemical weapons. Saddam was the little devil, Washington was his master. For Haider, freedom was not the saccharine of Hollywood movies or American pop, both of which could already be found in Baghdad. It was mass Shia pilgrimage and the public display of the revered trinity of Imam Ali, Prophet Mohammed's rightful successor, and his two sons, Hassan and Hussein, in place of the profane trinity of Saddam and his two sons, Uday and Qusay.

Come the last Saddam-era Ashoura, two weeks before war, Shia neighbourhoods sloughed off Baathist bans, as if liberating themselves. For the first time in decades, volunteers dished out funeral cakes and lentil gruel with rice, known as *timan wa qiwa*, in the alleyways. A few even dared challenge the official prescription on traipsing barefoot the 80-kilometre highway from Baghdad to Karbala. By daylight the rooftops of the slums of al-Thoura sparkled with a kaleidoscope of green, red and black flags, representing the colours of Shia saints, demarcating borders ahead of Saddam's imminent fall. The marketplaces morphed into a sea of bobbing black *chadors*, Iranian-style, clenched fast between female teeth. And by night, the slums reverberated to the shrill lamentations of women, as their men played banned tapes of chest-thumping incantations behind wooden doors. 'We're not cowards,' said Abu Felah, a local Baath apparatchik who even then was carving out a new identity as a Shia devotee. 'It's just that the *mukhabarat* would no longer dare touch our women'.

Hitherto a Baathist neighbourhood officer, Abu Faleh, ushered me out of his sitting room with its obligatory photo of Saddam into a windowless candle-lit annex festooned with Breugelesque posters smuggled from Iran. In his adopted fantasy world, he revelled in the scenes of Shia faithful avenging writhing Sunni tyrants strapped to racks over burning coals and strung on crosses at which bowmen shot arrows. Like most of al-Thoura, he explained, he was armed. The weapons he had stashed under the floorboards would be used not to fight Saddam, or America, but to defend Baghdad's new Shia enclave.

Iraqis – so long pummelled to abstain from politics – were cajoled into taking sides. As they retreated into their separate houses of worship to beseech the Most Compassionate, the Most Merciful to spare them the ravages of war, communal tensions grew. For all the ecumenical glue of intermarriage, Iraqis spoke of the sectarian strife that Saddam's downfall would precipitate. In Arassat, the Bond Street of Baghdad, shopkeepers hired armed guards to hold back the Shia mob anticipated to surge from the slums. The wrong surname, not to mention the wrong creed, could cost one one's life. 'Tragically,' said Professor Nadhmi of Baghdad University, 'Iraqis are now afraid of each other.'[25]

Slumped in his armchair, Nadhmi typified the dilemma of many. Despite his staunch secularism, he found his family being drawn into the world of Sunni preachers. He huffed that his daughters had begun praying with clockwork regularity and that his son was attending the rabid sectarian homilies of the Salafi mosque next door. 'People are surrendering themselves to God's will because they cannot influence Saddam Hussein and they cannot stop the Americans. If you feel you are so alienated from the affairs of your country it is natural to look to the spiritual. Religion,' he quoted Marx, 'is the spirit of the spiritless world.' But even he was unable to avoid the confessional pull. After the war, he was to emerge as one of the most effective spokesmen of the Sunni opposition.

Such sectarian tendencies were tempered by the realisation that, except for the well-heeled able to flee, Baghdadis shared a common fate. Tomahawk bombs, after all, did not discriminate between Sunni and Shia. But for most, religion was the only retreat left. By early March, Iraq's six neighbours had all began battening down their hatches. Most gruelling, Jordan – which for 12 years had dined on the gift of free oil from sanctions-ravaged Iraq – turned on Iraq in its hour of need, rounding up poor Iraqi migrants and barring entry to all but the rich. 'Jordan's king used to come and beg for money. This is how he repays us,' griped the owner of a haberdashery planning his escape to Damascus. 'Seek charity not from the fatted who were hungry, but from the hungry who were fat,' he continued, quoting the seventh-century Caliph, Imam Ali.

Queues at the passport offices spilled into the streets, as frenetic families panicked at how long the bridges would continue to span the Euphrates. US bombers launched daily attacks near Iraq's western border crossings, and the BBC and the Voice of Kuwait both broadcast US military warnings of the imminent dropping of 21,000-pound 'daisy-cutters', the latter with unconcealed Schadenfreude. Father Sharbil Elias, a Chaldean monk at a monastery in Baghdad's southern suburb of Doura, said a quarter of his congregation had shuttered their homes and fled from the capital. And bus companies reported an unexpected surge of interest in the annual pilgrimage to Damascus' Shia shrine of Lady Zeinab. Cars piled high with belongings queued at petrol stations, and the nights in Baghdad's smarter quarters hummed with the leaving parties of diplomats, UN officials and the well-to-do.

Cars crammed with suitcases and children swarmed up the Euphrates to Syria, which had pledged to keep its borders open in the name of Arab solidarity, only to find a taut metal chain strung across the dustbowl of Abu Kamal crossing. Beyond, bored Syrian security guards with assault rifles looked on nonchalantly, condescending to lower the chain whenever Syrian oil workers, favoured Iraqis or those wily enough to be driving heavy industrial equipment sought to pass. Cranes, oil-tankers and even an ambulance piled with luggage were all waved across. But in the 30-metre stretch of no-man's-land between two plinths bearing the smiling portraits of dictators Saddam Hussein and Hafez al-Assad, a Baghdad family bedded down under a battered Mercedes. Iraq and Syria shared the same ruling Baath party, the same ideology of Arab unity and (bar a third Iraqi star) identical flags; and, mocked the owner of the battered Mercedes, the same interest in humanitarian affairs. Pleas to the Syrians from the UN's High Commissioner for Refugees were met with the tart reply that the border was a closed military zone.

In such troubled time, Iraq's international partners proved no less ready to wash their hands of them. The Russians, recognising the end of an era as Iraq's prime foreign backer, closed the Russian school and airlifted hundreds of workers out of Iraq. The Philippine consul, Grace Princesa-Escalante, held a farewell karaoke party. And Spanish human shields took over their empty embassy. Muhammad Nazrul Islam, the Bangladeshi representative, feared he might be left behind for want of funds to evacuate. Only the Cubans, the Vietnamese, the Angolans and the Papal Nuncio vowed to stay.

Most disturbingly, UN staff, who had profited handsomely from Iraqi oil proceeds, also heeded American orders to flee. They had nominally been in the country to administer sanctions, but Iraq had been the UN's best bankroller in its history: it was the only case in UN history where the host country funded its own humanitarian programme. From 1996 until Iraq's demise in 2003, the UN's budget was augmented by $60 billion of Iraq oil revenues routed through its agencies. Thousands of expatriate staff lived off the proceeds, procuring, administering and monitoring Iraq's supply chain, sometimes for personal gain. Miniscule agencies, such as Habitat, expanded into multi-billion-dollar concerns, and the UN in New York required Iraq to pay $1 billion a year in administration costs alone. 'We're the outsiders here; we're eating their food and receiving their money,' admitted a UN head of mission. Iraq's Information Minister, Saeed Sahaf, put it more bluntly. 'They use our money for this programme after they steal part of it,' he said. 'Many parasite employees of the United Nations, who are doing more harm than good, live off this programme.'

Fearing the regime-change would butcher their cash-cow, UN bureaucrats issued hysterical warnings against the invasion. 'If there is a conflict it will be the biggest challenge the humanitarian community has been confronted with,' said the head of the UN mission in Iraq, Ramiro

Lopes da Silva, who brewed Baghdad's best espresso. Ten million Iraqis dependent on UN rations, he predicted, could starve: 'Iraqis have no coping mechanisms. There is total exposure.' Faced with the impending catastrophe, da Silva and his entire foreign staff rushed abroad to such luxury hotels as Amman Intercontinental and Cyprus' Flamingo Beach, again at Iraq's expense. To mask the impression of a holiday camp, UN staffers abbreviated the latter – some two seas and a desert from Baghdad – to 'FBH': short, they joked, for Forward Base Hoperations.

With the country all but abandoned from outside, Iraqi stoicism, which had pulled it through so many crises, teetered. A midnight thunder-clap heralding the mid-March rains was mistaken for the start of the US apocalypse. Hyper-tense drivers collided across Baghdad and pharmacies were inundated with prescriptions for tranquillisers. Even if they attended school, teachers let alone their pupils could no longer concentrate. 'We have to keep busy, always busy,' said Souad al-Sinawi, a local staffer at the UN's Development Programme in Baghdad with an air of Mrs Tittlemouse, who, having packed up the departing head of mission's paintings, was anxious for more work to keep the war from her mind. 'Otherwise we worry about the loss of electricity, about water. We worry about how smart smart bombs are, about Iraqi tanks ploughing into our neighbourhood and turning us into military targets, and about mass-hysteria.'

To stop their human shield in the cities from further thinning, the authorities closed most of the garages inside Baghdad a week before war, reducing traffic on the desert highways to a trickle made up of those paying black-market prices. Confined to their city, Baghdadis bunkered down, hoarding canned food and bottled water marketed at ever-inflated prices. There was a rush on car batteries and candles as Baghdad prepared to be bombed back to a pre-industrial age. Some converted their bathrooms into chicken pens, to ensure a food supply when the fridges failed. Housing estates pooled resources to store sacks of flour and build outdoor bakeries. Well-diggers and water pumps became a boom industry as Iraqis dug boreholes in their basements. The Baghdad stock-market stayed bullish, but dollar rates and land-prices soared, as Iraqis rushed to exchange their Iraqi dinars for something a little longer-lasting than a note bearing the imprint of Saddam. The Iraqi dinar, worth $3 dollars before the first Gulf War, touched $0.0003 on the eve of the second.

After the last Friday prayers before war, fathers thronged in their thousands to the animal markets in the old tumbledown Jewish quarter of

Shorja. Dog-handlers did a roaring trade marketing mangy strays as guard-dogs against looters. And aviculturists peddled caged canaries as the country's only popularly available detector of chemical weapons (only regime cadres had gas masks, and few believed their profuse denials that Iraq had non-conventional weapons). In brisk afternoon trading, Abu Mustafa, a French trained ornithologist, sold 400 canaries from Iran. 'You'll know when the air turns to Chernobyl', he said with a salesman's patter, 'because canaries take just ten minutes to die'. In plusher neighbourhoods, barrow-boys went door-to-door selling the birds as $16 'pollution alarms'. Iraqis were later surprised to discover that US troops in Kuwait strapped down-market chickens to their armoured cars.

In the final lull before the storm, there was a detectable shift in the popular mood. No doubt 'shock-and-awe' warheads primed on the capital felt distinctly less liberating than the more abstract notion of regime-change had four months earlier. But perhaps it also dawned on Iraqis that the first Arab state to win its independence in the twentieth century was to be the first to lose it in the twenty-first. A resilient population that had survived sanctions to rebuild Baghdad's bridges, museums and shrines now faced the prospect 13 years on of seeing them knocked down once again. 'I hate those palaces,' said Nadhmi, the politics professor. 'But they were built by Iraqis, and when I drive past I wonder does this destruction have to be?' The news that Iraq was bulldozing its most powerful conventional weapons system, at the rate of one per hour, foretold a greater emasculation to come – not just of Saddam, but Iraq. 'We can't hit America with these weapons; we can't even hit Israel,' said a burly Iraqi engineer, who like many had turned to taxi-driving to supplement his income. 'It's simply the law of the strong versus the weak.'

The final week of Iraq's Baathist siècle witnessed a cultural blossoming, part panacea against panic, part swansong to the end of self-rule, and part knee-jerk patriotic resilience in the face of foreign invasion. The streets buzzed in the Indian summer to a thousand parties, as lovers queued on the steps of hotels to get married, lest war stymie a union. Artists staged impromptu exhibitions, audiences packed theatre halls, poets penned new *diwans*, and the Iraqi Philharmonic orchestra took to the stage with much the same dedication as the quartet that played aboard the sinking Titanic. Iraq's intelligentsia flocked to cafes to debate Voltaire and the ethics of performing the works of British playwrights at a time when their compatriots were poised to invade. 'Their missiles are not armed with the works of Shakespeare,' said playwright Kathim Nazzar, a non-conformist Shia from Saddam City – the shantytown's transformation from leftist hotbed to millennial Shia stronghold had somehow passed him by. In his final play before war, entitled *Remnants of Love*, he defied the censors by portraying post-war Iraq under American rule. In the opening scene set in a seedy nightclub, the orphaned daughter of an Iraqi soldier killed in a US attack amused coalition troops. Despite the sharply divergent responses to war of Sunni and Shia religious leaders, it was not too late to believe that enough common identity remained to keep the country together. 'When it's all over', asked Nazzar, 'what will we think we have lost?'[26]

CHAPTER 3

Cracks in the Sunni Bulwark

While Iraqis oscillated feverishly between expectations of doom and deliverance, anti-war demonstrations could be found only outside Iraq. From Casablanca to Sanaa, black flags of protest fluttered from rooftops. In Jordan demonstrators braved water-cannons and tear-gas to chant for the closure of the American, British and Kuwaiti embassies, and the expulsion of western forces. Barefoot five-year-olds baited riot police with pebbles, playing cat-and-mouse round the warren of squalid unpaved alleyways of Palestinian refugee camps circling the capital, Amman. And a 13-year-old Palestinian Joan of Arc, Mays Chalash, led the masses with the battle-cry 'Close the streets'.

Garbed in a pure white headscarf and the shoulder-wrap of a black-and-white chequered *kifaya*, Chalash epitomised the humourless grit much of the Arab youth believed was key to purifying their world of occupation. From the steps of Amman's trade union headquarters, she whipped up the anger of the crowds by wailing chromatic scales like a siren. 'The palm trees of Iraq are bowed in sadness. The sky will be black with bombers. Freedom fighters of the World arise!' A chorus of girls in the audience took up her cry: 'Go out and revolt,' they yelled at their men. Even the state's supine institutions – the press and parliament – felt roused to serve as a safety valve for the discontent. 'We wish to see less silence,' said Abdelhadi Majali, the speaker of parliament and a former head of intelligence, one of 95 notables to demand the king declare the war 'illegal'.[27] Jordan's *al-Dustour* newspaper clamoured for a 'civilian jihad against the savage aggression US and British bombers are inflicting on fraternal Iraq'.

Why did Washington's cry for dictator-toppling strike so few chords in a region groaning under the autocracies of their own mini-Saddams? Even

Jordan, the most decent of the region's dictatorships, managed an all-pervasive network of intelligence agents who vetted an entire population. Employment in sectors ranging from banking to taxi-driving required their certificate of good behaviour – *husan sir wa suluk*. Students financed their way through the kingdom's universities by filing weekly reports on their colleagues for $7 per dispatch. The best informants won scholarships, and the promise of full-time jobs in unaccountable bastions of power.

To some degree, the protests may have been orchestrated. Even regimes implacably hostile to Saddam Hussein shuddered at Washington's hubris in toppling further heads of state, and were keen to prevent the campaign rippling beyond Iraq. But the protests also tapped into a well of opposition at the foreign overthrow of the Fertile Crescent's last major Sunni power. Ever since Napoleon Bonaparte first conquered the Nile Delta in 1799, western colonial powers had chipped at more than a millennium of Sunni Muslim rule, divvying the Near East out to non-Arab or non-orthodox satraps. Thanks to their intervention, Christians had won power in Lebanon, the Jews in Palestine, the Alawites in Syria, and most recently the Kurds in their safe-haven of northern Iraq protected by a no-fly ban America, Britain and France had declared on Iraqi aircraft without UN authorisation. Now America's neo-cons (less neo-conservatives than neo-colonials) were readying Iraq for Shia rule.

Moreover, much of the Arab world hailed Saddam as the latest and by no means the least in a long line of Sunni standard-bearers. In an Arab world of vassal states, Saddam remained defiant against US hegemony (all the more so since Libya's Colonel Qaddaffi had buckled) and resilient against the enemies circling Arabism: Persians, Kurds and Jews. He was the only Arab leader to have fired a missile at Israel in the previous 30 years. And he alone shielded the Sunni Arab hinterland from its traditional foe to the east, Shia Iran.

Ever since Cyrus the Great 2,600 years earlier, Iraq's scrub plains had served as a chessboard for armies from East and West. The coming of Islam had done nothing to defuse the tensions. The Abbasids, the Buyids and, half a millennium ago, the Shia Safavids had all arrived from the East to conquer Sunni incumbents in the flood plains of the Fertile Crescent. After the longest war of the twentieth century, Saddam had succeeded in stemming the Shia advance under Ayatollah Khomeini. And now western powers and their proxies threatened to undo his work, and restore Shias to power.

In addition to the demographic majority inside Iraq, the Iraqi opposition Washington cobbled together was almost entirely drawn from the ranks of Arab Shia and Kurdish militiamen. The Pentagon's favourite group, the Iraqi National Congress, could count just two Sunnis in its senior leadership.[28] The Sunni Arabs who did defect – Saddam's director of military intelligence, Wafiq al-Samarrai, his army chief of staff, General Nizar Khazraji, and General Najib al-Salihi – were for the most part lone-rangers, lacking an organisational base. Even Adnan Pachachi, an octogenarian former Iraqi foreign minister in the 1960s who had served as advisor to the UAE president Sheikh Zayed bin Nahayan for 30 years, kept the opposition at an aristocratic arm's length.

With Sunnis seemingly marginalised in America's plans for Iraq, preachers, journalists and officials across the Sunni Arab world conjured up the spectre of Iraq as the pivot for two Shia pincers – lobster-style – to encircle the remnants of the Sunni heartlands. From Iran in the east, one axis arched west through Iraq, Syria and Lebanon. The second enveloped the world's prime oil reserves, running from the Shia-majority Azerbaijan south through Iraq's Rumaila fields to the eastern coast of Arabia, another Shia preserve. Not since Saladin overthrew the Fatimids 800 years earlier had Shiites looked so ascendant in the Sunni Arab heartland.

In a rearguard defence, the Jordanian branch of the Muslim Brotherhood, the grandfather of modern Sunni movements, vowed to resist. In statements released from party headquarters, it threatened to wage a Jihad against traces of 'the American enemy of God' in the kingdom if Washington invaded. Gunmen shot dead a senior US aid official, Lawrence Foley, on the steps of his Amman home in October 2002. And on the eve of war, a second US diplomat was wounded in a drive-by shooting on a luxury hotel hosting US marines in the capital. Fearing widespread anti-western riots, British and American embassies rushed all non-essential staff and dependents out of the kingdom. The few who remained removed their diplomatic licence plates, and draped their car-seats with Palestinian headscarves. The American embassy provided staff with smallpox jabs for fear of a biological attack.

Non-Sunnis across the region lowered their profile in the face of Sunni revanchism. Catholics in Damascus and Amman moved their rumbustious open-air Easter parades and martial drummer-boys inside church walls. Iraqi Shias exiled in Sunni states went into semi-hiding, particularly in Jordan where a pre-existent Sunni refugee population jealously guarded their rights. While Palestinians comprised 60 per cent of Jordan's 5 million people and shared citizenship, employment rights and mosques with the host population, an impoverished community of 300,000 Iraqi refugees were denied work, citizenship and a place of Shia worship. In their sermons, Muslim Brotherhood preachers derided Shias as a fifth column of anti-Saddam polytheists, and Jordanian police hunting illegal migrants stopped Iraqis with the question – Muslim or Shia? 'We don't need more pagans in this country,' explained a Jordanian border guard.

Fearing an inquisition on the eve of war, jobless Iraqis who had once crammed the pavements and cafes of downtown Amman shrunk back to their tenements on the incline beneath one of the king's many palaces. Shia émigrés who dared welcome regime-change were denounced as traitors, and their children bullied at school. 'All day long we hear Palestinians eulogising Saddam, and we can't open our mouths,' said Jamal al-Hallaq, an Iraqi Shia poet who fled Baghdad with his family after the *mukhabarat* uncovered some of his poetry. Jamal's 12-year-old daughter, Norous, was forced by her Palestinian teacher to sing songs of praise for Saddam at school, and came home in tears. 'It's all right for them,' winced Jamal's wife. 'They're not Iraqi. They don't understand that Iraqis have suffered enough.' In the kitchen, the radio broadcast a call-in with Jordanian after Jordanian clamouring for Arabs to rise in defence of Saddam.

But the bravado was not simply raw religiosity. Jordanians had much to lose from the war. Ever since the Iran–Iraq war, Jordan had served as Iraq's prime trade conduit, binding the kingdom economically as well as religiously to the Baghdad regime. Jordan depended on Saddam for its entire oil consumption of 90,000 barrels per day, mostly supplied for free or as barter with Jordanian goods. From truckers ferrying medicines to the Hashemite royals who sold the oil to their subjects at market rates, hundreds of thousands of Jordanians owed their livelihoods to Saddam. So too did Jordanian journalists, who lived in a plush housing estate built by Saddam, and students who each year won scholarships by the thousand to Iraqi universities. To many, Saddam was less tyrant than sugar-daddy.

Far from weakening the relationship between Saddam and the outside world, UN sanctions reinforced it. Banned by UN resolutions from using its oil revenues to procure home-grown produce, Iraq imported supplies through favoured Lebanese, Syrian, Jordanian and Egyptian middlemen. The son of Arab League chairman Amr Moussa, one of the invasion's staunchest opponents, ran a highly profitable business exporting pharmaceuticals and food to Baghdad. Jordan's then prime minister, Ali Abu Ragheb, engaged in a similar trade. To circumvent sanctions, Amman became Iraq's banking capital in exile, fuelling the rapid development of the desert kingdom. In mid-2002, King Abdullah cut the ribbon on Le Royale Hotel, the country's tallest building, built like a ziggurat and financed from Iraqi funds. Amongst the Iraqi government clients with Jordan's Ahali, or National Bank – owned by the family of then foreign minister, Marwan Muasher – was Iraq's military intelligence.

Fostered over three decades, the Jordanian–Iraqi economic alliance was mutually beneficial. While some Iraqi Shia businessmen in Jordan did prosper (most notably the Khawwam brothers), the network successfully eliminated those who were seen as potential threats. In 1989, Said Nabulsi, the chairman of the Central Bank and a former head of the largest Palestinian bank, the Arab Bank, successfully engineered the commercial downfall of a rival Iraqi Shia entrepreneur, who within a decade had turned his bank into the second largest in Jordan. Ahmed Chalabi had arrived in Jordan in 1977 a smart if cocky 32-year-old with a Massachusetts Institute of Technology education, bent on reviving the role his family had established as royal bankers to the Hashemites prior to the 1958 Iraqi revolution.[29] To sweeten his path with the royals – particularly King Hussein's brother, Crown Prince Hassan, who also considered himself an intellectual – he offered to return some of the Hashemites' long-lost overseas assets and established Petra, a bank named after Jordan's rose-red cave-city of antiquity. By the mid-1980s, his bank was the second largest in the kingdom, Jordan's first provider of Visa cards and ATMs, and its first bank to open a branch in the Israeli-occupied West Bank. To the fury of the kingdom's traditionally Palestinian financial community, Petra was pinching their clients and the Chalabis were rapidly establishing themselves as the Hashemites' royal bankers. The Iraqi Baath regime had also grown concerned. According to Chalabi's spokesman, Zaab Sethna, he was 'using the bank to fund opposition groups and learning a lot about illegal arms transfers to Saddam'.[30]

To attribute Chalabi's downfall to an alliance between Baathist Baghdad and Sunni Palestinian bankers would be to ignore his own malfeasance. According to a 423-page charge-sheet prepared by the Jordanian authorities, Chalabi squirrelled $219.7 million into other parts of the family empire stretching from Beirut to Washington, and spurious projects including a Jordanian shrimp farm. Creative accounting disguised the bank's $215 million deficit as a $40 million credit. Parallel investigations in Britain, Beirut and Geneva resulted in the conviction of two of his brothers in absentia for falsifying documents.

But the continuing acrimony surrounding the case suggests that personal vendettas also played a part. Fifteen years on, Nabulsi continues to wage a campaign against 'the biggest bank robber in Jordan's history'.[31] When Nabulsi failed to get a court of first instance to convict Chalabi, the case was transferred to a military tribunal, which convicted him in absentia in April 1992 of 31 charges of embezzlement and sentenced him to 22 years' hard labour. Chalabi's assets were sequestrated, and his sprawling villa in Amman's elite Abdoun hilltop was mortgaged at a discount to Nabulsi's niece. A further nine of Chalabi's relatives were sentenced. All Jordanians on the charge-sheet were acquitted.

Despite the conviction, Crown Prince Hassan retained his personal ties with Chalabi. On 5 August 1989, friends of both men say he provided the getaway car, a Saab 9000, which spirited Chalabi to Syria, two days after Nabulsi launched his investigation.[32] A relative drove the car, after locking Chalabi in the boot. And even after Chalabi began lobbying for Washington to wage war on Iraq, the Crown Prince continued his contacts. In the face of fierce Jordanian condemnation, Hassan publicly joined Chalabi on the dais of London's Chelsea Town Hall in July 2002 to support an opposition rally for regime-change. Speaking to an audience of generals, clerics and politicians, Hassan called for the restoration of the values of his great-uncle, King Faisal I – 'the father of pluralism and modern Iraq'.

For his part, King Hussein remained abidingly loyal to Saddam Hussein for almost his entire 47-year reign. Alone of Iraq's neighbours and to the delight of his people, he opposed the war to oust Saddam from Kuwait.[33] His son and successor, King Abdullah, followed suit, dismissing the ecumenical niceties of his uncle. Mindful that over 95 per cent of his subjects were Sunni, Abdullah donned the mantle of Sunni defender of the faith, and jettisoned advisors who fell foul of Jordan's Saddam lobby. On the eve of war, he dismissed and then jailed his chief of intelligence, Samih Battikhi, who was trying to break the mercantile nexus between Saddam and Amman. 'Iraq was trying to spread through Jordan, to use Jordan for their illegal imports and I was trying to do my duty to stop these activities,' Battikhi claimed in June 2003, a week before a closed military tribunal sitting in the intelligence headquarters sentenced him to eight years' imprisonment for corruption. '[Prime minister] Ali Abu Ragheb was close to the Iraqis and I was an anti-Iraq hardliner. [I was sacked] because I protested at government policy.'[34]

Washington soon realised that it would only prise the kingdom from Iraq's clutches by outbidding Saddam. The auction cost America dear. King Abdullah required funding for his costly globetrotting lifestyle, gold-leaf private jet and penchant for foreign casinos. He was also hungry to rebuild his family fortunes after his exiled stepmother – the New-York born Lisa Halaby, better known as Queen Nour – inherited much of his father's foreign estate. In a thinly disguised auction, he sent his trade minister Mohammed Bashir shuttling between Baghdad and Washington. Saddam's offer to finance free trade zones in the kingdom was matched by Washington's creation of Quasi-Industrial Zones for tariff-free export to the USA. Jordan was the first Arab state to be accorded 'favoured nation trading status' by Washington. US aid poured into the country – up from $20 million to $1 billion in a decade. By the eve of war, the tiny desert kingdom had become the third largest recipient worldwide of US foreign aid and on the eve of war the king took delivery of six American F-16 fighters.

President Bush feted King Abdullah at the White House more often than any other Arab leader, heaping praise on his reform programme despite a delay in elections; he diplomatically steered clear of any comparison between Abdullah's fondness for palaces (he had four alone in Amman) and that of Saddam, and made his kingdom the first Arab state to be accorded 'favoured trading status'. His courtiers predicted more to come. In a report entitled 'Allocating the Spoils of War', a Jordan broker and royal advisor listed the kingdom's top ten of companies best positioned to profit from US-led reconstruction. 'War-profiteering is a horrible word if people get injured or harmed by it,' said Omar Masri, manager of Atlas Investments. 'But the positives outweigh the negatives, and to get there we have to go through this bloody and terrible war.'[35]

In exchange for US beneficence, the king rented out the eastern third of his kingdom, declaring a closed military zone over a belt running in places up to 100 miles from the Iraqi border. Within its confines, American, British and Australian Special Forces in unmarked vehicles sped along Iraq's border to the Saudi border town of Arar. Huge juggernauts of US military equipment, including mobile military hospitals marked Blood Bank, plied the roads, and vast transport planes flew out of the desert fog. Shepherds in the remorseless flint plains bordering Iraq swapped their flocks for more profitable jobs building bases round the clock, after swearing an oath of silence. 'If my ruler tells me it's not tea, it's not tea,' said a goatherd as he slurped from the cup.

Fearing a public outcry, the Jordanian authorities denied they were there. 'There is not a single foreign soldier on Jordanian soil, and Jordan will not be used as a launching-pad,'[36] Marwan Muasher, the foreign minister, incanted like a mantra. A censored press dutifully agreed, and foreign journalists who questioned otherwise were threatened with expulsion. (After my name appeared on an article in the London-based *Observer* in July 2002 reporting plans for entry of some 2,400 American troops, the British Embassy in Amman invited me for tea, and advised I make a hasty exit or face deportation.)

But by the end of 2002, the disguise was wearing impossibly thin. Car rental agencies in the capital ran out of 4x4 vehicles to hire. And on a hill behind Amman University, Ali's Laundrette worked round the clock washing uniforms sporting US Air Combat crests. 'They must roll around in the desert,' complained Ali of the sand-grit he had to clean from 1,200 fatigues a day. The arrival of a reported 6,000 US troops in early 2003 was dismissed as part of pre-planned 'routine training exercises'. And when the exercises continued for months, Jordanian officials insisted they were engaged solely in the defensive task of manning three Patriot anti-missile batteries the US military had stationed in the kingdom against any elusive Iraqi warheads heading for Israel. History, it seemed, was repeating itself. Just as the British had employed the Hashemites to expel the Ottoman Empire from the Fertile Crescent during the First World War, so the Americans had hired their descendants to topple Saddam.

While the king and his courtiers profited handsomely from the U-turn, his poorer subjects fumed at the threat to their livelihoods. In the first week of the war, 55 unauthorised demonstrations erupted kingdom-wide,[37] and their ferocity increased after King Abdullah acceded to American requests to expel Iraq's diplomats. 'Ninety-five per cent of Jordanians are with Saddam,' said Mahmoud al-Baidawi, an ex-Palestinian guerrilla. 'Unfortunately, the five per cent are in power.' The Iraqi ambassador in Amman received a pledge of allegiance from the chieftain of Jordan's powerful but frequently troublesome Beni Hassan tribe. And in his last visit to Jordan, Iraq's intemperate vice-president, Taha Yassin Ramadan, warned the king that if he continued to meddle with Iraq, Iraq would meddle with Jordan. At a football match between Jordan and Iraq in Damascus, Iraqi supporters spat insults against King Abdullah, mocking the

Sandhurst-trained monarch as British not Arab. Cartoons circulating on the internet but banned in the Jordanian press showed Arab leaders as voyeurs in dardashas, standing round a table on which a soldier was raping a woman. One recorded the act on video, another reported into a microphone, a third appealed to the soldier to take it easy, a fourth pointed an accusing finger at the victim, a fifth pinned down her ankles, and a sixth was a pimp counting his profits.

In response, the king's intelligence agents tightened their hold on the realm. Some took up editorial posts at the newspapers, and the king delayed elections and ruled by decree, promulgating amongst other laws a ban on the playing of religious cassettes in buses and taxis. The measures succeeded in quashing unrest, but exposed the sham of a western war for democracy, which demanded reforms from foes but feigned not to notice the abuses of friends.

For Arab leaders, the invasion was mercifully brief. Most of their subjects spent it glued to television screens rather than protesting on the streets. Arabic news studios kept the masses hooked with wishful reports of Iraq's heroic resistance. The day Baghdad fell, Jordan's state newspaper, *al-Dustour*, emblazoned its front-page with the headline: 'Republican Guard Enter the Battle'. Sidebars reported 'Iraqi Resistance Attacks on Fao' and the downing of a British helicopter. 'I think the stand of Iraq is phenomenal,' ululated Taher Kanaan, an academic at Jordan's premier government think-tank. 'Humanity should be proud that there are such peasants who can stand up to invasion.' Few dared to report that most Iraqis longed to be rid of Saddam. For 19 nervous days, Arab capitals lost their rhythm. Cafes opened through the night, as the spectators zapped nervously between declarations of *khabar ajil* (breaking news). Iraq's surprisingly prolonged resistance at the port of Um Qasr, a few hundred metres from the Kuwaiti border, evoked whelps of delight, as did the reported downing of an AH-64 Apache south of Baghdad by a pensioner. Even the repeated albeit grainy resurrection of Iraqi television from mobile broadcasters and the plucky press conferences of Information Minister Mohammed Sahhaf was proof of Arab survival.

The shock of America's entry into Baghdad was aptly likened to the 1967 war, when Israel defeated three Arab armies and conquered Jerusalem, the Golan Heights and Sinai in six days. Rather than report the defeat, the most popular Arab network, Qatar-based al-Jazeera, focussed attention on their gentle reporter Tariq Ayoub, killed by an American missile on the rooftop of their Baghdad bureau. While thousands of Shia Iraqis rejoiced in the streets, many in the Arab world mourned. After a three-week vigil at their television sets, audiences across the Arab world returned to Qur'anic dirges. The humiliation was brilliantly captured in a bitter-sweet play, *Goodbye Saddam, Welcome Infidels*, written and performed by a Palestinian impresario, Hisham Yanis, who portrays the Iraqi leader as a Wizard of Oz with a thin waspish voice who at the first sound of gunfire runs away. 'Forgive us, Baghdad,' wrote Egyptian playwright Mohamed Salmawy, of the Arab leaders who turned their backs on Saddam's crumbling Sunni bulwark. 'For not being brave, forgive us.'

SECTION 2

UNRAVELLING IRAQ

CHAPTER 4

The Scramble for Shia Succession

Following a day of bombing on 21 March 2003, Central Command sped through southern Iraq in a standard formation that bore all the hallmarks of a classic Second World War advance. From Kuwait, the British advanced anti-clockwise to the outskirts of Basra while the Americans traced an arc clockwise through the desert to the outskirts of Najaf. Special Forces advancing from Arar in Saudi Arabia and the Jordanian border seized the key strategic airfields at H-2 and H-3. And 1,000 paratroopers airlifted to the Kurdish enclave breached a fourth front from the north. Despite some heated paramilitary resistance along the Euphrates towns, and even across the Kuwaiti border at Um Qasr port in the first week, the dust-swirls were more of an impediment to the Anglo-American advance than Iraq's depleted military.

Once the weather cleared, US forces marched on the two Shia shrine cities of Najaf and Karbala. Within a fortnight they stormed Baghdad Airport in the last major engagement of the war. Basra fell to the British on 7 April, and two days later US forces symbolically toppled the Saddam statue in Fardous Square – conveniently positioned in front of the Baghdad hotel, which housed the world's press. Further north, Kirkuk on the edge of Iraqi Kurdistan fell to US forces on 10 April, and Mosul a day later. US forces captured the last bastion of Tikrit, 100 miles north of Baghdad, on 15 April. The most militarised regime in the Arab world survived barely three weeks. So wide was the chasm in technological capabilities that, using half the assault force of its 1991 war, America had conquered 20 times as much territory.

Predictions that Baghdad might struggle on valiantly as an Arab Stalingrad proved vain cant. Much of the Republican Guard encamped round the capital abandoned its positions at the first sound of sonic bombs. Charged with defending Baghdad, Saddam's son, Qusay, hastily ordered his troops that remained into the open fields outside Baghdad, rather than wage the planned guerrilla war once US troops entered the city. Too late, the army discovered that their rocket-propelled grenades so lethal against Iranian tanks were ineffective against the armour of US tanks. Nor was their ability to fight furthered by the regime's decision to disable the anti-aircraft guns for fear the artillery would be turned on the regime itself. The results were an American pigeon shoot, as old Russian tanks lumbered into the paths of America's video-gamesters. Facing overwhelming odds, Iraqi generals ordered surviving troops to change into civilian clothes and scarper. US tanks on a foray into the capital on 5 April met scant resistance and stayed. The regime fled.

It was a remarkable achievement. Iranian leader Nader Shah had invaded Ottoman Iraq in 1743 with 375,000 troops, and even then failed to conquer Iraq's greatest cities. During the First World War, the British devoted 600,000 men, almost 100,000 casualties and two and a half years to conquer Iraq. The US-led 200,000-strong coalition (double Rumsfeld's initial preference of 80,000 but still far short of his generals' recommendations) had proved more successful, but after galloping 700 kilometres from the Kuwaiti border euphoric US forces wanted no more than to rest their feet. Ensconced in the marble luxury of the Saddam palaces their government had long-mocked, the palace beds and swimming pools proved too inviting. They had come as invaders, not nation-builders – to topple not to reconstruct. Mission accomplished, America's soldier-governors lost the initiative, impervious to the population beyond the barbed wire.

One businessman in the city later called the ease of the victory 'a trap'. Certainly, it was less complete than presented by prime-time television. As General Tommy Frank's forces galloped north, they bypassed population centres, sidestepped towns, and left ammunition dumps unguarded. A plethora of well-armed local chieftains and religious leaders stepped into the vacuum, carving out a honeycomb of strongholds from the unitary state. From Ramadi in the west to Kut in the east, America was to spend the next two years fighting the war for control of the towns that it skirted in its dash to Baghdad. 'We controlled three Iraqi cities for one month before the US forces entered them,' claimed Hadi al-Amiri, a Shia militia leader. 'The governor and police chief belonged to our organization at the time, and during our presence in these cities, no single incident of killing took place.'[38]

In Baghdad, seven days passed before the first tank rumbled into Saddam City, the capital's Shia core. In the interval between the collapse of the regime and the arrival of US forces, a jubilant population liberated their shanty-town, and renamed it Sadr City, after the two Shia clerics who had preached the fall of Saddam. Tens of thousands of Shia men, some waving palm fronds, marched through the streets publicly observing the Shia rite of the lutm, or chest-beating, for the first time in their lives. Others used their shoes to beat Saddam's icons, their knives to gouge out his eyes, and their Kalashnikovs to blast out his many mouths. US forces may have chased away the regime, but in many towns and suburbs of the capital, Iraqi rather than American forces were the first to replace it.

Even in those areas which US forces did formally occupy, they failed to control. Though obliged by Geneva Conventions to maintain security, America's 3rd Armoured Division, which took Baghdad, stood glibly by as looters trashed Iraq's national monuments. The world's greatest collection of Assyrian art at the Iraq Museum, the archives at the National Library, and the ancient manuscripts in the Library of the Religious Endowments – all fell prey to the pillagers.

US Defence Secretary Donald Rumsfeld called the ransacking 'part of the price of getting from a repressed regime to freedom'. But the mob rendered redundant the care US commanders had exercised in targeted bombing. Unlike the 1991 Gulf War, bridges, power stations and oil installations (with the exception of the K3 pumping station near Kirkuk) were all spared bombardment. Two-thirds of the 29,000 bombs US forces dropped on Iraq were guided munitions, as opposed to one-tenth in 1991. Having acquired the world's second-largest oil pool in a lightning war for a pinch, US commanders threw its victory away to the pillagers.

Much was opportunistic. Looters hurled grenades into marketplaces, pillaging stalls in the mayhem that followed. But the scale suggested that a method lay in the madness. Court-rooms and government offices were torched. Court records, title deeds, vehicle licence documents and police files turned to ash in the regime's last act of a scorched-earth policy. The doors to the intelligence headquarters remained open for days (prompting Human Rights Watch to warn of the loss of evidence to track a litany of Baathist abuses). A regime that had kept files on each of its subjects was less changed than abolished. Baghdad was rendered ungovernable.

The sole ministry protected by US troops was the elephantine oil complex, but even there the invading army only secured control once the ministry's department of research had been stripped of Iraq's strategic data about virgin fields. Beyond the building, the country's oil infrastructure was plundered, and its water injection plants, filtration units and gas compressors disabled. Hospitals, water facilities and government food warehouses were ransacked, and the UN's vacated Baghdad headquarters at the Canal Hotel was divest of its documents, including the country's entire food ration list. 'What is horribly worrying about the looting, chaos and breakdown of order is that the systems we counted on may completely disappear or collapse. It would have taken a looter with technical know-how to do that,' said a senior UN official.[39]

Basic services similarly crumpled with the regime. In a country awash with oil, queues at the petrol stations snaked for miles. Electricity blackouts created a cloak for looters to dominate the unlit nights. Even in daylight, streets ricocheted to a cackle of gunfire as if a giant colony of crickets prowled the city. Car-thieves nabbed vehicles in front of police stations. The country's state industries, employing hundreds of thousands of people, lay dormant for years. A $20 handout aside, the country's 1 million civil servants went unpaid for three months. Civil servants bothering to clock in for work had nothing on their desks, if they had desks at all. In central Baghdad's wrecked Karrada criminal court, Judge Abbas Tamimi sat on the floor of the burnt shell of his courtroom like a half-wit, staring at the ash of his previous judgments that swilled in the summer breeze around him.

For months if not years, looting was Iraq's most active economy. Four times a week Fauzia went to Basra University armed with a machete, because in the oil-rich city she needed firewood to cook for her seven children. When she had finished chopping up desks, the mother-turned-lumberjack hacked at the university's grand arbour of eucalyptus trees. 'If we had dared chop down the trees in the past, Saddam would have chopped off our heads,' she said, as she made her way home past the stumps, bent double under her bundle of branches. On a larger scale, factories were gutted, high-tension copper wires were stripped from electricity pylons by the truck-load, and million-dollar tanks were sold for scrap for $200. The trade in Iraq's obsolete industrial complex quickly found global markets. Dozens of juggernauts poured daily over the borders of Iran and Jordan, each laden with 25 tonnes of copper turbines, pipes and high-tension cables. The royal warehouses in Jordan's free-trade-zone of Zarqa were piled 20-foot high with ingots of smelted Iraqi copper and aluminium for onward sale to Dubai, Bombay and Europe. 'It makes more money than drugs,' said a delighted Jordanian dealer, who netted $10,000 a truckload. Two years after their arrival, Anglo-American forces were still blaming blackouts on looters.

Iraqi old-timers who had seen many regime changes in the republic's 45-year history derided this as the most inept. In 1958, the Free Officers had declared an immediate curfew and, after killing the king and his family, opened the cinemas the following afternoon. By contrast, the US commanders took weeks to declare a curfew and longer to institute it, and in what had hitherto been a police state, entire cities were bereft of police. Donald Rumsfeld, the US Defence Secretary, had supplied enough soldiers to take Iraq, but less than a third of the 500,000 troops the US National Security Council judged were required to enforce the peace. The British sent a mere 48 military police to protect Basra's population of 1.3 million, a sum denounced by Amnesty International as 'astonishingly insufficient'. At the gates of Saddam's palace, the new British base, a well-to-do Christian woman tearfully begged for protection from armed militias on a witch-hunt for Baathists. 'Tell her it's not our jurisdiction,' they ordered their translators, and they waved her on. For months, the vast three-square-mile arsenal at Qa-Qaa complex, 25 miles south of Baghdad, provided a ready supply of heavy weapons to fend off any law-enforcers when the Americans finally set up a police force. International monitors claimed 140 tonnes of military-grade explosive was missing. And at arms markets, grenades sold for the cost of a few falafel.

By the time Iraq's Anglo-American administrators began to apply themselves, they had no state to run. Aside from the oil ministry, it took over a year to get government departments and courts back into rudimentary service. Four months after their arrival, British troops cut the purple ribbon on Iraq's first courthouse to reopen in southern Iraq. 'But the problem is we still have no paper, tables or books to convict,' said the presiding judge, Wael Abdel Latif, who later became Basra's governor. He and his fellow judges spent the day sipping tea in the court gardens instead.

The chaos undermined confidence in American omnipotence and begged unfavourable comparisons with Saddam's success in reviving services following the 1991 war. Despite far heavier bombing, defeat and an uprising in 15 of his 18 provinces, Saddam Hussein had his civil service back at their desks and the lights on after a month. Perplexed by their incompetence,

Iraqis asked whether the Americans had come not to liberate but emasculate their state. 'We waited 35 years for freedom, and now we are sad,' wailed a British-trained doctor at Basra general hospital. 'You thought you were saving the patient. Regrettably you killed him instead.'

The implosion of central authority left a vacuum that local powerbrokers moved quickly to fill. Local militias spilled out of the Shia slums ringing Baghdad to seize key institutions and substitute the former regime. Within days of Saddam's downfall, Shia clerics took control of health centres, schools and government warehouses with a smoothness that smacked of advanced pre-war planning. Posters of past and present clerical leaders replaced Saddam's. And by the end of April, clerics controlled two-thirds of the capital's clinics, and a third of its hospitals. International aid agencies applauded the efforts of incoming clerical administrators and their accompanying guards to restore security, reopen hospitals albeit chaotically, reduce medical fees for patients and find the wherewithal to pay doctors.

The hospitals were a financial attraction. In the final years of Saddam Hussein, the health sector became self-financing through the sale of medicines and heath-care. Flouting health ministry orders to hand over revenues, the clerics turned the hospitals into key sources of fund-raising, and instruments of control. A notice pinned over the portal of Baghdad's Hindi hospital warned 'Do as the Hauza instructs, and forsake what the Hauza forbids'. Doctors questioning the clerics who took charge (after in-house elections, they claimed) said they were beaten. Sheikh Abbas al-Zubeidi, a 30-year-old theology student, underpinned his authority with a calligraphic letter of appointment from a Najaf cleric, and a loaded pistol. Ensconced in his hospital, he lectured nurses to remove make-up, don veils, and in some cases work separately from men. 'Politics should be left to the politicians, religion to the clergy, and hospitals to the doctors,' protested Dr Taweel, the Baathist director evicted from Baghdad's Alwiya maternity hospital.[40]

Religious leaders quickly established vigilantes to requisition the loot. The mosques of Sadr City heaved beneath its hoard of air-conditioners, x-ray machines and arms caches. Forecourts doubled as car parks for the purloined UN and *mukhabarat* fleet. Bank vaults were stripped of reserves to pay fresh recruits, and appropriated state property daubed with the label 'Property of the Hauza', the term for the Shia Curia. In an ammunitions plant near Najaf, clerics with blow torches reportedly broke in on the grounds they were seeking a new site for a religious seminary.[41] Overnight young Shia novices morphed into liberation theologians, ruling that all state property belonged to God and his earthly representatives – themselves. They were, explained a cleric from Karbala, Robin Hoods redistributing the wealth of the rich to the poor. 'If the state has possessions, and the state is illegitimate, then its possessions belong to the people and their representatives, the Hauza,' pronounced Sheikh Khalid al-Qathmi, whose forecourt contained three new landcruisers, two Isuzu pick-ups favoured by Saddam's *mukhabarat*, and a 23-seater Nissan bus.

After years of suppression and often closure, the *husseiniya*, or Shia prayer hall, resurfaced as the hub of communal life. Baqir Mohammed al-Basri, who unusually had graduated in both theological and secular studies, converted his *husseiniya* in Baghdad's working-class Shia neighbourhood of Topji into a quasi-municipality. He had the power supply for a nearby textile factory rerouted for domestic consumption, and a bakery that had exclusively made bread for Saddam's court re-employed to bake for the masses. In the absence of functioning traffic lights, he paid young boys to direct the traffic through the gridlock at key junctions. Within a month of the war, he offered an adult education programme for women at his *husseiniya*, and assigned acolytes to reopen Topji's 15 primary and senior schools.

Some of his actions were tinged with revenge. Mirroring America's iconic toppling of Saddam Hussein's statue in the Fardous Square, he ordered a bulldozer to topple the local statue of Saddam's predecessor, Hassan al-Bakr, who had executed his father for propagating Dawa ideology 30 years earlier. Saddam's aphorisms were whitewashed from classroom walls, his image ripped from textbooks, and the daily lesson in *Wataniya*, or nationalism, replaced with religious tuition. Local Baath apparatchiks were allowed to keep their homes, but only on condition that they handed over their guns and remained under effective house arrest. Former regime cadres accused Basri of lording over a gang of toughs, though he claimed his neighbourhood watch was armed with no more than moral authority.

Though aged only 36, Basri was at the upper end of the age bracket of Iraq's nascent theocrats. A 29-year-old, Mohammed Fartosi, ruled over the two-million-strong township of Sadr City, and made undergraduates masters of its 90 sub-districts. The township's main mosque, al-Hikma, was made his administrative headquarters, replete with a framed photo of Ayatollah Khomeini and an array of Uday Hussein's torture implements (recovered from the basement of Uday Hussein's Olympic Committee) dangling from the roof. (Amongst them was a hollow iron frame shaped to fit a man from which naked electrocution wires protruded.) Crammed into the corridors, computers and photocopiers repossessed in the name of the Hauza churned out Fartosi's latest fatwas. And, to enforce them, Fartosi instructed clerical underlings to oversee *lijan*, or committees, to enforce liquor bans, repair television masts bombed in the war and collect rubbish with a 50,000-strong force of slum-boys, whose vests were embossed with the words 'Hauza police'.

The lawlessness only played into the hands of conservatives seeking to enforce puritanical codes. While women, predominantly exiles, demanded equal inheritance rights and the abolition of Saddam's laws sanctioning honour crimes or banning travel without a male guardian, the violence had reinforced the law of the patriarchs. Fathers locked their daughters and wives indoors after a rash of reports that girls had been kidnapped from cars stuck in traffic-jams and sold into prostitution. Girls stayed back from school, men did the shopping, and wedding parties dispersed before dusk.

As the representatives of the new order, Shia clerics soon began dispensing justice and adjudicating civil disputes in their mosques. 'Punishment committees' in starched white tunics distributed leaflets advising liquor stores and cinemas to close. Sinbad Cinema, which had used liberation to screen a soft-porn film titled *Mistress Pamela* opposite a playhouse staging Imam Ali's tragedy, was firebombed. In Basra – a port whose reputation as the Venice of Iraq had been due in the 1970s as much to its risqué cosmopolitan lifestyle of Egyptian bartenders, Kuwaiti punters and South Asian samosa pedlars, as to its matrix of canals – vigilantes prowled the streets. 'They want us all to wear the hijab, dress in black, and never celebrate a wedding. I'm too afraid to go back to work. They want an Arab Iran,' said a Christian student beseeching impassive British soldiers in Basra to intervene. At universities across the south, male and female students alike were instructed to cover their skin: girls with garments; boys with beards. Basra's 400 liquor stores – the staple trade of Basra's 1,000 remaining Christian families – closed down over night following a rampage in which two bartenders were shot.

God squads also targeted senior regime cadres, Republican Guards and non-Iraqi Sunnis from the city's prime real estate. Ousted from homes bequeathed by the Baath, Palestinians found themselves back where they had begun 55 years earlier – inside Red Cross tents. 'Even outside Palestine, the Americans are seeking to engineer the expulsion of Palestinians,' fumed Palestinian consul Najah Abderrahman, before US troops raided his embassy and locked him up too.[42]

Encamped on a muddy football pitch, the Palestinian refugees were a potent symbol of Iraq's new pecking order. Under Saddam, the Arab world's Sunnis had enjoyed residency rights in a state struggling to subvert the Shia majority. Partly with an eye on their Sunni inhabitants, Saddam had tried and failed to annex Khuzestan, the predominantly Arab province of south-west Iran, in the 1980–8 war, before setting his sights on Kuwait. On the eve of war, Iraq played host to 270,000 Egyptians, as many Sudanese, and 35,000 Palestinians. Many of the latter had circumvented a formal ban on owning cars, houses or a bank account (lest they abandon the dream of return) by joining the Baath party or such security forces as the al-Quds (Jerusalem) brigades.[43] To the Shia downtrodden, Sunni expatriates were Saddam's favoured beneficiaries who helped keep him in power. 'Palestinians and Syrians are criminals who defended Saddam,' thumped a Shia cleric, as he goaded his followers to launch a pogrom through Palestinian housing estates. Yasser Arafat Boulevard – the main artery along the East Bank of Baghdad – was renamed the Imam Mahdi, and a Sudanese club opposite the Turkish embassy was sledge-hammered to rubble.

The clerics busied themselves underground as well as above it. As the regime melted away, they broke into locked doors in underpasses concealing secret prisons. Inmates emerged blinking into the sunlight from the troglodyte world beneath, crazed from hearing the world drive by a breezeblock away while the drone of car engines drowned out their cries. Days later, the same crowds reassembled armed with shovels and unearthed pit after pit of mass graves dug by bulldozers in the aftermath of the 1991 Shia uprising, and handed them over to the clerical registrar.

In a former Baath party youth club in the southern Shia town of Musayb, a woman pulled the bows on one of 475 small white nylon sacks arranged in neat rows of ten and cradled its contents. She crouched on the concrete floor, stroking the remains of a skull still tied in a blindfold and kissed the skeleton's teeth. Strewn around her were the shreds of the clothes in which her son, Jassim, had died, along with a laminated identity card recovered from the remains of a pocket. 'My only son,' she burbled. 'God bring him back.' One by one the sacks were removed, stashed in a car boot or carried home like shopping on foot.[44] Similar scenes were repeated across southern Iraq. Karbala's mass grave had been dug in broad daylight beside a roundabout in the city centre. In the town of Hilla, a half-hour's drive from Musayb, grave-diggers recovered 2,000 more of the 300,000 cadavers Human Rights Watch estimated Saddam had had buried.

Shiites, whose faith is rooted in public commemoration of 1,400 years of persecution, revelled in their release from a silence in which every Iraqi had been forced to conspire. Iraq hummed with pent-up lamentation – compensating for the years when the regime had banned public displays of grief for its executed. From slums to palm groves, the country was shrouded in black cloth etched in yellow with the names of the dead. Husseiniyas – whose walls were plastered with the photos of missing congregants – staged wakes for victims unmentioned for decades. A host of journals and pamphlets circulated the streets devoted to recording their memory. A newsletter, *Echo of Freedom*, published in Najaf, claimed 5 million dead, another clerical paper claimed 7 million. Pavement booksellers fed the lurid obsession for uncovering the past by photocopying alleged confessions of Saddam Hussein's exiled intelligence officers, sold by the chapter, or even – for those of lesser means – by the page. From Basra to Baghdad, the highways were clogged with minibuses draped in velvet, bearing the coffins of the disinterred on their roof-racks for a second burial in Najaf's Valley of Peace, the world's largest graveyard, where the resurrection is slated to begin.

Further stoking the Shia awakening, religious merchandise poured across Iraq's borders. Tabriz carpets woven with the icons of Shia saints hung from the awnings of the capital's smartest shops. Liturgy long banned by the regime arrived by the lorry-load from Beirut and Tehran. Once imprisoned in Abu Ghraib for stocking Mafatih al-Janan, a manual of Shia ritual, Mohammed al-Bazzaini, a bookseller in Karbala, adorned his counter with brightly bound volumes of Shia liturgy.

Pilgrims as well as produce streamed over the borders. Freed from the fetters and wallets of secret police that had set up travel agencies to chaperone Shia pilgrims, Iranians in their thousands flocked to the shrine cities. When worried US administrators suggested a daily quota of 500 Iranian pilgrims, Tehran proposed an upper limit of 10,000. By August, tourism was earning the Hausa, the Shia Curia, and its related hotel and tourism business $8 million a day, an income second only to oil.[45] The few public parks surrounding Baghdad's Shia shrine of Kathimiya were hidden beneath a sea of picnicking *chadors*, and the streets reverberated to the lilt of Farsi. 'Iran is reviving our economy,' pealed the owner of Abu Ali, one of a host of restaurants which opened to profit from the trade. Within three months, he was working on a $50,000 extension. The façades of Najaf and the shrine-crammed city of Karbala were shrouded in a criss-cross of scaffolding as hotels rose from the rubble.

As money and clerics poured in, the Hauza laid plans for reviving its devastated seminaries. Armies of unemployed were lured into enrolling at makeshift colleges with the promise of free accommodation and stipends for students. By the summer of 2003 clerics claimed their theological colleges in Najaf bustled with 3,000 students, up from a few dozen students following the destruction of colleges in 1980 and 1991, although far short of the 12,000 students they claimed had once studied under their arches before the 1968 Baath coup. For the first time in centuries, Shia flags fluttered over Iraq. America's overthrow of the Baath – knowingly or otherwise – was spawning a Shia renaissance.

Like much else in Iraq, the sudden whoosh of clerical people-power caught the new occupiers woefully off-guard. US troops entering Najaf shortly after two days in charge beat a hasty retreat after protestors blocked their path, accusing them of violating ground sacred to 120 million Shia Muslims. Loath to ignite an anti-US front amongst the very population supposed to rise in support, the commander of the 101 Airborne ordered his men to angle their guns at their feet, kneel briefly on the ground, and then tiptoe backwards.

The Pentagon's own strategy for dealing with clerics had focussed on parachuting an émigré priest into Najaf to serve as interlocutor. Abdel Majid al-Khoi was not a bad choice. Although resented for fleeing the 1991 Shia uprising for a more comfortable future in London, he was the son of Iraq's most respected Grand Ayatollah of the twentieth century, Abul Qasim al-Khoi. He espoused his father's quietist traditions, opposed Khomeinism, which intertwined religion and politics, and in exile had developed warm personal relations with western politicians, including UK prime minister Tony Blair. 'Even if the Americans temporarily appoint one of their generals to be president of Iraq, the Shia will be fine with that,' he proclaimed.[46] On 4 April, US forces flew Abdel Majid al-Khoi to Najaf, and left him to lay claim to the Imam Ali shrine, the St Peters of the Shia's Vatican City. Two days later he was hacked to death by a Shia mob.

It is unclear how much easier America's venture in Iraq might have proved had Khoi survived. Possibly he could have engineered the promised welcome for American forces with flowers. But as there was no understudy for his role, US plans for the Shia were scuppered by his killing, which marked the opening shot in America's struggle for the shrine cities when they had been in the country for barely a week. Fellow quietists who might have been tempted to publicly embrace American hegemony recoiled

CHAPTER 5

Foreigners Come Gobbling

The attempted putsch of the adolescent theocrats did not go entirely unchallenged. Many had no desire to replace one dictator with another, still less to be told by a turban what to watch (one widely circulated fatwa said only Indian martial arts films were permitted). 'Iraqis just need some time to have fun,' said an artist from the relaxed riverside southern town of Amara, with a whisky bottle tucked under his jumper. Even he, however, could not have paid for his whisky were it not for a rush of commissions for clerical portraits to fill the billboards formerly filled by Saddam.

Ironically, America's best allies in stemming the slide to an Islamic state were the Baathists – particularly secular Shiite ones – and the Communists. Comrades from the Workers' Communist Party of Iraq (WCP), the smallest of three Marxist factions to surface after the war, staged coming-out parades for girls who shed the veil and black shroud (*abaya*). An energetic Canadian exile and wife of the WCP's leader, Yanar Mohammed, who called herself an 'ex-Muslim', was mistress of ceremonies. On the top floor of a looted Tigris-side bank which doubled as the party headquarters she opened a refuge for bare-headed rape victims, whose numbers had surged in the wake of the lawlessness. Like the clerics, her male comrades sported beards as bushy as Marx's and believed that property belonged to the state, albeit a secular not a theocratic one.

Iraq's battle of the beards dated back 45 years. During the regime-change of 1958, Marx not the mullahs was the Shia *marjaiya*, or source of spiritual authority. And when Ayatollah Mohsen Hakim, then the Shia spiritual leader, denounced communism as heresy, 45,000 women marched through the streets for their rights. But 50 years on, the flags that fluttered over Sadr

City were black and green not red. Comrades still daubed Marxist slogans on the walls, and in fiery debates a Trotskyite proposed Molotov-cocktailing a mosque for each liquor store or cinema torched by Islamists.

Amid the anarchy, ideologues aplenty gained a voice. Without a censor, nearly 250 newspapers and magazines, 25 of them dailies, went into publication in the first year of occupation. The old aphorism 'Cairo writes, Beirut publishes and Baghdad reads' once again rang through Iraq. Over the following 12 months, a third of Iraqi households acquired satellite dishes to tune into foreign (often anti-American) channels. Within months, the Qatar-based 24-hour channel al-Jazeera was Iraq's prime source of news.

Business practice was as liberal as the press. The collapse of customs transformed the entire country into a single free-trade zone. Money-changers played havoc with the exchange rates, revelling in a world where inflation was no longer capped by the chopping of profiteers' ears. With 15 years of pent-up consumerism to unleash, moneyed Iraqis went on a shopping spree. Fridges, washing-machines, televisions, fax machines and computers piled four metres high spilled out of storerooms onto Baghdad's pavements. Dilapidated hotels with broken sewage were packed with carpet-baggers. The cost of a ten-year-old estate car slumped from $7,000 pre-war to $1,500. Impromptu auctions sprung up across Iraq trading cars any self-respecting Saudi would have dumped on the roadside. Fleets of the world's mobile detritus were shipped into Jordan's port of Aqaba and, when demand still outstripped supply, via Israel across the River Jordan to Iraq.

Dismantling the old era was not easy. For months Saddam's aphorisms lived on in school textbooks and his palaces, where the occupation forces struck camp. For over a year, the four giant busts of Saddam wearing helmets modelled on Jerusalem's Dome of the Rock loomed over the Republican Palace, which the coalition made their headquarters. Saddam's dark stencil continued to poke through the whitewash of public buildings. 'We feel Saddam is still with us, listening and lurking,' whispered a hospital orderly, fearful the walls still had ears.

But despite the backdrop of chaos and the hidden paw of the Baath, in many ways these were Iraq's best days in decades. Iraqis and foreigners travelled the country without fear of the secret police. Fishermen rowed their dinghies on the out-of-bounds stretch of the Tigris that flowed opposite the Republican Palace, hauling catches of Iraq's famed fish, *masqouf*, and lit impromptu barbecues on the banks. Hawkers peddled assortments of previously banned religious CDs alongside Thai porn. Bootleggers, freed from restrictions limiting alcohol sales to Christians, set up stalls on the roadsides, peddling beers ranging from Turkey's Efes to Israel's Goldstar. Whisky dropped to $12 a bottle. Hope in the future had yet to dissipate.

Sadly this anarchists' utopia was an open house for predators. The collapse of border controls applied as much to people as goods. Using Kurdistan as their springboard, militias swept into the Iraqi plains from their mountainous north. An estimated 50,000 Kurdish *peshmergas* ('soldiers of death') took Mosul, Kirkuk and even Tikrit, 100 kilometres from Baghdad, defying US instructions to stay out pending the arrival of US forces from Kuwait. A further 8,000-strong force of Iranian-trained and -equipped Shia exiles, known as the Badr Brigade, fanned into central Iraq. And Ahmed Chalabi's 200 fighters, known as the Iraqi Free Forces, boarded a Pentagon airlift from their Kurdish hideout to the southern city of Nasiriya, where they lost their way and had to ask the US military for directions.

As in Lebanon, the breakdown of a central authority sucked in regional powers, anxious to mitigate their rivals' suspected ambitions. Each of Iraq's neighbours adopted local proxies 'to protect', earning a foothold in Iraq. Iran campaigned for the restoration of its fellow Shia, Turkey banged the drum for the Turkomen, Syria and Jordan strengthened their ties with fellow tribesmen across the border, and even Israel looked to defend the property rights of its few dozen Jews.

After the Kurds, Iranian-backed clerics were the fastest into Iraq. Bucking US efforts to forestall his arrival, the turbanned Mohammed Baqir al-Hakim – a Shia exile some 25 years in Iran – led an armed entourage across the former killing fields of the Iran–Iraq border and arrived in Basra on 9 May to rapturous frond-waving applause. For almost a generation, Iranian leaders had worked for the moment when Hakim would re-enact Ayatollah Khomeini's historic return to Iran to spark an Islamic revolution in Iraq. Not only was he one of Khomeini's favoured students, he was the son of a highly-respected Iraqi Grand Ayatollah. In 1982, Iran's Information Ministry held a press conference for Hakim to unveil the Supreme Council for Islamic Revolution in Iraq (SCIRI), which claimed to represent the million Iraqi refugees in Iran. Twenty years on the promised revolution seemed about to transpire.

Certainly the two Shia revolutions are intertwined. The late Ayatollah Khomeini himself had spent 18 years in Iraq's Shia shrine cities – from

October 1965 until four months before the Revolution – coining his theory of Islamic government at the same time as Dawa founder, Mohammed Baqir al-Sadr. One of three leading ideologues of the Revolution, Ayatollah Mahmud al-Hashimi Shahrudi, an Iraqi cleric from Najaf, headed Iran's judiciary. But by the time the convoy had reached Najaf, the expected uprising had largely petered out, as sceptics turned their back. For many Iraqis – Sunni and Shia alike, Hakim was the Iraqi quisling of an Iranian-led Shia Internationale. Instead of following Iraq's Ayatollahs, Hakim declared Khomeini and his more controversial successor – Ayatollah Ali Khamanei – to be Wali al-Faqih, the governing jurist with jurisdiction over not just Iran, but also Shias worldwide.

In part his arrival was a reflection of Shiism's new balance of power. By the close of the Saddam-era, Iraq's Hauza was a shadow of its former self. Battered by forced exile, the destruction of many of its institutions, and the atrophy of those that survived, Najaf's collegial system had withered to a few score novices. With Najaf in Baathist quarantine, Shia communities from across the world sent their would-be clerics and political exiles for training in Iran. By the close of the Saddam-era, the Iranian city of Qom, hitherto a minor pilgrimage stop – it housed the eighth Imam's shrine – bustled with some 50,000 clerical trainees, of whom over 2,000 alone were Iraqi émigrés. Iran also reached outwards, asserting its politico-religious authority across Shia communities in the wake of Najaf's retreat. In February 1985 Hizbollah's leaders declared Lebanon a province of Khomeini's *wilaya*, or jurisdiction, obliging its Shia to 'abide by the orders of the sole, wise and just command represented by the supreme jurisconsult, who is presently incarnate in the Imam, Ayatollah Khomeini'. SCIRI's leaders also declared their allegiance, and made their armed wing, the Badr Brigades, an adjunct of the Revolutionary Guard, fighting loyally with Iran against Iraq during the Iran–Iraq war.[48] For all Najaf's historical and religious pedigree, Iran had wrested control of global Shiism.[49]

Yet, though deflated and weak, Iraqi Shias were also loath to let Khomeini's claim to be *wali al-faqih*, or rule of the supreme cleric, ride roughshod over their own intellectual tradition. After the Islamic Revolution, Khomeini refused permission to Al-Sadr, who feared Saddam's brutality, to enter Iran, belittling his authority by referring to him as Hujjat al-Islam not Ayatollah. Uncomfortable with Arabs playing second fiddle to Persians, the largest Shia clandestine group in Iraq, Dawa, split from SCIRI in the mid-1980s, prompting its leaders such as Ibrahim Jaafari to move west. Tensions increased after the Badr Brigades abandoned Iraq's Shias in the 1991 uprising, withdrawing the few auxiliaries they sent as soon as Saddam counter-attacked.

Iraqi distrust of the incoming exiles' pro-Iranian sympathies was compounded by their haughty habit – apparently acquired in Iran – of lording over the locals.[50] Many arrived back with Iranian wives and Farsi-speaking children in tow, and addressed their countrymen with a detectable Persian air of snootiness and disdain for Arab vulgarity. Native Shia who had borne the full torment of Saddam's reign while their coreligionists fled abroad had no desire to surrender their liberation to the exiles.

Tensions erupted as soon as the exiles arrived, seeking to return to their homes. Hapless returnees found their homes had long since been auctioned at below-market rates, and now were no longer vacant. In a few cases, their new incumbents conveniently fled, after SCIRI's militia issued death-threats giving them 48 hours to leave. 'The killing of Baathists is lawful,' read graffiti daubed on the houses they wished to repossess. But others without Baathist connections refused to budge. Taqi Mudarassi, who had left Karbala a 28-year-old rabble-rouser and returned a venerable 55-year-old Ayatollah, spent months angrily bedding down on the floor of a former police station. 'Thousands of exiles are returning for the summer holidays, and there will be *fitna* [or civil strife], between locals and exiles if no solution is found,' warned his spokesman, Hassan al-Furati. 'The refusal to return confiscated property might lead to violence.'[51]

Iran's clerical leadership quickly understood they would need to do more to win the support of Iraq's Shias. By the summer of 2003, truckloads of Shia paraphernalia and medical supplies were pouring over the borders. Ignored by oblivious American troops, images of Iran's Ayatollahs dominated billboards. And while America struggled to cobble together a half-hour news bulletin, Iran launched its slick 24-hour Arabic-language news station, al-Alam, beaming news of the Shia revival direct to Baghdad from across the Iranian border. Tehran also opened consulates in Iraq's Shia shrine cities, ostensibly to oversee the welfare of the thousands of pilgrims-cum-tourists who each day flocked over the border, no longer chaperoned by suspicious Baathists. And in contrast to America's much hyped but repeatedly postponed trade fair, Iran monopolised the exhibition grounds of Palestine Boulevard to stage a vast book fair replete with stylised images of Shias reaping revenge on Sunnis.

Iran's apparent expansionism jolted Iraq's other neighbours out of their torpor. Their first move was humanitarian. Jordan and Saudi Arabia set up separate military field hospitals in the Sunni outskirts of Baghdad, and the Emirates took over Uday Hussein's hospital, Olympia, and renamed it after their leader, Sheikh Zayed. Turkey, whose military presence of 2,000 troops and 40 tanks predated the war,[52] bolstered its network of 'liaison' offices. Weeks after the war, it opened a fourth in the disputed oil-rich town of Kirkuk, penetrating deeper into its former Ottoman colony than at any time since the 1920 Treaty of Sèvres. And when the Kurdish parliament passed a resolution calling on Turkey to abandon their towering garrison across the road, the Turks responded by painting the external walls of their garrison sky blue, the colour of the Iraqi Turkomen flag. Having emerged from a decade of war vanquishing its own separatist Kurds, Ankara had no desire to see Kurds carve out their own irredentist state on their southern border. To justify extending their presence, Turkish foreign minister Abdullah Gull initially argued implausibly that the 1923 Treaty of Lausanne had ceded Mosul Province – including Kirkuk – to Ataturk. Then, in the summer of 2003, he turned to the Turkomen.

Unlike the Iranians, the Turks had shown no overt concern for their kinsmen during the dark years of Saddam. When the Baath pushed the Turkomen from their ancestral lands in the 1980s, Ankara evinced only a whimper of protest. Lacking foreign support, many Turkomen quietly signed Baath party declarations that they were Arabs to prevent the Baath taking their land. But in the aftermath of the invasion, Ankara gushed with new-found affection for the defenceless Turkomen, and its newspapers called on the military to save their ethnic kinsmen from the ravages of expansionist Kurds.

By post-war standards, Kirkuk was remarkably harmonious. Some Kurds Saddam evicted had tried to return, but polyglot locals still played dominos in the cafes, musically juggling Turkomen, Kurdish and Arabic phrases in a single sentence. Into this pluralist hotchpotch, the Turkish ambassador to Baghdad, Osman Paksut, arrived in Kirkuk to propagate pan-Turkic consciousness. He patronised a local political party, the Iraqi Turkomen Front (hitherto based in Irbil), helped oust its president, Sanan Aga (who questioned the wisdom of inviting foreign troops), and sponsored a series of conferences and lectures for its members to entreat Ankara to intervene as the protector of Turkomen. In pamphlets, the Front inflated the Turkomen population from 200,000 to 3 million, hailed Kirkuk as 'their Turkomen heartland', and accused Kurdish warlords of seeking to subvert 'their natural majority'. And on repeated occasions, demonstrations against the Kurdish influx turned violent. The 'Turkish liaison force' was deployed to escort a large delegation of Turkish journalists to Kirkuk to cover the Front's General Congress in September 2003. The event merited the lead story in Turkish bulletins – conveniently replacing news of US Secretary of State Colin Powell's visit to Iraqi Kurdistan, and an impassioned speech for regional reconciliation with the Kurds.

Israel also looked to the past to justify present involvement. Prior to 1948, Baghdad had been the most populous Jewish city in the Middle East. Fifty years on, only 36 Jews remained. Most had been transferred to Israel, where they grew into a 300,000-strong community preserving the memory of a pluralist Arab world where Jews were part of the cultural and business elite. A flautist, Albert Elias, who still kept his Iraqi passport, wept on the banks of the Mediterranean when he remembered his youth in the Iraqi Symphonic Orchestra. Shmuel Moreh, a professor of Arabic Literature at Jerusalem's Hebrew University, wrote poetry about his childhood before he swore allegiance to Baghdad's underground Zionist movement with a gun in his hand. And Samir Naqqash, an author, still wrote in Arabic and called himself Iraqi despite his transfer from Baghdad to Tel Aviv 50 years earlier; after his transfer aged 12 to Israel's transit camps, or *maabarot*, he had been captured by Israel's border guards trying to return to Iraq. After the invasion, a few Jews did try to realise the dream of return, for the most part in US military uniforms.

With little Jewish living left to protect, Israel began laying claim to Iraq's 2,500-year-old Jewish past. Mordechai ben Porat, a former Israeli minister and Mossad agent who organised the airlift of Iraqi Jews to Israel in 1950, called for the protection not of people but shrines:

> There are many Torah scrolls and tombs of Jewish Prophets in Iraq, but we are afraid that many are not guarded. The [shrine of] Prophet Ezra lies deserted, and I am afraid Jonah has been surrounded by a mosque, and that Muslims are trying to adopt it. The Muslims even want to share the Prophet Ezekiel with the Jews, but I don't know if I want to share him with another religion. If we could send guards to Iraq, we would have the power to say this is not yours, it is ours.[53]

Focussing on less ancient property, the coalition also employed Carole Basri, a New York lawyer and scion of a former head of Baghdad's Jewish community, who had written extensively on compensation for Iraqi Jews. She was entrusted with drafting a charter for a commission to process pre-invasion property claims from Iraqis expelled or forcibly displaced by the state.

Jordan also had its historical reference to press claims. Its Hashemite royal household harked back to an era after the collapse of the Ottoman Empire when it was the leading local power. Backed by British intelligence, King Abdullah's great-uncle had led the Arab Revolt in 1916 against the Ottoman yoke and briefly wrested control of five of the Middle East's great cities. Their conquest had not lasted long. The Hashemites managed to lose Damascus in 1918, Mecca and Medina in 1926, Baghdad in 1958 and Jerusalem in 1967, but memory of their brief dominion survived in their only remaining royal court atop the windy mountains of Amman.

Of all five, perhaps Baghdad – the seat of their forefathers the Abbasids – held the greatest lure. Under the terms of the Arab Union that had joined the Hashemite kingdoms of Jordan and Iraq prior to the 1958 coup, explained a Hashemite prince, the Jordanian monarch was the rightful heir to the throne of Iraq.[54] Their ambitions were variously nourished by such Iraqi opposition leaders as Ahmed Chalabi and Iyad Allawi, who were offspring of the Hashemite court in Iraq. Other courtiers touted a vision of Jordan – a geographical misfit – inflated into a powerful state controlling the world's second largest oil reserves. The aspiration was not without its Iraqi sympathisers. As the first rulers of modern independent Iraq, the Hashemites claimed a track record both for liberating Iraq from the clutches of western colonialism, and for presiding over three decades of political freedom relative to the dictatorships that followed. Moreover, a Sunni dynasty that traced its lineage to the House of the Prophet, beloved of the Shia, could help straddle Iraq's sectarian divide.

But the Jordanians were deluding themselves if they believed they could restore the Hashemite throne. After half a century as a republic, few Iraqis aspired to live in a feudal monarchy led by a foreigner. For many, particularly the Kurds, the Hashemites were remembered less as benign despots than as British protégés who had sanctioned the British aerial bombardment of Kurdish towns with poisoned gas.[55] In addition, the Hashemites were bitterly divided over the nomination for heir apparent. Having competed for the Jordanian throne in 1999, Prince Hassan bin Talal and King Abdullah both sought to deprive the other of the more powerful realm of Iraq. When Hassan began to promote his claim on US networks, his satellite uplink was mysteriously cut in mid-speech. And when Hassan joined Chalabi in London, he was publicly disowned by the state media controlled by the king. 'All Jordan's propaganda against Chalabi is not against Chalabi. It's against Hassan,' said Khalid al-Shammari, an exiled Iraqi businessman who advised Hassan on Iraqi affairs. 'The [royal] court is deliberately trying to undermine Hassan's integrity.'[56] (Chalabi, never one to shy from a fight, responded to King Abdullah's attacks by threatening to disclose photographic evidence of him and Uday Hussein frolicking with prostitutes.[57])

Initially, Abdullah backed a stalking but docile horse, Prince Raad bin Zeid, to test the depth of support for the monarchy. A survivor of the 1958 Revolution, Raad was a soft-hearted 67-year-old aristocrat, who still bore the title 'Head of the Royal House of Iraq'. His genteel manner could not have been less suited to Iraq's bloodthirsty politics. He spent much of the day tending his lupins in a garden more befitting a Shropshire village than the rocky steeps of Amman. For a would-be king, he was unhappily lacking in pomp and majesty. 'I hate the word I,' he said effacingly. He argued for the restoration of Arab kings not just in Iraq, but also in Egypt, Syria and Libya on the grounds of human rights. 'The abolition of the monarchy was a big, big mistake,' he said. 'I've witnessed 40 years of so-called republicanism, and all we've ended up with is dictatorship.' He had a royal disregard for political correctness that sadly put him out of touch with his constituents. He touted Iraqi recognition of Israel, and the reopening of the pipeline running from Mosul via Jordan to the Israeli port of Haifa. He added that he hoped to invite former Israeli defence minister Yitzhak Mordechai back to his Iraqi homeland.

Abdullah soon jettisoned Raad's bumbling to stake his own claim. The royal court took charge of the country's 300,000 Iraqi exiles, sending agents to émigré cafes, and offering a fast track for residence visas to those who signed up to their cause. And to heighten awareness of the Hashemite heritage, new bank notes were issued depicting the torsos of the five generations of Hashemite monarchs dressed in traditional finery. Then, on a balmy mid-May afternoon, he flew his helicopter down to the sands of Humayma, a rose-red mountain hideout 230 kilometres south of his capital. The scarp had twice been used by Abdullah's forefathers to rally troops for an assault on Baghdad, said his courtiers: first by the Abbasids in the eighth century, inaugurating a Caliphate that lasted five centuries; and again in 1916, when Faisal and Lawrence of Arabia had marshalled the Bedouin into the Arab Legion on their way to conquer Iraq. The third attempt had similar props. Travelling the last few hundred metres atop the rocking hump of a camel, Abdullah trotted into an encampment to cheers from 4,000 tribesmen assembled on carpets beneath camel-hair canopies laid out in the scrub. 'Since Mecca through the Abbasids to today, the Hashemites have changed the course of history,' a sheikh of the Beni Attiya tribe bellowed through the sound system. The Bedouin dutifully cheered – mindful perhaps of the 16 royal bodyguards who suspiciously rotated their guns at the crowd – and were then rewarded with *muncef*, a traditional Jordanian feast of sheep heads doused in goat's milk, as the entourage trotted off on its camels. 'Our plan is for the Hashemites to again be the monarchs of Hijaz [Western Arabia], Jerusalem, Syria and Iraq,' confided a Jordanian prince on the helicopter back to Amman. In the weeks that followed, tribal delegations were summoned from Iraq to Amman to discuss plans for an oath of royal allegiance. King Abdullah called for an Iraqi referendum on restoring the monarchy and began dipping into $1.5 billion of frozen Iraqi government bank deposits as if they were his own.[58]

Other Jordanians were more self-sacrificing – literally. With all the passion of 1930s European ideologues volunteering for the frontlines in the Spanish Civil War, young men crammed the buses and sports-utility cars (managed by Uday's company, al-Dhilal, or Shadows), and flocked eastwards to save Iraq from the predations of America – and the Shia. With the exception of Egypt, which formally closed its land borders, most Arab states responded with the same indifference they had shown their troublesome Islamists departing for the Afghan Jihad 20 years earlier. 'We cannot prevent people from choosing to commit suicide,' sneered Jordan's information minister, Mohammed Adwan.[59]

Islamist and Baathist movements from Syria to Algeria helped enlist the foreign legion. A month before the invasion, Jordan's Committee for the Defence of Iraq, a Baathist solidarity organisation, claimed to have compiled a register of 17,000 volunteers for the defence of Baghdad. Iraq's embassy in Amman was crammed with visa applicants. While the UN (wrongly) predicted a mass refugee crisis, most of the traffic was in the opposite direction. 'British troops are supporting America, why shouldn't Jordanians and Palestinians support Iraq?' said Rafiq, a 34-year-old veteran of the Palestinian Intifada who had spent a year recuperating at his uncle's in Amman. 'We'll make the USA regret their entry into Iraq, as much as they regretted Vietnam.'

Only a fraction of the thousands of Arab volunteers who signed up to defend Iraq against the Anglo-American invasion were hardened Jihadis, and many went home as soon as the regime collapsed. But the absence of controls at the border and order in Iraq ensured that migration of subsequent recruits went largely unchecked. A harder core of Arab Jihadis fleeing America's war in Afghanistan in 2002 travelled through Iran and found refuge in the isolated mountains straddling borders of Iran and Iraqi Kurdistan. By September 2003, the UN's Security Office in Baghdad was reporting the citing of 'groups of foreigner Taliban' further south, 'hiding among the local inhabitants in the region of Ramadi, Falluja and in certain quarters of Baghdad'.[60] In Washington, officials had finally found the link – albeit *post invasion* – that connected their war on Iraq to that on al-Qaeda. 'Foreign jihadists have arrived across Iraq's borders in small groups with the goal of installing a Taliban-like regime,' said President Bush.[61] In the global battle for Iraqi hearts and minds, America – tucked in Saddam's palaces – was almost nowhere to be seen.

CHAPTER 6

The American Shah of Iraq

Ever since the Prophet Isaiah first called on his followers to make 'straight a way' for Persia's Cyrus the Great to topple Nebuchadnezzar in 536 BCE, propagandists have hailed Iraq's conquerors as liberators. Fifteen times Baghdad was occupied by foreign armies, each entering with the same promise. In 1917 the British Major General Stanley Maude unveiled his march into Baghdad with leaflets promising release from the Ottoman yoke:

> Our armies do not come into your cities and lands as conquerors or enemies, but as liberators... Your citizens have been subject to the tyranny of strangers... and your fathers and yourselves have groaned in bondage. Your sons have been carried off to wars not of your seeking; your wealth has been stripped from you by unjust men and squandered in different places.

His troops stayed for the next 40 years.

Perhaps Iraq should have learnt from experience. Instead they again opened their gates with as much incredulity and faith in the American mission as the Berbers who heard America's Second World War broadcasts as they set foot on Moroccan soil: 'Behold we, the American holy warriors have arrived. We have come to set you free.'[62] While opposition to the invasion in the West focussed on the weapons of mass deception that Western leaders deployed to win backing for the war, Iraqis were far more perturbed by the coalition's broken promise of liberation. Just as in the occupation of 1917, Iraqis had been promised liberation only to fall under the mandate of the Great Power of the day, Britain.

By the summer of 2003, the invading coalition seemed just one of the many new bounty-hunters grasping for the spoils of Iraq. Anglo-American forces appropriated the country's best real estate, declaring state property from palaces to hospitals no-go areas for Iraqis. Baghdad's presidential complex – Saddam's forbidden city within a city, which occupied a four-square-mile enclave on the west bank of the Tigris – was turned into coalition headquarters, or in military parlance the Green Zone, and expanded. Military commanders who weeks earlier had scorned Saddam Hussein's 72 gold-plated palaces, Louis XIV furniture and private swimming pools now delighted in them. Saddam's throne-room became the coalition synagogue and chapel. US commanders struck camp in a further 40 sites across the capital, ranging from the Tigris-side Officer Clubs to Baghdad College, Iraq's Eton. Patients in al-Wasiti hospital's newly renovated wing were displaced to the lobby. The Basra palace, derided two months earlier as 'more extensive and sophisticated than Versailles, filled with exotic flowers and shrubs', became the British residence. In the North, General David Petraeus commandeered Mosul's palace on the banks of the Tigris crafted in opulent marble and teakwood, for which the city's masons and carpenters are famed. In Karbala and Najaf, the US army requisitioned the town's universities, and in Diwaniya nearby the medical school. Two years after the invasion, it was still a closed military base.

But of an administration there was scarcely a sign at all. The fledgling civil service the Pentagon had cobbled together sauntered into Baghdad almost two weeks behind the rest of the army, seemingly disappointed to have been finally forced from their luxury chalets in Kuwait's beachside Hilton. Its head, Jay Garner, was a retired 65-year-old general and arms-dealer who, according to his advisor Zalmay Khalilzad, had 'no interest, absolutely no interest, in ruling Iraq'[63] and seemed almost as keen as his chief-of-staff, Tommy Franks, to get home. He had an abhorrence of direct occupation, meekly naming his team the Organization for Reconstruction and Humanitarian Assistance, or ORHA, pronounced by Iraqis like the braying of an ass.

Given the immensity of the problem they faced, his team was woefully ill-equipped. His senior advisors had barely a satellite phone or email connection between them.[64] Their authority seemed to stop at the barbed wire of the palace enclosure, and even there they apparently had no idea who anyone was, so that journalists could wander in and out of their meetings. Beyond the perimeter razor wire, huge queues for petrol snaked round the capital, and looters roamed free. Garner's cultural advisor, the US ambassador to Mauritania, John Limbert, threw up his hands in horror at the looters at the National Museum pillaging the world's finest Assyrian artefacts – from the safety of his palace. With the promised showpiece of the new Middle East overrun with marauders and bandits, Iraqis asked where the superpower was.

One way to get Iraq back on its feet might have been to seek outside advice. In a country suckled for 35 years on state provision of basic services from electricity to food, the UN's expertise, though blemished, was unmatched. It had seven years' experience running Iraq's supply-side economy. But so determined was the White House to monopolise power, it even overruled a US Department of Justice request for international police. 'The UN can be an important partner,' said Deputy Defence Secretary Paul Wolfowitz, 'but it can't be the managing partner.'[65] Washington's neo-cons had not sent an army half way round the world to hand power to the same world body that had proved so vociferously anti-war. Nor did the politicians, punch-drunk on victory, understand the extent of the unfolding chaos. To the contrary, the ease of America's march into Baghdad had duped Washington into a sense of invincibility that considered the country a bit of a pushover. 'Regrettably, we fell victim to the ease with which the military campaign was conducted,' said Isam al-Khafaji, an exiled Iraqi economics professor the coalition hired to advise on reconstructing Iraq. 'Because of this and because of the euphoric mood after the fall of Saddam Hussein, the Americans thought: what's the need for Iraqis? We can do it on our own.'[66]

The night Jay Garner arrived in Baghdad, the White House took the decision to jettison him and his plans for indirect US authority facilitating a new Iraqi government, and opt for direct American rule. In came the neo-cons led by Paul Bremer III, a former head of the US counter-terrorism department. Like President Bush, Bremer was a graduate of Harvard Business School, and from a young age preferred to be known by his saintly middle name, Jerome, which he shortened to Jerry. He had the air of a man on a divine mission, who brooked no apostasy. After a bombing of the US barracks in Saudi Arabia in 1996, he publicly advised President Clinton to threaten Libya, Sudan, Iran and Syria with military action within a week.[67] He landed in Baghdad on 12 May 2003 with the aspirations of a Napoleon Bonaparte, determined to make Iraq the crucible for a new Middle East.

Initially, Iraqi insiders welcomed the decision to fill the vacuum. 'At least we knew who was in charge,' said Adnan Pachachi, a former Iraqi foreign minister who arrived in Baghdad from exile in search of a political role.[68] But Bremer's arrival signalled the transition from American liberation to occupation. Where Garner focussed on civilian needs, Bremer was security-orientated. Where Garner had spoken of a handover to Iraq starting within 120 days, Bremer declared indefinite American rule. And where the former had signalled his preference for leaving the regime largely intact, the latter promised a total overhaul of the state. Out went ORHA, and in came the more authoritative Coalition Provisional Administration. By the end of his first week he had purged his civilian staff of Garner and his advisors. Out went a State Department team of 140 Iraqis, called the Democratic Principles Working Group, which had spent months in Washington devising a plan for Iraq's reconstruction, and in came the Pentagon mandarins. 'There seemed to be no interest on the part of the coalition in involving Iraqis as advisers on the future of their nation,' said one of the Group's members, Professor Isam al-Khafaji, who resigned.[69]

Where Garner was consensual, Bremer was regimental and disciplinarian. Aged 61 with the appearance of a forty-something, he began his day with a 5 a.m. run, and went to the office in army boots. He demanded the same dedication of his 600-strong staff, a motley crew drawn from the ranks of Chicago police officers, Milwaukee students, mortgage brokers, defence lawyers and sales representatives all cobbled into Iraq's new civil service. Most had no knowledge of Arabic, and some had never set foot outside America. With the power of ministers overseeing vast projects by day, they lived as undergraduates at Baghdad High by night, drinking by the palace pool, cavorting on the palace roof, and retiring to sleep in the palace ballroom, which filled with bunk-beds became the unisex college dorm.

From the first Bremer ruled as a sovereign, decreeing with fiats which began with the phrase 'I hereby promulgate...'. In 13 months in the job, he issued 100 orders, 17 memoranda, 12 public notices and 12 regulations, as if good laws alone produced good societies. 'We as Americans like to put our template on things,' noted Garner, in a barbed interview after his departure, 'and our template's good, but it's not necessarily good for everyone else.'[70]

Of Bremer's 23 years as a career diplomat, none had been spent in the Arab world, and the little he knew of Arabs was largely as terrorists. Local culture was tolerated for the sake of public relations, but considered an inconvenience. Bremer distrusted America's State Department Arabists, and insisted on holding his weekly press conferences at dusk during Ramadan, despite the absence of Iraqi journalists breaking their fast. The Wild West names the coalition gave its bases suggested Iraqis were seen as Red Indians: Camp Headhunter, Camp Warhorse, Camp Gunslinger and Camp Steel Dragon.

If there was a foreign yardstick by which Bremer judged Iraq, it was America's previous colonial experience. He saw himself walking in the footsteps of two American architects of post-war reconstruction – General Douglas MacArthur, the 'American Caesar' of Japan, and John McCloy, the US High Commissioner in Germany. He kept a dateline of their decisions in his breast-pocket, against which he was obsessively comparing his performance. He repeatedly likened pre-war Iraq to Nazi Germany,[71] and considered the US blueprint for dismantling Hitler's regime – the three Ds of DeNazification, Demilitarisation and Delayed-democracy – an appropriate formula for Iraq.

Order No. 1 – 'the De-Baathification of Iraqi Society' promulgated four days after he arrived in Baghdad – mirrors minutely the Allied Control Council's Proclamation No. 2 – annulling the Nazi party, dismissing Nazi personnel, seizing Nazi property and funds and suppressing Nazi ideology. His second order, issued ten days later, demilitarising Iraq bears a striking resemblance to the Allied 'Dissolution of Entities', which abolished 'all German… military and quasi-military organisations'. With a stroke of a pen, he dissolved Iraq's armed forces, border guard, police, intelligence and National Olympic Committee, and its Ministries of Defence and Munitions. In May he declared a seven-point plan for political reconstruction in which America would continue to rule Iraq – as it had Germany and Japan – until it had implanted a democratic constitution and free elections. He offered no timeframe, but observers noted that in both Germany and Japan, US occupation had lasted seven years.

Iraqis were shell-shocked. Only two weeks earlier on May Day 2003, President Bush had stood aboard the flight-deck of the USS *Abraham Lincoln* anchored just off America's West coast and declared Washington would not treat Iraqis like defeated Germans. 'Military power [then] was used to end a regime by breaking a nation,' he said. 'Today we have the greater power to free a nation by breaking a dangerous and aggressive regime.'[72] Moreover, unlike Germans, Iraqis had not been defeated, but rather complicit allies in the toppling of Saddam. The war had lasted 19 days, not 2,174, the death-toll had averaged 200 a day, not 27,000, and there was no Iraqi surrender. Crucially, unlike post-war Germany, America also lacked the manpower to manage Iraq, let alone effect the sweeping changes it decreed. But in treating Baghdad as Berlin, Bremer transformed the bilateral relationship from one of partnership to one of colonial master against colonised capitulated servant. In his takeover of Iraq, Bremer alienated millions, and made armed resistance inevitable.

It is hard to underestimate the damage Bremer's application of strategies from the Second World War did to US support in Iraq. Before the war, no Iraqi had really anticipated that the Americans would have the arrogance to attempt to run the country without the skeleton of the existing regime. 'How are they going to run the country alone?' asked an information ministry minder, adding apologetically 'We had to be Baathists'. The initial decision by US commanders to limit their formal manhunt to the 55 most senior members of Saddam's inner circle – the pack of cards – seemed to confirm that assumption. Bremer's decision to opt for wholesale exorcism of the Baath made enemies of hundreds of thousands. Under his anti-Baath edicts – translated brutally into Arabic as *ijtithath al-baath*, uprooting the Baath – all party members exposed in the top three tiers of all government departments and all 35,000 members of the upper four echelons of the Baath were dismissed without pay. Appeals could be made to an Accreditation Review Committee run first by US military intelligence officers and then Iraqi exiles, who employed McCarthyite techniques of interrogation. Baathists simply stopped turning up for work.

America's purge of Baathists in Iraq was never as widespread as that of Nazis in post-war Germany, and was to prove far more short-lived. In Germany, US commanders dismissed 375,000 civil servants. In Iraq, less than a tenth that number lost their jobs. Nor did Bremer, unlike his predecessor in Germany, order the detention of all party members without trial. In addition, the policy had mass appeal amongst Shia religious factions who considered Baathism heresy, and the tens of thousands of state employees – such as teachers, previously sacked for 'poisoning minds' – who hoped to be reinstated. Doctors staged internal elections to unseat their hospital managers, and oil refinery workers held demonstrations to denounce their bosses as Baathists. The purge undoubtedly removed many officials most intractably opposed to working in post-Saddam order. Arguably, de-Baathification also helped defuse tensions that were turning violent. Mobs formed by Shia militias had taken the law into their own hands, lynching alleged lackeys of the former regime. Most were soft targets: a surfeit of academics and a saccharine TV pop-star who sung odes to Saddam were all killed outside their homes.

But second only to looting, the messy inquisition filleted the Iraqi state, which the war had left largely intact. It cast out a whole swathe of technocrats – travellers with the regime – who had bandaged the country together after the 1991 war and were experts in rebuilding Iraq. The decision to expel 1,200 senior managers and engineers from the oil ministry severely set back plans to rehabilitate the energy sector. And instead of being emasculated, the Baath party, which had been all but defunct, found itself reinvigorated as ousted revengeful employees rushed to advise the resistance on how best to sabotage the state. Former phonetappers in the Communications Ministry found work as taxi-drivers by day and clandestine couriers by night. Ex-employees of the oil ministry advised on which pipelines were most vulnerable.

The deBaathifiers purged not just people, but also books. A 60-person Coalition committee expurgated textbooks for paeans to and drawings of the Great Educator, Saddam Hussein, who had hailed children 'his radioactive agents'. So many Baathist references were removed that the censors feared there would be no textbook left. The course on National Identity, or *Wataniya* – in which Persian war-mongers stood accused of conspiring against Iraq from Nebuchadnezzar via the Classical Abbasid Caliphs to Saddam – was eliminated altogether. Belatedly, the Coalition commissioned the UN's child agency, UNICEF, to print some 70 million new textbooks with blank pages pruned by the committee, but they were not delivered in time. On the children's first day at school under American rule, Saddam still reigned in their books.[73]

Bremer compounded his mass sacking of Baathists by dissolving the country's largest employer – the security apparatus. The battalions of oil-police that had protected the pipelines were disbanded and their fields abandoned first to looters and then saboteurs. With another pen-stroke, Iraq's entire military-industrial complex was abolished, and its accompanying workforce, from doctors in military hospitals to blue-collar workers in munitions factories, dismissed. The army's hardware was similarly discarded in the desert as scrap. Metal-merchants scavenged the dozens of acres where the US dumped dissected tanks and fighter-jet engines, on which Saddam had lavished his oil billions, for highly-prized magnesium, copper and lead. 'We are turning swords into ploughshares,' claimed Mahmoud, a spotlessly dressed Indian from the Bohara Shia sect, who made a handsome profit shipping ores back to Gujarat.

US mandarins hailed the demilitarisation as an essential step on Iraq's transition to a model civilian state. Conscription, the bane of Iraqis for decades, was abolished, and the military removed from the circles of power. But in a country with an unemployment rate touching 40 per cent, the social consequences were devastating. All told, some 750,000 men lost their jobs. They were entitled to pensions of first $20 and later $60 a month, but claimants had to queue in lines a mile long in the Baghdad heat, a harsh and humiliating deterrent. As much as an economic catastrophe, the emasculation struck at the heart of the country's psyche. Nothing more symbolised Iraq's descent from a sovereign to an occupied state than the sound and sight of US military might rolling through the streets, while Iraq's armour rusted in the desert. For better or worse, the army had been the backbone of Iraqi society for at least half a century. Iraqis, reared on the belief they were the fourth largest fighting force in the world, felt castrated.

Dissolution of the military rendered Iraq dependent on inadequate American might for law and order, which Iraqis suspected was intended to delay a withdrawal. 'Why can't they bring back the traffic wardens? Are they also war criminals?' asked Professor Wamidh Nadhmi, who spent months in post-war depression. [74] In Jay Garner's words, the result was the creation of '400,000 new enemies'.[75] Without any formal process for rehabilitation or retraining, defrocked soldiers flocked to the resistance. Externally, the removal of border controls allowed Jihadis ready access throughout Iraq. The coalition assigned just nine Dutch soldiers to patrol the entire southern border between Jordan and Kuwait, and all but one of 14 pre-war border-crossings was left unmanned. Local Bedouin shepherds were able to smuggle their contraband on the backs of sheep into Saudi Arabia. Arms and drugs dealers disguised as pilgrims flooded into Samawa, a traditional caravan stop to Saudi Arabia (where the Dutch soldiers were based), and in its back streets, children popped acid pills.

Subsequently, US officials defended their decision to disband Iraq's army on the grounds that it had simply melted away. But unlike other state institutions that abandoned the regime in its final days, the Americans never had it recalled. Iraq's generals – not disingenuously – argued that the orders for their troops to scarper were proof of their readiness to work with America. And a year later, when fighting erupted in Sunni towns such as

Falluja, US forces discovered how difficult the conquest of urban centres could prove when Iraq's fighters did stand their ground. 'We opened Iraq's gates to the advancing US forces. We were their best asset during the war,' argued a general from Iraq's Special Republican Guard.[76] A rare Pentagon insider agreed: 'We spent a lot of money on psychological operations that urged the Iraqi army to remain out of the fight. They did, and what did we do? Rewarded them by throwing them out of work and denying them a living.'[77]

Even more than deBaathification and demilitarisation, Bremer's third D – delaying democracy – irreparably destroyed his credibility with Iraqis. Left to run the provinces under Garner, US field commanders sought to fulfil President Bush's declared dream for Iraq by organising elections. Days after President Bush's 1 May speech on the USS *Abraham Lincoln,* promising to help Iraq make 'the transition from dictatorship to democracy... and establish a government of, by and for the Iraqi people', the local marine commander, Lieutenant Colonel Christopher Conlin, went on local television to declare 5 June the date for local elections. Marines became the vanguard of America's democracy mission, hammering together makeshift wooden ballot boxes, printing registration cards and identifying polling stations. Lawyers and teachers claiming the backing of Najaf's clergy printed leaflets declaring themselves candidates of Iraq's first free elections in decades.

Six days before the vote, Bremer cancelled the polls. Summoning the candidates, a sheepish young captain assisted by a Lebanese-American translator explained there were problems with the size of the registration card, and it would take a further two months to print the cards. The voter lists, he added, would also need to be vetted. Outraged, the candidates pressed for a date, only to be told that the elections had been suspended indefinitely. 'Paul Bremer first wanted to make the country more stable before elections take place,' pleaded Major David Toth, and as the candidates began overturning their chairs and cursing the Great Satan's machinations, added 'we find that rather insulting'. He and his fellow marines were left preaching to an empty room. 'When we're working so hard for Iraqis and they speak against us, we just don't understand,' he confided. 'Being a parent isn't easy. Sometimes you have to correct your children even when you know it's tough love.'[78]

Viewed from Washington, the decision was perhaps understandable. Having lavished billions of dollars conquering Iraq, Washington shrank from transferring the country unconditionally to the representatives of

Ayatollahs who looked every inch like the leaders of Iran's Islamic Revolution. 'Elections that are held too early can be destructive. It's got to be done very carefully,' explained Bremer. 'In a post-war situation like this, if you start holding elections, ...it's often the best-organized who win, and the best-organized right now are the former Baathists and to some extent the Islamists.'[79]

Viewed from Iraq, it looked as if history was repeating itself. Just as European powers in the late nineteenth century had used the cry for the emancipation of slaves to wrest control of the raw materials of the non-white world, so too America had raised the banner of democracy over oil-rich Iraq. As their European antecedents, once in charge they appeared to rediscover the virtues of authoritarian rule and the shortcomings of democracy amongst the natives. Britain's administration following the First World War, which had justified its Iraq takeover as liberation, rigged the only elections held under their rule, awarding King Faisal 96 per cent of the vote in 1921. Moreover, the US suspension was not just inept, but critically short-sighted. None of the candidates standing in the Najaf elections were clerics. They were a motley crew of middle-class lawyers, teachers and merchants who could have provided a grassroots leadership indebted to American forces. Instead, the enthusiasm morphed into anger and demonstrations.

Similar scenes were repeated across Iraq. Plans for elections in Samara were derailed, and a host of self-appointed local mayors removed from office, including Baghdad's, Mohsen al-Zubaidi, who was arrested and charged with attempting to raid the Central Bank. In Mosul, General Petraeus ousted Mishaan al-Jibouri, a rich tribal leader and pro-Syrian Baathist, under whose brief tenure not a single US soldier was killed. The British in Basra ousted another self-appointed governor, Sheikh Muazam al-Tamimi, and appointed Brigadier Adrian Bradshaw, the British commander of the 7th Armoured Division – the famed Desert Rats of the Second World War – in his stead. 'They'll be taking orders from us,' said Ole Wohlers Olsen, a Dane who was Bremer's representative in the city. '[Bremer would] rather have a confrontation now than later. He was quite strict. He wants them out.'[80] Brigadier Bradshaw dismissed elections as a time-wasting distraction to 'getting utilities up and running', but proposed establishing a 'non-political civil forum' at some later date. Garbed in army-issue shorts, the British military lawyer, Colonel Nicholas Mercer, insisted he was civilising the natives by banning the beating of wives[81] (prompting

Amnesty International to protest that as the occupying power Britain was violating international law by altering sovereign law).

On 31 May, two days after a visit to Basra by British prime minister Tony Blair lasting long enough for him to hug photogenic children at a school adjoining a British base, the city erupted in protest. The people of Basra, Blair had told British troops, would 'remember what you did as the start of their future and a life of hope and the possibility of prosperity'.[82] Instead, 10,000 took to the streets chanting 'No to British rule over Basra' and 'We can rule ourselves'. Instead of Anglo-American rule, the organisers issued an appeal to 'all Iraqi political forces to quickly hold a conference under UN sponsorship' to determine Iraq's future.

It was soon apparent that the suspension of democracy was part of a nationwide plan. Four days after arriving in Baghdad, Bremer announced that his predecessor's plans for a national convention and a provisional Iraqi government under UN auspices had been scrapped. Sovereignty, he said, would only come at the end of a seven-stage handover of undetermined duration. To Iraqis, the language echoed that of other Middle Eastern autocrats who mouthed commitments to democratisation, but insisted security came first. Even America's pre-packaged coterie of exiles was indignant. 'The idea that for a year or more there will be no Iraqi state, no Iraqi sovereignty, is wrong,' protested the patrician Adnan Pachachi. In an attempt to calm his critics, Bremer proposed appointing 30 Iraqis to a talking-shop. He favoured the title 'Advisory Council', although conceded after intervention from the UN special representative in Baghdad, Sergio de Mello, that it be called a 'Governing Council'. He insisted, however, that he hand-pick its members in a process devoid of even token Iraqi ratification. It had 25 members, nine of whom he named rotating presidents. Each spent a month at the helm, ensuring the Council remain a rudderless divided body.

Despite its powerlessness, London and Washington touted the Governing Council as the most representative body in Iraq's history. It comprised 13 Shia Arabs, five Sunni Arabs, five Kurds, a Christian and a Turkoman; and for the first time in centuries Shias had a majority.[83] But for the vast majority of Iraqis, the Council did not represent them at all. It was dominated by exiles, particularly nominees of the 'Group of Seven' opposition groups long financed and cajoled by Washington, some of whom had not been to Baghdad for 35 years. At least five had spent a lifetime under American tutelage, starting from when they were pupils at the same private school, Baghdad College, then run by Bostonian Jesuits.

Moreover, Bremer ensured that even those politicians who did have a constituency, such as the Kurds, were poodles. He controlled their travel plans, and demanded a veto over their decisions. If individual members dared contradict him, he 'would lose his cool' and thump the table, according to one of the 25 summoned to Bremer's office for a ticking-off. And while he occupied Saddam's mammoth presidential palace, he assigned the Council a squat bungalow which had formerly served as a munitions ministry outhouse. 'The Council is just a façade,' said Loulouwa Rachid of International Crisis Group. 'How can you run a council with people who have no budget and no infrastructure?'[84]

Equipped with absolute powers, Bremer at times veered dangerously close to acquiring the attributes of the regime he had come to replace. His forces acted with impunity; his administration grew obsessed with control; and, as his predecessors, he embarked on expanding his palace. Fifty years earlier under the monarchy, Baghdadis recalled driving past the gates of a modest mansion which served as the centre of government. In the 1960s, the Free Officers of the Revolution rerouted the traffic, and their successors, the Baath, added two marble wings to the building. After taking power in 1979, Saddam adorned the roof with four vast likenesses of himself and built two triumphal arches a mile north and south of the palace to cordon off the grounds into a 41-acre enclave.

The biggest expansion, however, occurred under American rule. Within weeks of their conquest, they had established a city within a city they called the Green Zone. Surrounded by concrete megaliths stacked like gravestones, it encompassed the capital's prize monuments, including its best hotel, the Rashid, the zoo where Uday Hussein kept his tigers, a museum and its former National Assembly. Off-limits to ordinary Iraqis, the vast territory – which included a bridge and an underpass linking east with west Baghdad – reduced Baghdad's traffic to gridlock. But inside, Bremer embarked on plans for refurbishment. Iraqi trade minister Ali Allawi was shocked to discover Bremer had prioritised the off-loading of $40 million of new palace doors while food rations for Iraqis waited to dock at Um Qasr.

In their stance on the media, the coalition also quickly picked up local habits. Bremer's order abolishing the 5,000-strong information ministry was hailed as inaugurating a new era of free expression in the Arab world, but all it did was to transfer control over the media from Iraq to Bremer's own propaganda arm, Strategic Communications – Stratcom for short. By coalition standards, Stratcom was intensively staffed, often by highly placed

Republicans.[85] It pumped out daily bulletins, with such turgid Soviet headlines as 'Farmers' Unions in South Central Iraq Attend Agricultural Conference'.[86] Content had to be deciphered for half-truths. A release headlined 'Insurgents Attack Hospital'[87] neglected to mention that it occurred after US troops had occupied Mosul's largest hospital and evacuated its patients amid an outcry from doctors. Insurgent attacks were routinely attributed to incoming 'foreign fighters' without a trace of irony. Under Order No. 14, 'Prohibited Media Activity', reporting contrary to coalition guidelines was a criminal offence. The authorities were empowered to imprison for up to one year any journalist said to support resistance against US forces. In September the CPA enforced a two-week ban on the two most popular Arab satellite channels, al-Jazeera and al-Arabiya, and on occasion Bremer's British spokesman, Charles Heatly, tried to ban British journalists penning articles deemed unfavourable, including this author. Located in the inner sanctum of the palace opposite Bremer's office, Stratcom served as the Cerberus warding off unwelcome journalists. Officially, meetings with coalition officials could only take place in their presence and with their approval. 'The American and British military don't tend to like journalists working independently in Iraq,' said the Reuters Bureau Chief in Baghdad, Andrew Marshall.

Despite promising to remove military rule from the region, the military dominated proceedings. The email addresses of Bremer's staff ended in .mil not .gov. Bremer decreed an end to the Iraqi executive control over the judiciary, except for crimes against the coalition, for which he set up a separate Central Criminal Court inside the US-fortified Green Zone, whose judges were appointed by the coalition and subject to guidance from US military legal advisors. Rather than abolish the notorious Abu Ghraib prison camp, US forces revived it as their prime detention centre, detaining tens of thousands in the first three years of occupation. Torture was widespread, it emerged, first from the Red Cross and then from the photographs US soldiers sent to websites in exchange for porn.[88] US forces declined to reveal their rules of engagement, but a civil administrator with US forces, Christopher Varhola, cited activities 'condoned by the chain of command' as including 'shooting at Iraqi vehicles on major highways, destroying walls that have anti-American graffiti painted on them, collectively detaining all males in a given area or village for up to several weeks or months, and detaining preadolescent family members of suspects in an effort to force suspects to turn themselves in'.[89] The army was used as a standard instrument of local law enforcement without due legal process. 'If the armed thugs who have taken over the hospitals don't stand down, we may have to rely on coalition forces to return them,' warned Stephen Browning, the coalition official in charge of the Health Ministry. US tanks were deployed at Baghdad's Alwiya maternity hospital to oversee the restoration of a former Baathist, Mohammed al-Taweel (whose office walls were discoloured with 21 patches where he had previously hung photos of himself and Saddam). And international aid workers were banned from working with hospitals under clerical management to starve them of medical supplies. The coalition, aid workers complained, had turned the health sector into a battlefield.

In another echo of the past, while preaching the virtues of decentralisation, Bremer battled to concentrate powers in Baghdad. Empowered by Congress to spend up to $100 million without their prior approval, he insisted Coalition representatives in the provinces obtain his signature for expenditures over $50,000, regardless of the logistic complications. After field commanders ran out of the billions of Iraqi dinars they sequestered from Saddam's palaces to pay salaries, Bremer used the tight control he exercised over finances to enforce his dictat. British officials struggling to maintain a quasi-autonomous enclave in the southern three provinces derided the US proconsul for his 'absolutism' and 'Bolshevik tendencies'. Some suspected him of being so angry with the British claims of superior management of the occupation that he withheld the payment of salaries to Basra to stoke unrest, and delayed the reopening of Basra airport until the Americans opened theirs in Baghdad. Even the Kurds, who enthused at American patronage, feared Bremer was seeking to undo a dozen years of autonomous existence, and restore legislative authority to Baghdad. When the US proconsul discovered that a small oil-field at Tactac was prospecting for oil without the authorisation of Baghdad's oil ministry, he had it capped. A sugar refinery the Kurds had converted into an oil refinery seven years earlier to power their autonomous zone was also shut down for failing to obtain Baghdad's approval.

Even in matters of foreign policy, Bremer acquired local traits. Like Saddam, he would rail against Syria and Iran, and on occasion Kuwait. In one outburst he reprimanded the emirate for refusing to cancel its Saddam-era debt and forgo its payment of punitive Gulf War reparations. 'I have to say that it is curious to me,' snarled Bremer, 'to require a country whose per capita income, GDP, is about $800 ... to pay reparations to countries whose per capita GDP is greater by a factor of ten times.'[90] Such a statement might have made Saddam Hussein proud.

Ultimately, Bremer's vaulting ambition to be America's Middle East Caesar o'er-leapt itself. So full of hubris was his administration that it mistook Iraqi silence for acquiescence, repeating an earlier mistake of the British. In 1920, the then Oriental Secretary had confidently written to the British military authorities that 'the stronger the hold we are able to keep here the better the inhabitants will be pleased. They can't conceive an independent Arab government. Nor, I confess, can I. There is no one here who could run it.'[91] Two months later, Iraq rose up against the British. Bremer felt similarly cocksure. Having launched his political blueprint, he turned his attention to the economy and its conversion to Iraq Inc., USA.

CHAPTER 7

The Reconstruction Myth

> The conquest of the earth, which mostly means the taking it away from those who have a different complexion or slightly flatter noses than ourselves, is not a pretty thing when you look at it too much. What redeems it is the idea only.
>
> (Joseph Conrad, *The Heart of Darkness*)

The infertile salt-encrusted banks of the Dead Sea were not the most auspicious place to launch Iraq's economic revival. This after all was the land where Sodom and Gomorrah, earlier ventures in materialism, had been obliterated and across the water from where a suicide squad of rebel fanatics at Masada had refused to submit to Pax Romana. But it was also the place where John the Baptist had preached deliverance, and where Bremer chose to proclaim his message of salvation.

The Swiss-run club of the world's political and business rulers, the World Economic Forum, relocated from the snowy heights of Davos to the sweltering depths of the Dead Sea to hear the word in June 2003. The mobile air-conditioning units inside the marquee struggled impossibly against the Dead Sea's summer heat, and kings, CEOs and ministerial delegations summoned from 30 assorted states flapped their programmes in a limp attempt to produce a breeze. But Bremer himself was impressively unflappable. Rigid in his trademark sand-coloured army boots and a pin-stripe suit, he had swanned through far fiercer temperatures in the Iraqi deserts to the east, and never once mopped his brow. Even the guest-list defined him as Iraqi.

Bremer was at the height of his powers. Exactly a month earlier the UN Security Council had passed Resolution 1483, ending Iraqi sanctions and investing Bremer as Iraq's civil administrator with authority over Iraq's oil revenues. To the assembled audience, the invasion seemed an attractive investment – with an estimated 100 billion barrels of oil in the ground, Iraq had assets of 5 trillion dollars waiting to be realised. In his address to delegates, he unveiled his plans for Iraq's 'reconstruction', resurrecting the same term the Washington-led North had used to integrate the American South in the aftermath of the American civil war. Disregarding the fact that America was a signatory to the Geneva Accords prohibiting an occupying power from making any permanent changes to the state or its laws, he promised to 'refashion… Iraq's Soviet-style command economy'[92] and convert it to the free market. Subsidies would be slashed to ensure 'a level playing field' with the private sector. Inefficient industries would either close, or be transferred 'into private hands'. Tariffs would be officially lifted and the entire country converted into a free trade zone. Iraq's rationing system – on which 60 per cent of the population depended either in part or total for their food – would be replaced with monetary benefits, targeted at the poor. Iraq's oil revenue would be paid out to its citizens as dividends. Instead of scrounging on the state for food, gas, electricity, petrol, telephone calls, education and healthcare, Iraqis would be elevated into stakeholders in Iraq Inc.

Though disguised as free trade missionaries, many of Bremer's auxiliaries had more personal interests. Many of the project managers rotated in the doors that revolved between US company boardrooms and government departments. Contracts worth billions of dollars were awarded without public tenders, and non-American firms were ruthlessly excluded. Halliburton, the company Dick Cheney ran prior to his appointment as vice-president, secured the contract for the restoration of oil installations, securing control over the oilfields. Reconstruction was a euphemism for the takeover of the Iraqi economy by US companies.

To oversee reconstruction, President Bush appointed his former campaign-fundraiser and Harvard Business School classmate Tom Foley, who, like Bremer, came from the millionaires' neighbourhood of Greenwich, Connecticut. Michael Fleischer, brother of the President's spokesman, Ari, was appointed to help him. He arrived promising to liquidate Iraq's 192 state-owned enterprises, and flew 18 of the architects of Eastern Europe's conversion to capitalism to Baghdad to preach the virtues of rapid reform. 'The first six to twelve months of any new administration are the window of opportunity where 90 per cent of the foundation of success is laid,'[93] declared Yegor Gaider, economic mastermind and prime minister of Russia's transformation under Boris Yeltsin. The CPA's economic advisor, and later Polish prime minister, Marek Belka, reminded his audience that Iraq, which 30 years earlier had had a higher per capita income than Australia or Italy, had sunk to the level of Congo.[94]

Even with the best advice, reviving Iraq was a near impossible task. A decade of sanctions had sapped the regime of its instruments of power as was their intended purpose. But the unforeseen consequence was that the USA inherited an anaemic hollow state. Sanctions fostered a criminalised economy, corrupted the bureaucracy, impoverished the middle class and broke the infrastructure. Adding bull-in-the-china-shop economic reform was more than the ruined state could cope with. 'Privatisation... that's just one fight that you don't have to take on right now,' cried Bremer's predecessor Jay Garner from the sidelines, after Bremer gave his Dead Sea address.[95] But tucked in his palace, Bremer aspired to utopia. In place of a new deal, Iraq got job-cuts. The suffering was the mere labour pain of Iraq's rebirth, or, as Bremer put it, 'short-term sacrifices', and a vital economic counterpart to the political reconfiguration he planned for Iraq. To paraphrase the French revolutionary Maximilien Robespierre, 'one could not expect to make an omelette without breaking eggs'.

Within weeks Iraq's public sector, which provided 70 per cent of the country's manufacturing output, was gutted. Subsidies were duly slashed. Electricity was diverted from heavy industry to domestic demand, and factories left fallow for scavengers to strip. In the absence of customs controls, tariff-free imports flooded the market. And contracts for anything from the cement blast-walls that reared up round Baghdad like gravestones to vegetables to feed the US military were also placed abroad, at great expense. While demand for cement fortifications soared, production at Iraq's 14 cement factories collapsed from 10 million tonnes in 2002 to less than 2 million tonnes in 2003. By the end of the year, half of the Industry Ministry's 80 factories were still moribund, including Basra's steel mills and Mosul's sulphur plant. Unemployment soared.

The cut in subsidies fell particularly hard on the 7 million Iraqis – one in three of the population – who worked on the land. Under pressure from America's grain lobby anxious to resume shipments to Iraq, Bremer's treasury officials cut agricultural subsidies, worth $250 million under Saddam, by 60 per cent in their 2004 budget. 'Within four years subsidies will be reduced to zero,' said Sawsan al-Sharify, a US-trained Iraqi agronomist whom Bremer appointed deputy agriculture minister.[96] Under Order No. 81, Bremer banned Iraqi farmers from sowing any foreign corn varieties they harvested because it infringed world patents. And farmers facing bankruptcy were advised to lease their land to foreign investors. Iraq's first post-war wheat harvest fell to a paltry million tonnes, its lowest for half a century and a quarter of its 1980s peak. To make up the shortfall, the UN's World Food Programme loyally shipped American wheat to Iraq for the first time since 1991, in sacks mockingly stamped 'from the generosity of the American people'.

While the coalition escorted journalists around the replenished marshlands that Saddam Hussein had drained, the reality according to the UN's Food and Agriculture Organization was that land under cultivation had receded to a mere 38 per cent of its 1980s high. Not only did the state cut supplies of seeds, fertilisers and pesticides, but the electricity outages were too numerous and the infrastructure too damaged by US bombs to pump water to outlying fields. One of Iraq's largest cooperatives at Qusaiba, an hour's drive through the palm groves south-east of Baghdad, was returning to desert scrub after an American missile ploughed into the turbines powering the irrigation system. Despite near record highs in the water-table, the livelihood of its 16,000 people was in jeopardy. After six months of occupation, Qusaiba's farmers took up their pitchforks and, led by the wizened local tribal chief, Sheikh Jassim Sumermed, marched on the nearby Ukrainian base. 'We need water,' protested the farmers. The Ukrainians responded they had no means to help.

Iraqi businessmen in Baghdad found it equally hard to make their voices heard. To make an appointment, they had to queue in the scorching sun beneath tank turrets and between lines of barbed-wire outside Iraq's former parliament, renamed the Convention Centre, which became Iraq's main interface with Bremer's administration. Each visitor was subjected to five separate body searches. Phones proved of no avail because Bremer had replaced government telephone numbers with American dialling codes. 'It takes two months to get an appointment with the Americans, and when we finally meet them they have no information,' said Adil al-Rawi, a besuited merchant who stocked irrigation pipes for agricultural use.

Frustrated in their attempts to meet the coalition in Baghdad, he and several dozen other indefatigable Iraqi businessmen drove 700 miles to Jordan to locate Bremer's chief procurer, Admiral David Nash. They found him fronting a Reconstruction conference in the ballroom of a five-star hotel filled with hundreds of western, Turkish, Israeli and Jordanian contractors. The proceedings opened to a fanfare of Yankee Doodle Dandy. And the only Iraqi official present, Governing Council member Songool Chapak, protested she had been invited by a Dutch delegation, not the Americans. 'You are speaking as if Iraqis are not there,' interjected an Iraqi when it came to question time. 'Why are Iraqis not being given a role?' Nash, who had the retiring disposition of an elderly post-office clerk, tried to laugh off the unscripted criticism. 'It seems I'm in trouble,' he said, and explained that American firms with government contracts were seeking regional partners who would then contact Iraqis. 'As long as I am spending American taxpayers' money, I have to be answerable to the United States,' he said.

But, for the most part, Bremer's administration was spending Iraqi not US funds. Though after much wrangling, Bremer secured a grant of $18.44 billion from US Congress – dubbed 'the boldest, most generous and most productive act of statesmanship in the past century' on a par with the Marshall Plan,[97] the package was so ring-fenced with accounting conditions that Bremer found it far simpler to spend Iraqi funds. The UN Security Council assisted. Under Resolution 1483, it lifted sanctions and transferred all unspent and new oil revenues into a Development Fund for Iraq, the DFI, to which it gave Bremer access. Added to the funds in Saddam-era bank accounts which were unfrozen after the invasion, Bremer established an Iraq chest of some $20 billion – about as much as Congress' supplemental, but unencumbered by tiresome auditors.[98] By the end of his 13-month tenure, the DFI was all but empty. Just 2 per cent of the Congressional supplemental had been spent.

Billions of Iraq's oil revenues were channelled to American contractors, the US Army Corps of Engineers, and western mercenaries, in deals that were vague on where or what work should be done. Contracts were issued without competitive tender[99] and, as under Saddam, reports of backhanders abounded. Contractors double-billed for work and exaggerated their labour costs. And without functioning banks, trucks and helicopters hauled plastic-wrapped bricks of 100-dollar bills across Iraq with scant cross-checking. Bremer's staff claimed that Iraq's needs were too urgent to adhere to standard contracting procedures. But an audit by the CPA's Inspector General completed after the CPA's demise found that the administration had failed to account for $9 billion of its $20 billion expenditure.[100] Testifying before Congress, a former CPA official, Franklin Willis, compared the CPA's accounting procedures to those of 'the Wild West'.[101]

Not only did US companies benefit from lax accounting procedures, they were also spared the long arm of the law. Under a public notice issued by Bremer in June, coalition personnel and their contractors were granted immunity from 'local law or the jurisdiction of local courts'. They were, however, given the benefit of Bremer's laws. In September 2003, Bremer decreed a raft of legislation hailed as 'the most far-sighted investment climate in the Middle East'.[102] President Bush also released US contractors in Iraq from liability from prosecution in American courts.[103] As a further safeguard from public scrutiny, most coalition contractors operated behind a military cordon protected from journalists by barbed wire and US forces. Calls were referred to offices in Atlanta.

Perhaps not since the East India Company ran the Indian sub-continent had foreign companies enjoyed such a free rein. In what *The Economist* called the 'capitalist dream', Iraq's economy was carved out amongst corporate America. Halliburton, the oil-services company run during the Clinton era by US vice-president Richard Cheney, was contracted to manage the country's oil infrastructure. Dyncorp took charge of police force training, and Vinnell Corporation the army. To circumvent military restrictions on interrogating under duress, an Arlington-based defence firm, California Analysis Center Incorporated (CACI), and Titan Corporation of San Diego, California were commissioned to interrogate detainees, not least in Abu Ghraib.[104] Companies seeking to compete without US partners found their businesses damned. Three months after the war a Bahraini telecom company, Batelco, launched Baghdad's first public mobile network, a vital utility in a capital where US bombing had destroyed the terrestrial exchanges. Six days later, Bremer closed it down, following furious demands from US senators that Iraq use American products. Iraqis had to wait six more months for a company using American Motorola equipment to launch a mobile service.

Rooted in America's military-industrial complex, many of the US contractors proved culturally inept, and managerially incompetent. Profit took precedence over service delivery. Creative Associates International Inc (CAII) of Washington DC, contracted by USAID to reform the education ministry, allocated $4 million on a programme to delete Qur'anic verses from a model Arabic grammar textbook.[105] Science Applications International Corporation (SAIC), a major defence contractor claiming expertise in what its website called 'information warfare', proved as poor in running Iraq's national broadcaster as the BBC might have been manufacturing a weapons system. SAIC, whose television channel was dubbed the Pentagon's *Pravda*, employed the same artists who sang praises to Saddam to sing paeans to Iraq's new age of freedom, relayed Bremer's press conferences in full, and censored interviews with Iraqis lest they prove too anti-American. Reporters were required to use formulaic Newsspeak in their reports, blaming 'anti-Iraqi terrorists' for attacks on the US military. Iraqis rushed to buy satellite dishes. Not that SAIC cared much for audience figures. While Iraqi staff received $100 per month, SAIC netted tens of millions paid from Iraq's oil revenues.

The biggest corporate winner was Richard Cheney's former company, Dallas-based Halliburton. While US forces were still en route to Baghdad, it won a contract worth up to $7 billion to revamp Iraq's oilfields. Its oil profits, however, were dwarfed by the contract its subsidiary, KBR, won to serve as the coalition's quartermaster.[106] By December 2004, the two contracts had earned Halliburton over $10 billion, four times more than its nearest corporate rival, Bechtel, and its share-price had soared 92 per cent since the war. Though resenting the profits, the US military welcomed the deal, which freed up a vital 20,000 troops.

The obvious losers in the corporate conquest were Iraqis. Since KBR took a percentage on its purchases, the more expensive a product, the greater the profit. Iraqi labourers and produce priced themselves out of the market by being too cheap. The cement for Bremer's vast blast walls came from Turkey and Mexico and the milk for his Kellogg's cereal from Saudi Arabia. His shirts went to Kuwait to be ironed. Each day KBR imported 1.23 million pounds of food, 570,000-litre bottles of water, and 12 convoys of caravans, which cost more to assemble than the construction of an Iraqi house. Fortunes were spent supplying luxury sport-utility vehicles to contractors and coalition officials, replete with the ludicrous frills such as wing-mirrors with flashing red indicators. The cars were so conspicuous they quickly became a target for insurgents and had to be restricted to cruising the few hundred metres within the Green Zone. In the much smaller base of Basra, officials raced round in Golf buggies. 'We would have been much better off with a small fleet of discreet used cars, and a bicycle for every Green Zone resident,' bemoaned a jaded US official. Not one contract went to a state-owned Iraqi industry.

KBR's labour market was even more distorted. Rather than soak up the unemployment precipitated by Bremer's political and economic revolution, KBR imported migrant labour en masse to increase its mark-up. Advertisements appeared in newspapers across small-town America enticing mini-bus drivers to the Green Zone for $8,000 a month, when Iraqis would have cost $80.[107] Truck-drivers testified before Congress that they had been instructed to bill 12-hour days for seven days a week on their timesheets when they had spent weeks in country with virtually nothing to do. Given that the American taxpayer was footing the $1 billion per week bill for US armed forces, it was perhaps not unreasonable that Americans should be the prime beneficiaries. But Iraqis were deriving scant benefit from the American presence. 'The expenditures are a lot of money for Iraq,' fumed a British advisor at the CPA. 'It's a lot more if the multiplier effect is in Iraq not the States.'

From their Houston skyscrapers, KBR justified their exclusion of Iraqis on the grounds of security. What would happen, asked contractors, if Iraqi caterers poisoned the American army, or laced the water with arsenic? 'From a force protection standpoint,' agreed Colonel Damon Walsh, the head of the US Defence Contract Management Agency overseeing KBR's operations, 'Iraqis are more vulnerable to a bad guy influence.'[108] Iraqi food, added a catering contractor, fell short of military specifications. For manual labour deemed too lowly for Americans, KBR's sub-contractors imported migrants from the Indian sub-continent by the planeload, much as their British predecessors had mobilised Indian sepoys. The outhouses of Baghdad's Republican Palace acquired Asian trappings. Cooks erected signposts in Urdu and Bangla and festooned the walls with the posters of the snowy peaks of Nepal. While their expatriate bosses lodged in hotels, the migrants – TCNs (third-country nationals) in KBR parlance – were grouped 12 to a portacabin, whose soft-skinned roofs left them vulnerable to mortar attack. Many lived like indentured labourers. They were forced to surrender their passports along with their rights on arrival at Kuwait airport, and earned less than $50 a month.

As migrant work spread throughout the coalition operation, Iraq was increasingly acquiring the attributes of a Gulf rentier state. In the state-owned oil sector, a Kuwaiti sub-contractor drafted 1,200 Pakistani and Indian oilmen into what had hitherto been exclusively Iraqi fields. Iraq's truckers found themselves relegated to the bottom of available workers from America, Jordan, Syria, Bulgaria and Pakistan. Iraqi day-labourers gathered at the gates of American bases, only to be told that the arrival of Bengalis meant their services were no longer required. 'US contractors import in the labour and export the benefits,' grumbled Hakim Awad, one of dozens of hopeful Iraqi managers who had set up camp at the gates of the closed military zone of Baghdad Airport, the largest American base in Iraq. 'Where's the benefit for Iraq?'[109]

Equally unnerving was the influx of businessmen from neighbouring states flush with US contracts to manage Iraq. Bremer gave Jordan's loss-making airline, Royal Jordanian, a monopoly on the operation of commercial flights out of Baghdad. Dyncorp went into partnership with Jordan's Public Security Directorate to train Iraqi police in a deal worth $1.2 billion. (Not a cent of the intelligence department's earnings appeared in the Jordanian budget.) And KBR awarded another of King Abdullah's close associates a contract to truck fuel to Iraq, a bizarre if telling reversal of the pre-war flow. 'We want to rebuild ourselves and will not let some Lebanese, Syrian, Kuwaiti, Emirati or Jordanian company do the job, make the profit and take that profit out of the country altogether, as they did during the embargo,' fretted Mahmood Bunnia, a corpulent scion of Iraq's largest family. 'Before, Saddam Hussein took our money out of the country and now the big corporations do. What's the difference?' As under the UN's oil-for-food programme, foreigners were again the prime beneficiaries of Iraq's oil revenues.

Inside their palace enclaves, US officials fine-tuning their PowerPoint timetables for recovery enjoyed a surreal world of uninterrupted fuel supplies, 24-hour electricity, free-flowing water for their swimming pools, and within two months of the invasion their own private network with US dialling codes. In the world beyond, known as the Red Zone, the blackouts and water-outages grew ever more acute. Queues for gasoline many miles long clogged Baghdad's streets and highways like giant question marks left hanging over American management. Highwaymen plagued the roads in and out of Iraq. Medical stocks ran low, exhausted by a surfeit of victims of worsening lawlessness. 'We're writing prescriptions we know the chemists can't supply,' said Dr Munaf Mohammed of Basra hospital's intensive care unit.[110] Doctors were equally scarce, as middle-class families fled the mayhem either to the safer Kurdish north, or out of the country.

Iraqis who had already rebuilt their country after two wars in the past 20 years watched in disbelief at the inability of the world's leading corporations to jump-start their country. Bechtel, the CPA's public works contractor, spent the first four months after invasion compiling a needs assessment for Iraq, and the next two months vetting contractors. After a year, its only tangible achievement in road construction was the routing of a rubble bypass round one of the 49 bridges downed by American missiles. 'Iraqis rebuilt their bridges after the 1991 war,' barked Samir, my driver, above the klaxons. 'Saddam could have done better.' Most government ministries were still wrecks two years after the war. A rapid rotation of the civil service serving three-month tours of duty only exacerbated the mismanagement. By the time a staffer had completed his feasibility study, he was replaced by another who began the work over again with fresh coloured graphs.

Moreover, the shortages could boost corporate profits. Rather than restore Iraq's refining capacity of 700,000 barrels per day, the US Army Corps of Engineers commissioned KBR to truck fuel from neighbouring states in an operation costing Iraq's budget $2.5 billion a year. 'Never in its history has Iraq had to import its oil,' said former Iraqi oil minister, Essam Chalabi, exiled in Amman. 'Now they import a third of Iraq's consumption needs and the country's still queuing for its gasoline. It's a tragedy.'[111] But not for the US vice-president's former company. It billed the Iraqi government at rates for fuel that were so inflated the US Justice Department investigated.[112] Deliveries went direct to black-marketeers rather than local garages. And, according to high-placed Iraqi officials, tankers arriving from Kuwait returned before unloading in order to double-bill or triple bill, a process Iraqi traders called recycling.[113] 'It's as if they put the gasoline on the *Queen Mary* and take it around the globe before they deliver it,' said Phil Verleger, a California oil economist and the president of a consulting firm.[114]

The mayhem was alienating even the initially welcoming Iraqi bourgeoisie. 'The prerequisites for business are transport, communications, electricity and security,' said al-Rawi. 'We lack all four.' Military commanders tried to mollify the growing ranks of the disenchanted by dispatching patrols armed with satchels of cash to chuck dollars at passers-by. Bremer's more managed version of the hearts and minds operation was to declare a manifold increase in salaries for public sector workers. Doctors' pay rose from $13 a month to $300; teachers from $4 to $180. The increases triggered a consumer boom, prompting US officials to claim they had enabled the launch of 10,000 new businesses in the six months since war, an accomplishment US Defence Secretary Rumsfeld lauded as 'without historical parallel'[115]. But the earnings spent on a rush of duty-free imports did not rebuild Iraq.

In an attempt to get Iraq back to work, Washington entrusted Bechtel with a massive programme of public works. 'If the work can be done by an Iraqi firm at a competitive price that's who's going to do it,' said Francis Caravan, a Bechtel spokesman in Baghdad, presenting the package as a panacea to an unemployment rate which had climbed to 60 per cent. Battalions of street-sweepers and gardeners on $3 wages a day were dragooned into such 'quick-impact high-visibility projects' as beautifying Baghdad. Iraq's war detritus of burnt-out tanks and artillery guns was hauled from the streets. And work began on the refurbishment of 1,200 schools at $30,000 apiece. But without proper monitoring by US supervisors, the projects compared poorly to a UN programme to refurbish schools a year earlier. Some contractors did no more than whitewash Baathist graffiti of missiles blazing over Jerusalem's Dome of the Rock. Others installed Syrian fans, and made off with the Japanese fans they replaced. Iraqi businessmen quipped they had exchanged sovereignty for broomsticks, and were feeding from the scraps of the corporate table.

To a large but little-acknowledged extent, Iraq's insurgency began as a battle for jobs. The first labour protests in June 2003 were only a few score strong. They consisted of dismissed workers from the disbanded munitions factories, who gathered at the barbed wire barricades to the Green Zone, demanding attention. 'Don't talk to them,' chided the US soldiers in their tanks, when Iraqi officials tried to engage them. 'You'll just encourage them.' But the workers understood they would simply have to shout louder. The following week they returned in their thousands, with the same result. On their third attempt, they were met with tanks. 'They are pushing me to become a time-bomb,' said Abdel Emir Hassan, a senior engineer at the military industrialisation ministry and a Baath-party member, as he headed home.

By August 2003, the rallies had mushroomed into nationwide riots. In Amara, the second largest town under British control, British troops opened fire on protestors hurling rocks at their base. Further south, British tanks rolled into the oilfields to break up a strike called to protest at the hiring of Pakistani and Indian engineers. In Basra, decommissioned Iraqi soldiers, some in wheelchairs, who had waited in vain for long-promised pensions, charged the palace gates of the British base, crushing razor wire, smashing arc-lights, and setting fire to tyres. Desperate Fijian mercenaries manning the gates hurled back the concrete blocks that flew through the air, as their white commander bawled at them to hold their positions. 'Go home, Go home,' chanted the crowd at the palace walls. Men with megaphones asked whether their British counterparts would tolerate such abuse of its war veterans. As the violence escalated in September, British troops shot dead three demonstrators in Basra who had refused to disperse. Seven more were killed the following month in Amara as anti-British protests swelled.

Basra's riots were testament to how brittle the occupation had become. No city had been more downtrodden by Saddam Hussein's dictatorship and scarred by his wars against nearby Iran and Kuwait. Unlike the Americans, British officials also had the advantage of a historic relationship. The British East India Company had won its first concessions in Basra in 1639, and British rule had marked the high tide of the port-city's fortunes. Basra's main mercantile families still prided themselves on being the local representatives of British corporations – once the engine of its empire.

And yet, for all their experience, the British administrators proved as inept as their American counterparts. The full quota of 120 foreigners appointed to run the civil service took eight months to arrive, by which time most preferred to hunker behind the blast-walls of their palace cocoon. Three years after their arrival the hulks of sunken vessels from the Iran–Iraq war still rendered the waterway impassable. The promenade along the banks of the Shatt al-Arab – once the haunt of Gulf Arabs dining in its restaurants – oozed with sewage. Foreign office mandarins who played down the size and severity of the protests were contradicted by their own troops. 'It's more dangerous now than when we invaded,' confided a soldier in late 2003, before he was reprimanded for speaking without authorisation. As British troops recoiled from the streets, Iraqi paramilitaries in balaclavas bristling with weapons filled the vacuum.

In the rural flatlands, the resentment was if anything greater. Incessant convoys bearing goods for the first-world of the coalition hurtled through the malnourished hamlets of the third. Shepherds gawked as the juggernauts emblazoned with the logo 'Property of the US Army' sped by like impossible prizes in a televised game-show, carrying caravans, hamburgers and provisions of Heinz mayonnaise. The inequalities were destined to clash. A Jordanian manufacturer of tissues, called Fine, lost all of its 14 trucks around Kut. And at the bottleneck of Samawa, where the Baghdad–Basra highway narrowed from six lanes to two, youths passed the day hurling found rocks. KBR, which maintained the supply routes, responded by kitting their truckers from Connecticut and Karachi in helmets and armoured vests, and provided army escorts. Stretches of highway were declared military zones off-limits to Iraqis and converted into fortified service stations for coalition convoys. But the attacks only intensified. 'People see all this material carried through their territory and they're not getting a penny,' said a Kurdish hauler of liquor, anxious for his deliveries coming from Kuwait. 'It would make more sense to pay locals a transit tax for the use of their land and have them secure the route, rather than treat them as spectators in their own land.'

By December 2003 attacks on civilian and military convoys had risen to 250 a month, said the coalition. The roadsides were again littered with graffiti proclaiming 'Long live Saddam'. For fear of ambush, $85,000 juggernauts that broke down were driven off the road and torched to prevent locals reaping the benefit. The smouldering hulks of KBR's detritus littered the scrub pastures of southern Iraq.[116] 'If they hadn't set fire to the truck, we'd have earned $10,000 a truck, not $2,500,' moaned a shepherd as he squabbled with colleagues over the previous night's detritus. Local markets were filled with shepherds in white tunics auctioning spare parts that survived. But scrap was a meagre return for the cost of occupation. Counting their day's profits over mint tea in the paraffin warmth of a roadside teahouse, the shepherds exchanged excited tales of uprisings further north. They too were restless, but their religious leaders had yet to declare a Jihad. 'Just one word from Ayatollah Sistani,' said one, 'that's all.' Ultimately, only sectarian rivalry spared America a nationwide uprising.

CHAPTER 8

The Quiet Ayatollah's Regime-Change

Given America's military might, Washington's viceroy could cope with violence. What ultimately toppled direct US rule was not the sickening cycle of car-bombs, assassinations, kidnappings and beheadings, but the still small voice of an Ayatollah. Freed from Saddam's shackles, his popular appeal exposed the hypocrisy of a war waged in the name of democracy. When Bremer handpicked Iraq's representatives, a simple edict from Sistani brought hundreds of thousands onto the streets. Should Iraq ever emerge as a sovereign democracy, it will be primarily because of an elderly, unarmed, unassuming, foreign cleric, who under Iraqi law had no right to vote.

Grand Ayatollah Ali Sistani made an unlikely Gandhi. Unlike the London legal training of the father of Indian independence, Sistani had scant exposure to western ideas. The Curia where he had spent his life was alien to people power. Under the British occupation in the 1920s, Ayatollahs had boycotted Constituent Assembly elections and declared a Jihad. They expected their followers to accept their fatwas on faith, and pay tithes without asking where the money went. And their administration of the clergy was deeply hierarchical. Novices eked out a living on pocket-money and a diet of deep-fried falafels while senior clerics supped in style. The most luxurious meal I ate in Iraq was as a guest of Sistani's corpulent advisor, Mohammed Haqqani, waited on by minions who perambulated with an Arabian Nights' feast of 40 salads piled around a succulent catfish. Sistani's views on personal conduct reflected his cloistered upbringing. He forbade chess, music and permanent marriage to non-Muslims, although plastic surgery, oral sex (provided no liquids were swallowed), and temporary 'enjoyment' marriages were permitted.

His right to represent Iraq was at best tenuous. He was born 800 miles to the east in the Iranian shrine city of Marshad in 1930, and only went to Iraq for the first time aged 30. He passed his youth in the Persian seminaries of Isfahan and Qom. And both he and his son, who in the nepotistic tradition of the clergy served as his spokesman, spoke Arabic laden with a Persian accent.

He was singularly introverted. His fatwas were written in the pinched scrawl of the recluse, and fellow clerics considered him 'uncharismatic and humble'. His sad watery moon-eyes – the product of years spent under house arrest – were so deeply recessed in their sockets that his face seemed perpetually cast in shadows. From 1960 onwards, with the exception of a year's trip to Iran after the Islamic Revolution, he confined himself to Najaf. Saddam considered him of such minimal threat that he spared him the slaughter of the 100 senior clergy after the 1991 uprising, and subjected him to a mere two months in prison. Baath agents stationed in a caravan at the end of his alleyway kept him under house arrest thereafter, but even after the collapse of the regime he rarely ventured out. He shied from public appearances, even sermons, and never rebuilt his mosque, which Saddam had destroyed in 1991. He received his stream of besuited visitors in a ragtag house, whose walls and stairwells subsidence had skewed at impossible angles, in a shabby black robe and turban, sitting cross-legged on floor-cushions in the dim light of a windowless room. His one air-conditioner was reputedly broken. When a visitor donated a new one, it was said he asked it be given to the poor.

His own town was as threadbare as his home. Within its grubby honeycomb of ramshackle crumbling alleyways, the donkey cart remained as common as the car. For over a generation, Saddam had ravaged the city of scholars, shrines and religious endowments. Jewels and treasures bequeathed by Indian and Iranian pilgrims were purloined by the state. After the 1991 uprising the ancient solid gold doors of the Najaf shrine were replaced with gold-leaf – in the name of restoration – and smelted into ingots. Alms-giving networks were plundered, and Shia assets diverted to fund the construction of gargantuan Sunni mosques and soirees by Egyptian starlets. Strapped for resources, student numbers collapsed from a peak of 12,000 before the Baath coup of 1968 to a few score on the eve of the 2003 war. Other towns – particularly Iran's Qom – spoke in the name of Shia Islam, as Najaf's clerics eked out a living selling legal prescriptions, much as the Catholic Church had once sold indulgences. Couples reluctant to pay the stamps for a registry office wedding sought clerical approval for a backstreet rate of 25 cents.

And yet, within weeks of the invasion, this backwater produced Iraq's *deus ex cathedra* of Muslim democracy. His adopted town broke loose from the scrubbiness where Saddam had moored it to reassert its spiritual power as the font – the Vatican – of Shia Islam. To a large part, it owed its prominence to the fact that its own message dovetailed so closely with the creed of the newcomers. Sistani used his religious authority to brand Shia tradition as a democratic creed, declaring the casting of ballots as a religious duty on the grounds that the popular will was an expression of the divine.

Though he emerged as the most powerful man in Iraq, the success of this mosque-less, militia-less almost tatty cleric in rallying Iraqis was never assured. Although Shias aspired to be led by a single Ayatollah, for most of its history the Hauza had been a papacy without a pope or dynasty. Under the umbrella of the Hauza, clerics competed for spiritual leadership by appealing to the lay masses. The larger a cleric's popular following the greater his authority. Candidates for the title of *marja mutlaq*, or source of emulation, appealed to lay Shias on the basis of their writings or manifestos. Of the dozen Ayatollahs or so worldwide who claimed the title of *alam al-ulama*, the most learned of the learned (five alone were in Najaf), Sistani was the most popular. A rival claimed 90 per cent of Shiites worldwide and 60 per cent in Iraq followed Sistani.[117]

Crucially, for a town seeking to restore its shattered primacy, Sistani's rival Ayatollahs rallied behind him. While Najaf's three other Grand Ayatollahs retained their individual claims to supremacy, they formed a loose collegiate body, which tacitly accepted Sistani's status as *primus inter pares*. They reactivated their battered network of country- and worldwide representatives to distribute their fatwas – hitherto censored prior to release – and revive the system of tithes, enjoining each Shia to pay his *marja*, or spiritual referee, a fifth, or *khoms*, of his or her annual income. The use of previously banned leaflets, billboards, the press and the internet further funnelled their message.

The wheels of the Curia began turning even before the Americans reached Baghdad. A week after its capture, Sistani delivered a lengthy fatwa laying the ground-rules for his subsequent interaction with the occupiers. He was not, he insisted, seeking power – 'the Supreme Marjaiya [Shia source of spiritual authority] is by no means whatsoever looking to establish itself as a political authority in Iraq'[118]. But he claimed that the role of supra-political guide ensuring Iraq's future direction conformed to Islamic law, and provided a roadmap for future governance, including what Bremer later termed deBaathification: 'One must be careful that former government staff and others who have tortured and persecuted people do not creep back into government posts.' Alms should also be tax-deductible, added his advisors, and Iraq's new judiciary recruited from clerical ranks.

Iraq's new rulers were caught off guard. Lulled by Sistani's silence under Saddam, US commanders had labelled Iraq's leading cleric a quietist. 'The vast majority of locals follow Grand Ayatollah Sistani's edict that clerics should stay in mosques and out of politics,' said a hopeful Marine commander ensconced in the holy city of Karbala.[119] Even a casual glance at the history books could have corrected such wishful thinking. When the British had invaded 90 years earlier, the Hauza had declared first a workers' strike and then a Jihad. And even under the Baath, Najaf had been at the heart of most revivalist or revolutionary movements in the Shia world. Lebanon's activist clerics, Mohammed Hassanein Fadlallah and Hizbollah's Hassan Nasrallah, Ayatollah Khomeini, as well as leading Iraqi revolutionary clerics such as the two Sadr, had all fashioned their political theories in the shadow of Imam Ali's shrine. In an age of civil liberties that America's rule was supposed to inaugurate, Iraq's ecclesiastical body was bent on exercising its rights.

The parameters of clerical power, or *wilaya*, had been fiercely debated in Najaf for over four decades. After the monarchy was overthrown, Mohammed Baqir al-Sadr had proposed Iraq be a *wilayat al-Hauza*, or governance of the Hauza. Ruhollah Khomeini, his contemporary in Najaf, had adapted the theory into the rule of a single cleric, *wilayat al-faqih* – himself. Traditionalists on the other hand – led by another Najaf-based Iranian, Grand Ayatollah Abolqassim Khoi – limited clerical authority to *al-wilaya al-khasa*, matters of personal status, ritual and morality. Carving a third way, Mohammed Fadlallah, who later proclaimed himself Lebanon's Ayatollah but retained great weight in Iraq, advocated Khoei's limited *wilaya* during times of peace and Khomeini's total *wilaya* in war.

Lay Shiites had long been accustomed to dividing their clerics into traditional (*taqlidi*) and political priests (*natiqi*). But the reality was a shifting shade of grey. Even the meekest of Ayatollahs had proved Sphinx-like masters of non-cooperation under the Baath. For over two decades, they had refused to bow to Baghdad's introduction of summer time, derisively dubbed *tawqit saddami* – Saddam time. Even Khoi, the supposed father of the apolitical school, had delved into politics during the 1991 revolt, issuing a communiqué authorising the establishment of a nine-man clerical council to administer Najaf's 13-day self-rule. His fatwas railed against communism, and hailed both Algeria's colonial struggle against the French and the Palestinian Intifada. His *Practical Guide for the Faithful* included a chapter on Jihad. And he counted not just Sistani amongst his disciples, but also the activist clerics of Sadr and Fadlallah, whom he appointed his representative in Lebanon. At least one of Najaf's quartet of Ayatollahs, Bashir al-Pakistani, openly espoused Khomeini's interpretation. And Sistani's son, Mohammed, accepted there were circumstances when *wilayat al-faqih* was applicable.[120]

In his fatwas, Sistani gave the Anglo-American military presence the benefit of the doubt. Legally, the occupation forces were neither *halal* (permitted) nor *haram* (sinful), but rather *mshbouh* (questionable), a necessary evil to fill the security vacuum. The nuance earned him opprobrium from the followers of young radicals, who after killing Ayatollah Khoi's openly pro-coalition son, Abdel Majid, the day after Baghdad fell, besieged Sistani in his Najaf office. Whether out of pragmatism or principle, Sistani thereafter eschewed direct contact with US forces. Dialogue was maintained through a network of Iraqi intermediaries, including at least one – Said Hakki – who was Bremer's religious-affairs advisor.

From the first, Sistani opposed US attempts to impose direct rule. In a fatwa of 26 June 2003, he responded to Bremer's cancellation of local elections by demanding that an elected body of Iraqis draft a constitution. 'There must be a general election so that every Iraqi citizen who is eligible to vote can choose someone to represent him in a foundational constitution preparation assembly,' he lectured the Americans. It was a remarkable fatwa. Ever since 11 September 2001 American neo-cons had been searching for a religious leader to preach the compatibility of democracy and Islam. But rather than rejoice, the administrators of Pax Americana back-peddled in shock at a Muslim cleric brazenly meddling in politics. Bremer's battalion of spin-doctors organised 'background unattributable press briefings', a favoured form of backbiting, to warn his 'Iranian' origins had generated concerns he was a Khomeini in sheep's clothing. Iran's chief mullah, they nervously noted, had also adopted the language of human rights as he swept the despotic Shah from power. Many secular Iraqis – Shias and Sunnis alike – sympathised, jittery that the clerics had emerged from the woodwork to transform Iraq into an Iranian-style Islamic state. 'It's a problem for democracy when the masses transfer their right to decide to an Ayatollah,' said Wamidh Nadhmi, a Sunni academic. 'If Sistani says Ahmed Chalabi is a thief and no one should vote for him, in one swoop he will lose 60 per cent of the vote.'

But Sistani was not a Khomeini. Where Khomeini sought power, and favoured those who hailed him the precursor of the Twelfth Imam, the Shia Messiah, Sistani remained hidden, almost occult. He was a reformer, not a revolutionary, and wanted to be linesman not captain. He opposed the appointment of clerics to official posts, and declined requests to nominate a minister of religious affairs. 'Whoever you choose, make sure he's not wearing a turban,' he told one of Bremer's advisors.[121]

For over a year, Sistani and Bremer battled like shadow-boxers, never meeting. The showdown pitted the world's most advanced media machine driven by 'strategic communicators' against the hand-written responsa of an ageing Ayatollah. While Bremer promulgated decrees weighty with legalese, Sistani's fatwas were modest, terse and curiously without Qur'anic embellishment. Brylcreemed Bremer strutted the televised stage, while Sistani shied from giving a single interview. And yet Sistani's captured voice was the louder. His portraits covered southern Iraq with almost Saddam-like ubiquity. He was the archetypal turbulent but inscrutable priest.

And Washington's rule depended on him. As the non-violent custodian of Iraq's largest community, Sistani kept 15 million Shias from open revolt. He shielded them from radical clerics who lambasted his pacifism and warned that the sole language occupiers understand his force. While threatened by his aura, America's neo-cons did their utmost to ensure none other emerged in his place. Advisors addressed him as 'Supreme' Ayatollah as if they were his *muqallidun*, or supplicants. They sought his blessing for their rulings and selected three of the nine rotating presidents on the Governing Council from his circle. The son of a clerical ally was made oil minister, and the clerical enclave encompassing the Imam Ali shrine was quickly declared a no-go area for American troops.

But US attempts to court Sistani were regally rebuffed. He never abandoned his call for America to restore Iraq's sovereignty. Within a month of the invasion, he demanded Washington submit Iraq to UN trusteeship as a first step to independence; unlike Bremer, the UN special representative to Iraq, Sergio de Mello, was received in his home. After the August 2003 bombing of their headquarters in Baghdad and the killing of de Mello and 19 others forced the UN's effective withdrawal, he demanded Bremer transfer Iraq to an elected national body. The authority, he said, should draft a constitution for his – rather than the viceroy's – utopian state, and clerics not Americans should play an advisory role. Incensed by his impudence, Bremer asked the Governing Council to handpick a Constitutional Committee, led by a Sunni Kurd who Bremer hoped would stymie clerical interference.

With the finesse of a consummate diplomat, Sistani invited the committee to Najaf and gently questioned their legitimacy to draft a constitution on behalf of the Iraqi people. Would they not need an elected authority? At least one Kurd, deputy Kurdish prime minister Sami Abd al-Rahman, was convinced,[122] but when others demurred, Sistani suggested they tour Iraq to take popular soundings. A single trip was enough to scupper the exercise. Heading to the Shia town of Hilla, the Committee was greeted by angry protestors, rattling sabres and cudgels and braying insults. 'Sistani has called for elections,' shouted the townsfolk. 'We have nothing left to discuss.' Sistani had had his first taste of people power.

Not only had the Ayatollahs confounded a key stage of Bremer's blueprint for Iraq, but the growing insurgency, and the downing of a US helicopter with the first major loss of American lives, was eroding the proconsul's credibility back home. In early November 2003 he returned to Washington to tender his notice, and within 48 hours was back in Baghdad to announce direct American and Coalition Provisional rule would end by 1 July 2004. It would be succeeded by a caretaker Iraqi government, and after six months Iraq would vote for a constitutional assembly. Bremer's plans for an open-ended US custodianship had crumbled. Sistani had toppled direct American rule.

But Sistani mistrusted the smallprint. The sub-clauses of the 15 November agreement provided for Bremer and the Council to draft a 'Fundamental Law' to lay the foundations for a future state. Although it was later dubbed a Transitional Administrative Law, Sistani rightly suspected it was Bremer's ploy to coin a temporary constitution by the back door. The complicated process of selection of the post-CPA government – a series of provincial caucuses adapted from a system once used in Chicago – also smacked of an attempt to finagle his favourites into position. Within two weeks, Sistani rejected the agreement. 'Each and every Iraqi,' he said, 'should vote for their government'.

Bremer's arguments against democracy sounded uncomfortably like those of neighbouring dictators. A host of procedural and security obstacles prevented an elected assembly, he said. 'Elections that are held too early can be destructive. It's got to be done very carefully,' said Bremer.[123] Moreover, he added, Iraq lacked an electoral roll, and sufficient security to conduct a census. The Ayatollahs responded by suggesting he make do with the database for the UN's distribution of rations, which listed every Iraqi man, woman and child. Bremer protested it contained forgeries, though not without dissent in the ranks. 'We have a working hypothesis that you could manage an electoral process within the timeframe, the data and the security available,' said Dominic D'Angelo, the British spokesman for the CPA in Basra. A British provincial governor voiced similar views.[124] When they finally did take place a year later to scenes of American jubilation, the elections exposed the expediency of America's objections. There was no census, the electoral list was the database, and the violence was far worse than it had been a year earlier when Bremer declared insecurity prevented staging elections.

The first of the Hauza's mass demonstrations set off in January 2004 from the same mosque, Abila, where in the early spring of 1991 the Shia had launched their rebellion against the Baath. Hundreds of thousands of Basraouis took to the streets, said British officials, armed this time with placards demanding the vote, not Kalashnikovs. The demonstrations spread north, up the Tigris via Kut, and the Euphrates via Karbala, before sweeping into Baghdad a week later. For two days, Baghdad's middle class rubbed shoulders with its slum dwellers, some donning crucifixes in a show of ecumenical mass action. Sistani had galvanised crowds on a scale never seen in the Arab world except at funerals, and done so peacefully. Horrified coalition officials tucked in their fortified enclaves made comparisons with Iran's Islamic Revolution. More favourable comparisons were made to Gandhi's salt marches, which had tolled the bell on the British Empire in India. Iraqis had opted for civil action in a struggle without precedent in the Arab world, to effect change without bullets.

Armed with the voice of the street, Sistani again appealed for UN arbitration, this time to determine a date for elections. Bremer, increasingly desperate to break the impasse, accepted the offer. After lobbying the UN headquarters in New York, Bremer agreed to the dispatch of a UN delegation led by Kofi Annan's special envoy Lakhdar Brahimi (an ex-Algerian foreign minister who had previously done America's bidding in Afghanistan). In return, the Ayatollah agreed to call off the demonstrations. A month later, the UN delivered its verdict: Iraq should conduct National Assembly elections in January 2005, but Bremer would hand over to a non-elected provisional government in June 2004.

It is perhaps worth speculating what might have happened had elections occurred while the CPA was still ruling Iraq. Sunni leaders – still dazed by the military defeat in April 2003 – might well have embraced rather than violently opposed the polls; Shia radicals would have bided their time; Iraq would have acquired a legitimate government, quickly filling the vacuum in its post-invasion leadership; and the fragmentation of Iraq might have been averted. A smoother path to democracy might even have persuaded neighbouring states to follow suit.

In the meantime, religion continued to be the tool Iraqis deployed to chip at American rule. On 29 December, Abdel Aziz al-Hakim, the leader of SCIRI and the then president of the Governing Council, smoothly convened a meeting to pass Law 137 cancelling Saddam's code of legal status – 'one of the most westernised in the Muslim world' – and replace it with 'the provisions of the Islamic Sharia'. Through the pages of the *Washington Post*, Bremer condemned obscurantist clerics for attempting to overturn the Baath's ban on child marriages, arbitrary divorce and male favouritism in child custody and inheritance disputes, but letting others appeal for the restoration of enlightened despotism. Women's groups and liberals beseeched the viceroy to exercise his veto of the Council's law. After two months of filibustering, Bremer ushered a gaggle of secular women's activists into a Council meeting called to review the Law. Eight Shia members of the Council stormed out in protest, and Law 137 was overturned.

Parallel brawls between occupiers steeped in a *mission civilatrice* and clerics loath to relinquish their newfound authority raged across Iraq. Sistani's representatives in the shrine city of Karbala continually frustrated the efforts of Bremer's corpulent governor, John Berry, to build his *Civitas Dei*. Few men can have appeared better equipped for the job. An eccentric retired schoolmaster from Maine, he had run an Arabic language school in Cairo and spoke Arabic – as Iraqis say – like a bulbul, or nightingale – a skill rare in the occupying authority. Steeped in classical Arabic literature, he portrayed himself as a successor to the non-Arab sultans of medieval Baghdad – the Seljuk Turks and the Buyid Persians – who had patronised Iraq's Golden Age. He designed plans for a National Library in Karbala (which, he explained, would cater for religious sensitivities by not stocking *Lady Chatterley's Lover*), to be a new Beit al-Hikma, the House of Knowledge established by the great Abbasid Caliph Al-Mansour. Just as the ninth-century think-tank had translated the philosophers, grammarians and theologians of Classical Greece which nurtured the Arab renaissance, so its successor would revive the Arab world with Americana.

Berry's dreams of grandeur were less well received by his subjects. Within days of his arrival in September 2003, he dissolved the local Karbala council and readvertised their 40 posts. For the next two months, the ex-schoolmaster personally subjected 144 candidates to oral examinations in Arabic lasting three to six hours, grading their responses on a sliding scale from A to C. He discriminated positively in favour of tribesmen and women, hopeful they would prove less susceptible to the prescripts of the clerics. Forty scored A-minus or more, including 17 peasants and 11 women. 'By rights,' he said, disappointedly, 'women should have been half.'[125]

The shrine city's clerics and mercantile elite were outraged. The town had been snatched from them by a patronising colonial officer bent on ruling through pliable women and country bumpkins. Berry's tinkering, they said, was as offensive a concept as a Muslim reshuffling the Vatican's College of Cardinals. Sistani's representatives rallied to their cause. Sitting cross-legged in a black gabardine in his humble lodgings near Imam Hussein's shrine, Hojetalislam Abdel Mehdi Kerbalai declared Berry's nominations 'illegitimate'.[126] Fourteen of Berry's councillors promptly backed out. 'We follow His Eminence Ayatollah Sistani and if he tells us to resign we will resign,' said one of the tribal appointees.[127] Councillors less open to reason suspended their participation after threatening phone-calls. When the old council refused to vacate their offices which the US army had decked with green carpets and large televisions, Berry called in the troops.

For the next six months Berry and the clerics shadow-boxed in a local rendition of the national struggle between Sistani and Bremer. From the pulpit, Kerbalai accussed Berry of calling appointments elections. 'What's to stop the religious militias in the villages stuffing the ballot box, or intimidating the voters?' snapped back Berry. 'We didn't come all the way here to make another lousy dictatorship.'[128] To erode the clerics' powerbase, he drew up plans to limit their sources of finance by seeking control of the booming pilgrimage trade. He drafted schemes for local taxes on pilgrimage hotels and the diversion of alms from the holy sepulchres to municipal rather than clerical coffers. He refused planning permission for the international airport the Governing Council had approved in Karbala to accommodate pilgrims. 'The downtown elite,' he bristled, 'cared more for their pockets and prestige projects than children shivering in schools in outlying areas, and villages surrounded by sewage.' A year after President

Bush called on Shias to rejoice in their religious freedoms, he banned saints-day rites lest they degenerate into political rallies. The Americans, mocked the clerics, had installed a second Saddam.

As hundreds of thousands of pilgrims prepared to descend on the city for Ashoura, Kerbalai declared 'a popular confrontation' against Berry. In the annual enactment of Hussein's passion, his followers delivered the ultimate humiliation on a man who had devoted his life to understanding the Islamic world, casting Berry as the tyrannical Caliph Yazid who had butchered Karbala's Shiites.

Increasingly isolated, Berry sought reinforcements. On a fleeting tour of the town, Bremer surrounded himself with women – many cloaked fully in black – and swore to defend liberalism from the dictats of canonical and patriarchal law. He cut the ribbon on the former Baath party branch revamped as a women's centre. The women clapped somewhat more enthusiastically than their husbands behind. But Bremer had too many problems of his own in Baghdad to offer much more than token support. Abandoned again, Berry tried unsuccessfully to impose another council, inviting 160 notables – most from outside the city – to 'choose' a 40-strong provincial council. But the climate was increasingly hostile. Under attack from mortar attacks, snipers on rooftops, roadside explosions and suicide bombings, he retreated from his office in the Council building in the city centre to a coalition base on the outskirts. Lacking a long-distance telephone and surrounded by a Polish corps with whom his English and Arabic proved redundant, he spent his days in a portacabin penning increasingly hysterical messages back to base. He was not sure, he warned with the air of General Charles Gordon defending Khartoum from the Mahdi's hordes, how long he could hold out. In a rare interview holed up in his base, he spoke of reconciling himself to the prospect of dying in Karbala. He hoped future generations might visit his grave.

Berry left Karbala alive, but an irascible, superannuated failure. Perhaps he was unlucky to be landed with Karbala. In contrast to conservative, mercantile Najaf, Karbala had a long-cherished reputation for activism. The Baath had only controlled the city with tanks and helicopter gunships, and even then its police stations had been repeatedly sacked. Its honeycomb of alleys – subsequently levelled by Saddam – had spawned the Islamic Action Organisation, founded by a rabble-rousing 20-year-old, Mohammed Taqi al-Mudaressi, who traced his revolutionary pedigree back four generations. His uncle, Hassan Shirazi, had first established ties with Khomeini in the

1960s and a more distant descendent, Ayatollah Mirza Shirazi, had led a tobacco boycott in the late 1890s, until the Shah of Iran stripped the British of a tobacco plantation concession.

But Berry's prime failing was his inability to grasp that he was dealing with forces far more powerful than himself. By early January 2004, Sistani's fatwas surpassed Bremer's in weight. Truckers who blithely ignored Bremer's decrees against copper smuggling halted business when Sistani pronounced earnings from smuggling as sinful. In hitherto secular ministries the veil became de rigueur for women, and a beard an advantage for men. The balance of power had shifted the way of the clerics.

All the same, America's interaction with the clerics contrasted markedly with Britain's colonialism, when Shia clergymen were consigned to a second-class status and in some cases expelled to Iran, and Ashoura rallies banned. 'A theocratic state,' wrote Gertrude Bell, a British orientalist serving in Baghdad in the 1920s, 'is the very devil.' No doubt American strategists were influenced by the demographics, and figured it was better to pander to a clergy that kept two-thirds of the population in check. But for all his failures, by accepting a cleric as Iraq's leading powerbroker, Bremer reordered Iraq's and the region's sectarian balance.

CHAPTER 9

America's Exiles Carve Up the Spoils

America compounded its error in discriminating between the sects with its choice of representatives. Of its nine rotating presidents on the Governing Council, all but one was an exile. A third of its 25 members were imported from a single city, London – amongst them two doctors, two businessmen, an architect and a one-time Chevron rep. That some should have been exiles was a given. Four million Iraqis – one in seven of the population – had fled into exile under Saddam, including much of its colonial-era leadership. But Washington was unashamedly predisposed to the émigrés. It assumed that their western exposure made them best suited to transplant western institutional norms and a budding democracy to Iraq, seemingly unaware that their long absence had cut them off from the communities they were appointed to represent.

After shuttling the migrants to Iraq, US forces gave them free run of the city. Within two days of the fall of Baghdad, the initials INC – Chalabi's Iraqi National Congress – were scrawled across the pick of the capital's real-estate, including the city's abandoned intelligence headquarters, a complex of presidential palaces on the banks of the Tigris and the defunct flour-mill that the Chalabis had owned under the monarchy. Chalabi himself bedded down in the lugubrious bar of the haunt of Baghdad's elite, the Hunting Club. More followers moved into the ransacked Boat Club, another favoured playground of Saddam's eldest son, Uday, in whose secluded bullrushes he would ravage the girls his henchmen plucked from the streets. 'One day it might be opened to the public,' mused Hikmet Thawr, a guard Chalabi had left at the entrance, 'but not yet.'

Four houses down from the Boat Club, Kurdish leader Jalal Talabani took up residence in another riverside palace and stationed his guards in the nearby mansion nestled amidst the palm groves of Saddam's secretary, Abdel Hamoud al-Tikriti. Two villas downriver, the turbanned Badr force leader, Abdel Aziz al-Hakim, requisitioned the home of Tariq Aziz, Saddam's deputy prime minister. A pro-American Shia cleric flew from Dubai to take up residence next door in the lodgings of Saddam's vice-president, Ezzat al-Douri. Across the river, Saad Jannabi, a former cigarette trader, arrived from Washington to make another of Uday's pleasure pavilions his own, replete with a fleet of vintage Rolls-Royces and an Excalibur saloon with the plate number Baghdad 1, which he parked in the stables. To startled Iraqis promised a new era of equality and rule of law, their first taste of the country's new rulers was as avaricious squatters.

The incoming exiles responded that land-grabbing was an essential component of building a power-base. Every Arab ruler, after all, relied on patronage to sustain his support base, and the émigrés-who-would-be-presidents were no different. Those who sought to play by the books largely fell by the wayside. Adnan Pachachi, a patrician who modestly rented rather than looted his mansion, failed to garner a single seat in the January 2005 elections. Moreover, some had outstanding claims from previous dynasties. As the scion of a pre-revolutionary landlord, the Chalabi were the historic proprietors of an entire eponymous Baghdad district, Chalabiya. The house he made his home was once his sister's, before Saddam's agents turned it into a brothel.[129] Nevertheless, rather than press his claims legally, Chalabi and his ilk took what they felt was rightfully theirs, and these acquisitions prompted comparisons with Iraq's bygone rulers and compounded their reputation for pilfering.

Bremer pandered to their lifestyles. He housed those who had not purloined property in a riverside complex shaded by eucalyptus trees where Saddam had hitherto kept his ministers. The corridors of the former Ministry of Munitions were converted into their private chambers. One councillor, a natty London architect called Samir Sumaidy, who sported a silk kerchief in his blazer, furnished his office with a fridge, a three-piece suite and a tasteful collection of paintings.

The coalition's attempt from the outset, in the transitional institutions it created, to measure precisely and to exactly reflect Shia and Sunni (and Arab and non-Arab) proportions of the populations for the first time in the country's modern history elevated sectarian and ethnic identity to the rank of primary organising political principle. As in the Lebanese system of *nidham al-muhasasa al-taifiya*, posts were parcelled out according to ethnic and sectarian group for the first time in Iraq's history, unleashing the country's latent sectarianism and creating a communal state.[130] Since 80 per cent of the population were declared to be Shia, Christians or Kurds, they secured 80 per cent of the seats. Sunni Arabs, who made up 20 per cent of the population, were assigned five of the Council's 25 seats. Of those, three were exiles. And of the two who had been in Iraq before the war, one transpired to be a Kurd (Islamic Party leader Mohsen Abdel Hamid) and the other had an Ottoman name, suggesting Turkish origins (Nassir Chaderchi). The Sunni Arab power-base that had governed the country for centuries was disenfranchised from America's new Iraq.[131]

Subsequent appointments only compounded Sunni alienation. As they set about building their fledging administration, the Governing Councillors cloned themselves in their mushrooming bureaucracy. For all their pretensions to western norms, the exiles catapulted their nephews, cousins and sons into ministerial, ambassadorial and bureaucratic posts. Iyad Allawi, the Council member who chaired the Security Committee, parachuted his son-in-law, Nouri Badran, into the post of interior minister.[132] Ahmed Chalabi, who ran the Finance Committee, slotted his relatives into the positions of trade minister, Trade Bank chairman and the Rafidain Bank president. And Chalabi's nephew, Salim Chalabi, a solicitor at the London offices of Clifford Chance, took charge of the Iraqi Special Tribunal, responsible for trying Saddam.[133] A Kurdish representative on the council, Jalal Talabani, made his son-in-law, Abdel Latif Rashid, water resources minister, and, not to be outdone, his Kurdish rival, Massoud Barzani, backed his nephew, Hosheyr Zebari, as foreign minister. Another councillor, London-based cleric Mohammed Bahr Uloum, threatened to resign unless his son, Ibrahim, became oil minister. 'Hopes that nepotism would fade with Saddam have been dashed,' moaned an oil ministry technocrat.[134]

As their patronage grew, so too did their demand for control over contract tenders, thinly disguised as a campaign to restore Iraq's sovereignty from America. Nassir Chaderchi, a minor member of the Council who ran the committee for designing a new flag for Iraq, awarded his London-based brother the $100,000 contract.[135] More influential members disbursed far larger sums. Abul Hoda al-Farouki, a former Palestinian business partner of

Ahmed Chalabi's, won a $327 million deal for supplying uniforms to the new Iraq army and refurbishing its bases. In an attempt to raise capital, the finance committee of the Governing Council (another Chalabi-led body) even considered mortgaging futures in oil production to four western banks, three of them American, for $1.4 billion.[136]

The more power they won, the more they squabbled over the spoils. The Council's first public tender – the issue of Iraq's first mobile licence – was split between three consortia, each with its own territory and political overlord. A business associate of Kurdish warlord Jalal Talabani won the northern licence and Chalabi's deputy, Mudhar Shawqat, and his son – émigrés from Canada – won the southern.[137] DeBaathification fell by the wayside in matters of business. Chalabi recruited a network of bodyguards, contractors and intelligence officers loyal to Saddam's son, Uday.[138] One of his associates, Mortaza Lakhani, a Pakistani-born Canadian with a pukka English accent who had traded oil for the Swiss company Glencoe under Saddam, resurfaced after the war seeking inroads with Chalabi's oil advisor, Nabil Moussawi, who amongst other offerings he had flown to London for a medical check-up.[139]

Other councillors were no less averse to using their offices for securing favourable deals. Nouri Badran, the Interior Minister and son-in-law of prime-minister-to-be, Iyad Allawi, awarded Lakhani a $12 million advance to buy a German plant manufacturing armoured cars, paid in new Iraqi dinars even before the currency had been made public tender. 'The Americans had vests and armoured cars, and the Iraqis had nothing but bad clothes bought by CPA contractors. So I decided to provide the leadership and asked a contractor to provide armoured cars immediately,' explained Badran.[140] Flushed with cash, Lakhani moved to Cyprus' plushest hotel, the Meridian, where business associates claim he treated visiting Iraqi officials and middlemen to the services of Russian escorts.[141] One year later, Lakhani had delivered only eight of the 100 armoured cars commissioned, and dozens of officials who might otherwise have survived assassination attempts were dead.

Oil supplies afforded even richer pickings. Conservative estimates claimed 120,000 barrels of crude oil a day, close to 10 per cent of the output, were smuggled abroad.[142] Even more lucrative was the import of refined products, in which Allawi's brother, Sabah, had a stake. In September 2003, Red Alert Group, an Atlanta-based company, appointed him director to 'greatly facilitate our foreign activities', in the words of its website, and within months had acquired contracts squirrelling liquid petroleum gas from Iraq's Beiji refinery to Gulf markets, despite critical shortages inside Iraq.[143] Others joined the smuggling ring, hauling fuel earmarked to relieve petrol queues overland to Jordan, via Kurdistan to Iran, or south to Iraq's Um Qasr port, where, according to transport minister Bahnam Boulos, Chalabi had appropriated one of the berths to sidestep official docking fees.[144] Far from instituting clean government and western concepts of transparency, the new regime stood accused of perpetuating industrialised smuggling for personal gain.

Even their own cadres were aghast: 'What is different between them and Saddam's sons?' asked one of Chalabi's closest advisors, who abandoned the movement in disgust after a few months in Iraq.[145] 'Many Iraqis appointed by the Americans know they have no constituency and are seeking the maximum benefit before getting out. The amount of corruption has never been seen even in the darkest days of Saddam Hussein.' The Council's reputation for kleptomania was so prevalent it became an in-house joke. At the signing ceremony of the Transitional Administrative Law, Jalal Talabani was overheard chiding Chalabi: 'Ahmed, leave the pen'.

For the most part, US officials allowed their protégés to operate unfettered, hoping they might increase their potential for patronage. In rare instances, the Coalition did tepidly intervene. Badran was forced to resign as interior minister following allegations of currency-smuggling, but left free to drive out of the Green Zone in a cream Cadillac and on to Dubai, where he resumed his work as Iraqi middleman – this time peddling insurance. Belatedly, in February 2004, Bremer's administration nudged the Governing Council to establish a Commission of Public Integrity to investigate official misconduct. But Muwaffaq al-Rubaie, the Council member arm-twisted into unveiling the Commission, stopped short of naming its members, and the Finance Ministry procrastinated in the transfer of funds to pay salaries.

Spared official scrutiny, the Governing Council sought to shield itself from public accountability as well. Though it claimed to be Iraq's legislative body, none of its sessions were broadcast and members sidestepped demands that they make a declaration of interests. Their aversion to criticism could be intemperate. A Voice of America correspondent was banned after questioning a Council member's integrity, and journalists constrained from making their own enquiries. 'Reporters have no right to ask that,' huffed Chaderchi when asked about his role in a tender, before terminating the interview. The Council backed the creation of an independent regulator for the country's broadcast media, but like Bremer insisted on a place on the board from where they needled hapless editors.[146] While professing its belief in a free press, the Council in September 2003 shut down two of the Arab world's most popular satellite channels on the grounds they incited violence.

To divert attention, the Governing Council focussed attentions on the iniquities of the former regime. In September 2003, Bremer handed the Governing Council responsibility for the deBaathification portfolio, and named Ahmed Chalabi its chairman of what became under his tenure a Star Chamber. Ministries led by mainly Shia exiles scoured files in a witch-hunt for apparatchiks who lurked in the woodwork. 'The Baathists all changed their identities and fiddled their files on the eve of war,' said Haider Abadi, the communications minister who joined the government from the London suburb of Neasden.[147] Baath party property was requisitioned 'in the name of the Iraqi people'.

From the fifth floor of a Green Zone office-block, the Committee took charge of the school syllabus, removing Saddam from the textbooks, and festooning classrooms with banners proclaiming Baathism = Nazism. Another department oversaw a programme of 'economic deBaathification', blacklisting recalcitrant beneficiaries of the former regime who shied from working with Iraq's new elite. 'All those who benefited from the former regime have to be prevented from gaining more business,' said a Chalabi cadre.[148] 'We are going to uncover those who have dealt with the previous regime and stop them gaining more contracts.' Conveniently, the committee focussed on deals in which Chalabi and his followers had an interest, notably the Baghdad mobile licence, in which Nadhmi Auchi, Saddam's alleged banker, had a stake. The Amman-based Arab Bank, the Palestinian bank whose former chairman, Mohammed Nabulsi, had ended Chalabi's banking career in Jordan, found its licence to operate in Iraq strangely blocked.[149]

The lords of deBaathification revelled in their newfound power. Chalabi delved into a backlog of files hunting for incriminating data to blackmail his political and commercial opponents. In January 2004, *al-Mada*, a post-war Iraqi newspaper, published a leaked list of 270 politicians and businessmen from 47 countries who had been issued coupons by the pre-war Energy Ministry to sell oil shipments through middlemen in the UAE. Amongst the alleged recipients were former French interior minister, and confidante of

Jacques Chirac, Charles Pasqua and the UN head of the oil-for-food programme, Benon Sevan, who subsequently fled to Cyprus in disgrace.[150]

The axe fell harshest on the weak. Within a month of Chalabi's takeover, over 15,000 teachers had been sacked. 'You can't fire 900 teachers and give them no incentive to support the interim government,' General David Petraeus, the commander of US forces in northern Iraq, reproached Chalabi on a rare visit by the latter to Mosul, whose population equated deBaathification to a plot to subdue Sunni Arabs. 'Every Sunni family had at least one member in the senior ranks of the Baath, or the intelligence services, or the Special Republican Guard,' said one of its townsmen, Mithal Jibouri, a Sunni tribal leader and Baathist.[151] 'We would rather have a civil war than accept that Arab Sunnis be jailed or expelled from government for being Baathists.'

The notion that the Baath was the sole preserve of the Sunnis was mistaken. Even in its latter years, the party still attracted secular Shias, mistrustful of Iran and the clerics. Though Saddam's clan of Tikritis controlled decision-making, Shias proliferated even in the senior ranks,[152] and almost certainly comprised an absolute majority of its estimated 1.5 million members. But the Shia overlords of deBaathification gave their coreligionists a chance to repent when they were discovered, while summarily sacking Sunnis. And while Shias readily found a new home with Shia religious parties, Sunnis in the new order often found themselves cast under a cloud of suspicion. For many Sunnis, deBaathification was synonymous with de-Sunnification, and thus an essential centrifugal force separating Iraq into its confessional parts.

While the Governing Council was entrusted with reconfiguring civilian affairs, the US coalition protective of its monopoly on the use of authorised force insisted the military remain off-limits. Three years after the invasion, Iraq remained without a status of forces agreement. Bremer only appointed a defence minister in the dying months of his tenure, carefully selecting a businessman devoid of military experience – Ali Allawi, a cousin and ally of Ahmed Chalabi. The skeletal force he succeeded in mustering remained subject to US command. While their American mentors patrolled in mortar-deflecting tanks, vulnerable Iraqi trainees trailed after in soft-skinned pick-ups supplied on the cheap from Eastern Europe (as part of another contract with one of Chalabi's associates).

Had Bremer worked to rebuild a central military force, Iraq's subsequent fragmentation might have been averted. Instead he spurned Iraqi participation, outlawing both the army and the militias – with the crucial exception of Kurdish *peshmergas* forces – while lacking the manpower either to secure Iraq's politicians and its population, or to enforce his decrees.[153] In response to the assassination of SCIRI leader Mohammed Baqir al-Hakim in Najaf, in August 2003, thousands of armed SCIRI fighters in black – the Badr brigade – took charge of the funeral, frisking passers-by and manning the rooftop of the Imam Ali shrine. They were, said party leaders, the 'sharp sword defending the Iraqi people'.[154] In the ensuing manhunt, a local Baath chief, Karim Ghaith, was tortured to death in SCIRI's party headquarters, 'in name of the people of Najaf'.[155] US forces hid from sight.

SCIRI's mobilisation prompted rival Shia groups to launch their own squads, if only to compete with the Badr. A few miles north, militiamen loyal to Hakim's rival, Muqtada Sadr, erected checkpoints at Kufa, and Dawa fighters manned more checkpoints nearby. Another Najaf cleric, the half-blind Bahr al-Uloum, threatened to resign his seat on the Governing Council unless it financed a force. 'A militia is a last choice, not the best choice,' said the 78-year-old cleric, sitting beneath the portraits of some 17 relatives murdered under Saddam. 'But I have the right to protect myself.'[156] The interior ministry was too weak to intervene. Of its 2,500 police, only 400 were armed, and of those, said police, half were broken. And anyway, rival members of the Governing Council had no faith in them. 'How can I trust the INA [the party of interior minister Badran] to run Iraq's security?' said Chalabi's deputy, Mudhar Shawqat.[157] 'Individual ministries need their own security forces.'

Iraq was soon aflush with private liveried armies. Shawqat himself hired a force in a business partnership with Terry Sullivan, a US Navy Seal and ex-CPA official. Chalabi's allies in the oil ministry paid themselves out of oil revenues to assemble a 14,000-strong oil installation protection force named Erinys after the Greek God of Fury. Amongst the directors were ex-SAS mercenaries and Faisal Sadoun, son of Chalabi's loyal confidante, Tamara Daghestani. Its men, in part, came from Chalabi's Free Iraqi Forces,[158] as well as Kurds from Sufi brotherhoods. Irate Sunni Arab ex-policemen – who under Saddam had guarded the oilfield – found new jobs with the insurgency, and promptly proceeded to target the new staff, including a genial elderly cousin of Jalal Talabani, shot dead in June 2004.

Sometimes, the Shia and Kurdish forces appeared set on expansionist agendas. In December 2003, during the rotating presidency of SCIRI leader

Abdel Aziz Hakim, the coalition agreed to mobilise a 1,000-man battalion selected in equal numbers from the five dominant factions of the Governing Council, who all (not by chance) were Shias and Kurds. Amongst their first operations was an attack on Falluja, the core of the Sunni insurgency. 'If the parties send their militias to the Sunni areas in the centre it is war,' said Mishaal Jabouri of the Homeland Party.[159] Even Ghazi al-Yawar – a leader of the powerful Shammar tribe and appointed the first post-invasion president – warned of Iraq's Lebanonisation. 'We are back in an age of warlords,' he declared.[160] His uncle, Mohsen al-Faisal al-Jaber, was one of them. By the end of 2004, he was master of a private military company, Action, comprised of 2,200 Sunni tribesmen and Jordanian recruits.[161] Largely inadvertently, America's Iraqi appointees were fragmenting the state they claimed to protect.

And yet even as their country was crumbling, they craved the power they had. While publicly praising Sistani and his call for elections, the Governing Council highlighted the procedural obstacles for a poll that might oust them from office. Before elections could be countenanced, the franchise had to be defined, a census conducted, and Saddam's Decree No. 666 of 1980, stripping deported citizens of their nationality, revoked to ensure Iraqis abroad regained voting rights. 'Democracy cannot be achieved and the elections will not be honest unless these citizens and other citizens return to the homeland,' said Samir Sumaidy, a dapper council member who most days sported a bow tie, and had no greater desire for elections than Bremer.[162] Equally threatening to their political careers was Bremer's deadline for dissolving not just the CPA but also their Council by 1 July 2004. 'Keeping the Governing Council is vital to give the country a sense of continuity,' protested Muwaffaq Rubaie. The Council should be the 'guarantor of power', he said, in a country spinning out of control.[163]

Though the Council itself was abolished, its members succeeded in temporarily securing their futures. Many were appointed to the government that followed Bremer's departure, until a series of elections whittled most from public view.

For all that, they were not bloodthirsty and most were dedicated. They championed Sistani's admonitions against revenge killings, and displayed markedly more restraint, pluck and nous than America's imported administration. In the insurrections that started in April 2004, Sunni council members shuttled between tribal patriarchs in the Sunni triangle and occupation administrators; Shia members did the same in the south. Almost all suffered repeated attempts on their lives, two fatally.

And yet by representing exclusively ethnic and religious constituencies, they nurtured the seeds of the sectarianism that was to be Iraq's undoing. Shia ministers turned their ministries into bastions of power for their various factions, and party membership ensured if not a job, at least a fast-track up the rungs of the civil service. One minister, Jamal al-Din Sagheer, turned the mosque where he preached into a recruitment office.[164]

Government offices were festooned in the bunting of Shiism Triumphant, and the images of Ayatollahs grew almost as prevalent as those of pre-war Saddam. As Bremer walked out of the health ministry, the first to be handed back from coalition to Iraqi control, its new owners proudly unfurled a four-storey black banner over the portico victoriously proclaiming 'Hussein's Revolution'. At the gates to Mustansiriya University, hitherto considered the capital's most emancipated college, Shia god-squads turned back women students and lecturers sporting trousers and tank-tops. Unveiled women risked insults, or worse, on the streets, and though ministers denied it, female civil servants defying reprimands against showing their hair risked dismissal. Men switched from duplicating Saddam's thick moustache to sporting salt-and-pepper beards, Iranian-style, and the televised call from prayer from the Sunni to the Shia rite. For the first time in Iraq's history, a Shia ran Iraq's *awqaf* – religious trusts – which numbered 10,000 in Baghdad alone, and which were held to be the country's most valuable asset after oil. Shias commandeered 18 Sunni mosques, including two in Karbala and Najaf, prompting Sunnis to coin the term 'sectarian cleansing'. 'Emptying Najaf and Karbala of the Sunni presence is a grave phenomenon akin to the Balkanisation of Iraq,' protested Sheikh Abdelsalam al-Kubaysi, the spokesman of the Muslim Scholars Council, a Sunni lobby.[165]

The Council's foreign policy underwent a similar conversion. In December 2003, it formerly accepted Iraqi culpability for the eight-year-long war with Iran's Islamic Republic, and offered to pay reparations, despite Iraq's crippling foreign debts. Ibrahim Bahr al-Uloum, the oil minister and son of a Najafi cleric, signed an agreement to lay a pipeline to the Iranian port of Abadan, the first link in a plan to join the grids of historic adversaries in a project which surprisingly won US acquiescence.[166] As Iran responded with copious support for the Council's legitimacy,[167] the Arab League – a largely Sunni club – turned its back on the country, relegating the Council to observer status devoid of legality. With the exception of the emir of Kuwait, Arab leaders who had unfolded red carpets for the previous regime only met its members in a private not official capacity.

But the most dramatic change was on the streets. Iraq's first post-invasion Ashoura was a celebration of Shia revivalism, and an end to almost 80 years of censorship. The forecourts of *husseiniyas* morphed into stages for cavalry charges pitting Sunnis against Shia. Even Baghdad's premier commercial theatre staged a *teshabeeh*, or passion play, re-enacting with gory detail the 680 CE massacre, replacing spears with Kalashnikovs. Iraq's American-financed television beamed enthusiastic footage of the self-mortification of young children lashing themselves with chains. And banners embossed blood-red with the name of Hussein hung the length of state institutions. Non-Shias too were dragooned into honouring Ashoura. Christian restaurateurs and the Sunni Hashemite scion Sherif Ali bin Hussein all doled out the traditional Ashoura gruel, *timan wa qima*, from vast vats along Baghdad's main roads.

Even the massacre of 150 dead in simultaneous bombings in Baghdad and Karbala at the height of Ashoura failed to quell celebrations. Within hours of the attacks, the ecstatic chants were again echoing through the shrines. Baghdad's Sunni chattering classes muttered that Iraq's Iranophiles had at last got their comeuppance, but faced with the paradigm shift in Sunni–Shia power politics after 1,000 years of supremacy, they were increasingly acting like a minority, anxious to retain their own rite. Their religious leaders chose separate days to mark the end of the month of Ramadan, and separate times to mark the end of the daily fast, flaunting their cigarettes a quarter of an hour before Shias to emphasise their differences, and more ominously discharging a hail of gunfire into the air. Amidst the confusion over which rite to follow, civil servants yearned for past simplicities, when Saddam Hussein declared the end of the month according to his shifting relations with Tehran and Riyadh. 'Then the state religion was politics,' grumbled a director-general at the communications ministry. 'Today, the state politics is religion.'[168]

Section 3

Balkanisation of the Broken State

CHAPTER 10

From Baathism to Jihad

There was nothing inevitable about a Sunni revolt. The USA had faced less resistance in Sunni provinces it captured than in Shia, and as the southern provinces they could have been integrated and hence largely pacified earlier. And as long as US forces limited their manhunt to the 55 names on the pack of cards there was scant communal backlash. Many Sunnis, in particular Sufi groups, had been active in intelligence gathering for the Americans before the war, criss-crossing the country with Thurya satellite phones recording the coordinates of key American targets. But a series of post-invasion decisions rapidly awakened the population to the Shia revolution Washington had in store. To Sunnis, Bremer's institutional steps – abolition of the armed forces, deBaathification and Shia supremacy on the Governing Council – amounted to collective punishment and relegation to the back of Iraq's new pecking order. Under the bayonets of the region's conspirators, Britain and the United States, the cradle of the Caliphs had fallen prey to traitors bent on dispossessing Iraq's traditional primates, the Sunnis.

Stunned by the intensity of its collapse, the Baath took time to regroup. No American soldier was killed in the first six weeks following the toppling of the regime, and the army waited to be recalled, and even offered their services, only to be spurned. But within weeks, the climate had changed. Days after the UN Security Council recognised the Governing Council as Iraq's representative body, Sunni militiamen struck the UN headquarters in Baghdad on 19 August 2003, killing the UN special envoy, Sergio di Mello, and 19 others. And the northern mainly Arab town of Mosul, which had enjoyed months of relative quiet under General Petraeus, emerged under the pressures of deBaathification as a haven for armed discontents.

Locked down in their Baghdad enclave, American spokesmen derided insurgents as FRLs – former regime loyalists – and 'deadenders'. The resistance, they confidently predicted, would peter out once the regime's leaders were captured. By early December, US forces had captured all but 15 of the 55 faces on their pack of cards. And on 15 December, America's jubilant proconsul took to the carpeted stage of the Convention Centre to grin at the cameras 'We got 'im' – a reference to Saddam Hussein. To rub in their triumph, American soldiers displayed the underwear, chocolate treats and the home-made sausages the Ace of Spades had strung from the walls of his coffin-size hideout. The accompanying reduction in the death toll of US forces – from 80 in November 2003 to 40 in December – gave grist to their claims that the back of the rebellion had been broken.

Had the occupation been more sensitively administered, Saddam's capture might indeed have proved a turning point. But fuelled by burning resentment, the insurgency had acquired a momentum of its own, beyond the command of the Baath's senior brass. Saddam's refuge in the palm grove of his cook, Qais Namaq, contained no communications equipment, and only two lacklustre guards defended the entrance, robbing the taking of Dark List One of an action-packed climax. 'We had intelligence that there would be an underground facility... We expected something better constructed, not something so humble,' said James Hickey, the US commander who led the assault at Doura, across the river from his hometown of Oujda. A stash of $750,000 notes suggested that he had either spent most of the $1 billion filched from the Central Bank vaults as Baghdad fell, or others had control of the money.

But the insurgency had already found a home: on a hill overlooking the hive of activity at the hideout, local leaders kept vigil under the arches of a new marble mosque. 'Our prayers are not acceptable in the eyes of God under occupation without Jihad,' said a former Iraqi intelligence officer now garbed in white religious robes. 'The Prophet Mohammed and his Companions died, but Islam lives on.' After evening prayers, they exchanged accounts of Saddam's capture embellished with a religious reverence Shias reserved for fallen Imams. So intoxicating was the gas used to smoke their leader from his hole that birds in the vicinity dropped dead from the sky. American soldiers kept watch near the hideout to prevent it becoming a shrine.

But aside from the odd demonstration in Sunni parts of Baghdad, the only towns to openly lament Saddam's incarceration were those like Doura, near his birthplace. While some fellow tribesmen sought to rebrand their president as a Sunni leader, many others cast him as the mother of all cowards for meekly surrendering to US forces while goading Iraqis to give their lives. Far from extinguishing the rebellion, his capture allowed anti-US forces to free themselves from a tarnished association with Saddam. The rebellion was acquiring a new identity. The prevailing graffiti changed from *Aish Saddam!* – Long Live Saddam – to *Aish al-Mujahideen*. 'The army of Falluja is the army of Islam not Saddam,' cried the city's walls.

The process of Islamisation was patchy, localised and frequently contradictory. Unlike the Shia, Sunnis lacked a *marjaiya*, or central source of spiritual authority, and proved far slower to regroup nationally than their Shia counterparts. Also unlike the Shia, their institutions had long been entwined with and dependent on the state. By early 2004, community leaders counted 36 atomised Sunni groups, loosely gravitating around three broad schools: Sufi, Muslim Brotherhood and Salafi activist.

All three trends had a history that predated the war. In the 1990s they had to varying degrees been co-opted by the Saddam regime, particularly its vice-president, Ezzat al-Douri, who had risen from hawking ice on a cart to overseeing the regime's religious affairs. Before and after the war, street traders peddled CDs of al-Douri and Qusay Hussein gyrating and chanting at a *takiya*, or Sufi séance, in western Baghdad, particularly those of the Rifaiya order, with whom he had blood ties. Douri had overseen the garish restoration of many of Baghdad's old Sufi shrines – including those of Abdel Qadir al-Gailani, the founder of the Qadiriya order, and Sheikh Maarouf, an eighth-century mystic revered by the Naqshbandiya order. The Kasnazaniya order, an offshoot of the Qadiriya, had provided the bodyguards of senior regime cadres, including Saddam.

The regime's relationship with the Muslim Brotherhood was equally involved. Founded in Egypt in 1929 as a movement to build an Islamic state, the Brotherhood struck roots in Iraq 30 years later after the fall of the monarchy. It quickly attracted the interest of the Baath, not least as an instrument of Iraq's foreign policy. To counter Egyptian influence, the first Baathist president Abd al-Salam Arif offered to give sanctuary to Sayid Qutb, the Brotherhood's radical mentor, following his arrest by Egyptian president Gamal Abdel Nasser. And subsequently, the Brotherhood joined cause with the Baath in its struggle in Palestine and against Syrian Alawite rule. In return for its support in the 1968 Baathist coup, the Brotherhood was rewarded with a cabinet seat, and the Iraqi

Islamic Party was gradually subsumed into Baathist institutions, particularly the universities. Its leader, Muhsin Abd al-Hamid, was a professor at Baghdad University's Education Faculty and as part of the regime's *hamla imaniya*, or faith struggle, the Brotherhood was granted control of Baghdad's southern suburbs.

Traditionally, the Muslim Brotherhood eschewed violence, except where, as in Palestine and Alawite-ruled Syria, it deemed non-Muslims occupied Muslim land. In US-occupied Iraq, the Brotherhood was initially undecided. Following the invasion, it split into two groups. Abd al-Hamid's Iraqi Islamic Party called for dialogue and accepted a seat as a presidential member of the Iraqi Governing Council. Its rival, the Association of Muslim Scholars, proclaimed a Jihad against American rule. The two wings competed for control of Iraq's 5,000 Sunni mosques. While Abd al-Hamid shared a platform with America's proconsul, the Association chastised Iraqi collaborators from their headquarters in the towering Um al-Qura mosque, whose four minarets Saddam had sculptured as ballistic missiles. 'How long will the infidels continue spreading corruption in our lands, rape our sisters, and kill our innocents?' thundered one of their preachers, calling Iraq America's graveyard.[169] 'If we dared do otherwise, the people would kill us,' apologised the sheikh after the sermon.[170] Relief parcels earmarked for Sunni villages under US attack lay piled in the mosque forecourt, some of them ripped open after an American raid. Statistics showed attacks peaked after Friday prayers, and sometimes mosques or their environs doubled as launch pads for mortar attacks.

The Association was led by the Dharis, a clan based between Baghdad and Falluja, whose battle with Anglo-American imperialism dated back four generations. While most Sunni tribes had found common cause with British rule of Iraq, the Dharis alone had rebelled, shooting a British Colonial Officer in Falluja, Colonel Gerard Evelyn Leachman, an act later celebrated in a film Saddam funded starring Oliver Reed. 'Muslims were against British occupation then, and they are against the Anglo-American occupation now,' said Muthanna Dhari, the young scion and spokesman who called the Association 'the political arm of the resistance'. Using tribal solidarity, or *assabiya*, to facilitate cross-border smuggling, the Dharis cemented a network spanning key sections of the Baghdad–Amman highway. Khan Dhari, the Dhari's tribal territory, was a hunting ground for abducting foreigners, and his tribe a favoured address and financial conduit for negotiating hostage releases.

The Salafis were the third Islamist trend fuelling the insurgency. Their school called for blinkered adherence to the way of Islam's *salaf*, or forebears – the Prophet and his Companions. Of the three, it was the youngest and smallest, both because the regime had hounded and jailed its members since its inception in Iraq in the late 1950s and because it was isolationist and exclusive. Rival groups, including the Association, were dismissed as lily-livered. 'They are just spoilt former regime loyalists,' said Fakhri Qaissi, a spokesman for the Salafi front, the Higher Commission for Call, Guidance and Fatwa in Iraq, who had spent years in Saddam's jails. 'They were professors who doled out PhDs to whoever al-Douri told them to.'[171]

In the immediate aftermath of the US invasion, Iraq's Salafis preferred to remain above the fray. Fakhri retained his job as a doyen of the Baghdad Dentistry College, an almost cuddly eccentric who wore a white hospital overall instead of a Salafi tunic. After long years of incarceration in Baathist prisons, he spent his weekends with the pro-American Kurdish leader Jalal Talabani and was keen to meet US officials. 'We wanted them to liberate us,' he said while invigilating a practical examination on teeth drilling. 'But it should have happened with dignity, not in this way.' Iraq's Salafis, he insisted, followed the teachings of Mohammed Abdou, a reform-minded Egyptian chief *mufti* appointed by the British in the late nineteenth century, not those of Saudi Arabia. To prove he opposed Saudi-style sexual segregation, he teased the female nurses in the hospital wards.

Juxtaposed with this older Iraqi salafism was a younger more virulent strain – which had arrived from Afghanistan in the mid-1990s. Fashioned out of the eighteenth century theology and practice of Sheikh Muhammad Ibn Abdel Wahhab, a revolutionary purist from the central Saudi outback of Najd, his disciples had applied his thought anew first in the early twentieth century to carve out the kingdom of Saudi Arabia and sixty years later in Afghanistan. After victory against the Soviet-backed rule, they had headed home, seeping into Iraq's peripheries – particularly along the upper Euphrates Valley – where their access to Saudi petro-dollars helped them strike roots amongst the sanctions-afflicted population. So prevalent did they become, that in places they supplanted Iraq's traditionalist Hanafi and Shaafi schools, until the regime – in need of allies – moved to co-opt it.[172] In the run-up to war, al-Douri oversaw the construction of Wahhabi mosques in the Shia holy city of Najaf, as well as in Baghdad and Mosul. Their anti-Shia diatribe complemented the regime's predictions that a US invasion would transfer rule from Iraq's Sunnis to an unholy alliance of foreign infidels and Shias, or, in Salafi parlance, *Rafida*, or rejectionists.

A New Year's Day raid on the Salafi's Baghdad base at the massive Ibn Taymiya mosque, another product of post-invasion loot, helped fuse the two strains – old and modern – of Iraqi Salafism. After uncovering an arms cache, US forces detained its Imam, Mehdi Sumaidy. His detention transformed the movement. From his prison camp, Sumaidy proselytised amongst bored inmates, supplanting their diet of Baathist and Arab nationalist ideology with the Salafi creed of puritanical Islam. 'I was happy in Abu Ghraib,' Sumaidy said after his release in June 2004. 'I created a prison *madrasa* with hundreds of students studying Qur'an and Sharia six hours a day. It was a spiritual high.'[173] US soldiers only too anxious to keep their inmates occupied provided four tents, Qur'ans and rosaries by the boxful, and even a megaphone for Friday prayers. 'We aren't stopping anybody in the compounds from practising their religious freedoms, and allow religious leaders to take services, regardless of what their messages may be,' said a US prison guard.[174]

Sumaidy's corner of Abu Ghraib morphed into a production line of Salafi activists. After study sessions, he staged demonstrations, which US military contractors countered first with dogs and then 'chicken torture', a stress position in which his head was hooded, and his arms and legs pinned behind his back in handcuffs and strung from a chain. To compound the agony, guards beat him and chastised him as Bin Laden as he rotated. In solitary confinement he continued to preach – this time to American guards, one of whom he claimed to have converted. 'I told her she had beautiful eyes,' he said. The compliment earned him the much-prized gift of a pen, which he used to write fatwas on the stickers of coke bottles, since paper was banned.

If Sumaidy had entered prison an individual puritan, he emerged in June 2004 as a group activist. He took to the pulpit castigating Iraqi policemen protecting the American order as *muwali*, or servants of apostasy, for whom God's punishment was death. 'If the resistance discovers that someone is cooperating in any way with the Americans, it kills that person. They are unbelievers. It is forbidden even to carry water for them,' he said, courteously smiling. In his sermons, he erected a mental as well as physical wall around Sunni identity, removing them from their new environment, redefining the sect as a distinct community. He envisaged the creation of a strict Sunni emirate, in which believers were sanitised from the strays who sullied themselves from infidel contact. But the result was that from its previous suzerainty of Iraq, Sunni Islam geographically was in retreat.

At the same time, a third core of Salafi activists had established a mountain retreat in the vacuum that followed the establishment of the Kurdish safe haven. By the end of 2001 up to 500 ex-Afghan veterans, including 100 Egyptians, had journeyed from Central Asia through Iran to the mountainous frontier posts of the Islamist Kurdish movement, Ansar al-Islam.[175] Replicating their lifestyle along the Pakistan–Afghan border, they established *diur al-diafa*, or guesthouses, and under the command of a former Egyptian army colonel, Muhammad Makkawi, who had overseen al-Qaeda's training programme in Afghanistan, and reinforced Ansar positions against attack from the PUK, the US-backed secular Kurdish party claimed control of the region.

Amongst the new arrivals was Ahmad al-Khalayilah, better known by his alias Abu Musab Zarkawi after his Jordanian birthplace, Zarqa, a mainly Palestinian town near Amman with a reputation for militancy.[176] He was an awkward loner; few could have predicted a future career as, depending on your viewpoint, 'the delight of the eyes of the Mujahideen' or Washington's second most wanted Islamist with a price-tag of $25 million. Even the soft-spoken Lebanese boarding-school-educated Usama Bin Laden was said to have found him obsessive, and kept him at arm's length.[177] He arrived in Afghanistan in time for the battle of Khosht in 1991 in the closing months of the Afghan war, and thereafter found refuge in a guesthouse west of Kabul with a group of 30 Jordanian Muslim Brothers under the patronage of Gulbedin Hekmatyar. Jailed on his return to Jordan in the mid-1990s, Zarkawi derided even fellow Islamist convicts as non-Muslim,[178] and on his release headed back to Iraq. Suggestions that the Iraqi authorities kept track of his whereabouts were strengthened by Jordanian claims that in 2002 a Baghdad hospital treated his leg wound.[179] Following an operation, he moved to Anbar province where – again quoting Jordanian officials – he plotted attacks on Americans in Amman. Anticipating the US invasion, he also assembled a network of cells based on tribal ties, which post-war emerged as Jama'at al-Tawhid wal-Jihad, the Group of Unity and Jihad.

Zarkawi may well have owed his success in moulding Iraqi Salafis and Afghan veterans into a new force, Jihadist Salafiya, to American bombing. In the wake of US attacks on Ansar al-Islam positions during the April 2003 invasion, Jihadis fled Kurdistan for Sunni Arab towns in the Euphrates

Valley. Saddam's last-ditch invitation for Jihadis to join the defence followed by Bremer's abolition of the border guard facilitated the unimpeded entry of further recruits. Throughout the CPA's tenure, only three of the 36 checkpoints Saddam had maintained along the Saudi border, and only 11 of the 270 countrywide, were manned.

The non-Iraqi accents on Jihadi videos circulating in Baghdad's markets gave clear evidence of the extent of foreign organisation. An Ansar al-Sunna video warned 'the brokers of the West' their Jihad would continue 'until we get back [the Jerusalem mosque of] Al-Aqsa and Andalucía [Spain]'. 'I will sacrifice every drop of my blood in the cause of Allah and tell Muslims everywhere to rebel against the Arab rulers, the traitors and agents. May Allah accept it from me,' said Abu-Salih, in a last will and testament before driving his 'car of death' at Kurdish offices in Kirkuk. Another entitled *Hidaya al-Eid*, the Holiday Gifts, featured sheikhs bearing Saudi accents and Hijazi tribal names such as al-Ghamdi. 'We tell our brothers from the Al-Qa'qa, Tariq and Death Brigades that they must now head for Iraq to support the brigades stationed in the land of Mesopotamia,' proclaimed the Brigade of Abu Hafs, the *nom de guerre* of a Saudi veteran of the Afghan Jihad. Another titled 'Heading the Convoy' had Zarkawi in the lead role. 'Here is America among us. So, come take revenge on it and quench your thirst with its blood,' he incanted.

There was no shortage of supply. Death notices on Jihadi websites recorded martyrs hailing from the Chinese province of Xingjian to Britain. Amongst them was a 22-year-old Yemeni asylum-seeker, Wail Abdelrahman, from Britain's northern industrial town of Sheffield. He had been the ultimate sleeper. He sported no more than a wisp of a goatee, and had fought for England in international Tae Kwon Do competitions, and celebrated after games down the pub. His coach tipped him to join the British Olympic Squad.[180] And the only hint of political activity known to team-mates was two trips he took to London to take part in marches against the Iraq war. Before leaving for Iraq, he told friends he was flying to Dubai to escape the white youths who dumped trash through his letterbox.[181]

Nevertheless, compared to earlier deployments, particularly Bosnia which attracted hundreds of British Muslims, Jihadi head-hunters in Europe found the Iraq war a hard sell. Europe's security forces increased their surveillance and Arabs had fewer visa problems; Yemenis, for instance, could enter Syria without a visa, and Algerian embassies, anxious to export their own problems, were said to be issuing passports to would-be recruits.[182] Volunteers in the West were also pricing themselves out of the market. 'For the cost of equipping and transporting a British fighter into Iraq – about $2,000 – we can shift two dozen guerrillas from Arab states and Chechnya into Iraq,' complained a retired Jihadi field officer in London.[183]

The bulk of foreign recruits came from neighbouring states, particularly Saudi Arabia where preachers sometimes backed by state institutions gave moral support. The kingdom's chief justice, Sheikh Salah al-Luhaidan, joined the call for believers to defend the Sunni realm with the same pioneering spirit with which two decades earlier they had defeated the Soviets.[184] By 2005, Saudi researchers estimated that a few thousand Saudis were fighting in Iraq, comprising perhaps half of the total non-Iraqi guerrillas waged against US forces.[185]

Averse neither to complicating American's mission for regional regime-change nor to sending troublesome Sunni Jihadis to kill themselves in Iraq, Syria, too, had an interest in facilitating their passage. Damascus became a key conduit for funds and a rear base where insurgents went for rest, recuperation and rendezvous. More than once former Vice-President Douri was reported to have met Iraqi tribal leaders near Aleppo, together with Baathist commander Mohammed Yunis al-Ahmad. Syrian intelligence, too, may have advised on the lessons learnt from the 1980s, when car-bombs forced US troops out of Lebanon. In its foreign addresses, Damascus denied all connections with the insurgency, but reports in local papers were more nuanced. 'According to moral standards, backing the resistance is dictated by the human conscience and is the duty of every free man in the world,' proclaimed its official press.[186] On condition they steered clear of Syrian affairs, imams in Syria were given free rein to preach the Jihad.

The foreign Jihadi presence played into the hands of American officials, who had long argued they were fighting al-Qaeda, not the Iraqis they had come to liberate. Preliminary investigations of attacks (few investigations were completed) were said to implicate a foreign hand. The New Year's Eve bombing of a smart Baghdad restaurant, Nabil's, was blamed on a Palestinian whose family reportedly received $10,000. The simultaneous attacks on the Kurdish offices in Irbil, which killed 150, were ascribed to a Yemeni. Interim Justice Minister Malek Dohan al-Hassan waved a list of 25 non-Iraqis to justify the assumption of the emergency powers.

But Iraqis needed little foreign instruction and less incentive in fighting. Despite American warnings of Falluja's takeover by foreign Jihadis, less than 30 of the 2,000 detainees captured in the US offensive of November

2004 were foreigners. More broadly, of 20,000 detainees US forces captured in their first two years, almost 99 per cent were Iraqi. And even the protestations of US commanders and their Iraqi allies that car-bombing was alien to the Iraqi mentality[187] clashed with the suicide-bomber parades Saddam staged in Baghdad on the eve of the war, and the fact that an Iraqi girl had launched the first suicide bombing when she rammed a US checkpoint at Najaf before coalition forces had reached Baghdad.[188] All told, no more than 10 per cent of the 30,000 estimated insurgents were thought to have come from abroad.[189] Zarkawi's killing in June 2006 exercised no noticeable restraint on the resistance.

Nevertheless, foreign influence may well have been greater than their numbers suggest. The influx of Jihadis rekindled the spirit of Iraqi resistance and anti-Shiism at a time when the collapse of the regime and the humiliation of Saddam's capture might have been overbearing, and offered a new activist ideology when Baathism seemed defunct. In exchange for membership and absolution, Baathists brought the money sequestered before Hussein fled, legions of former intelligence and military officers with logistics expertise, and large stockpiles of weapons.[190] The former regime provided the safehouses and the explosives and the Jihadis the recruits for self-sacrifice. US military spokesmen dubbed it a 'marriage of convenience', but the Iraqifying of al-Qaeda thought may have been a more accurate term. A movement ostracised to the caves of Afghanistan had found a homeland in the heart of the Middle East.[191]

The insurgency rebounded with a vengeance. A week after Saddam's capture, a wave of suicide bombers struck US positions near Mosul and north of Baghdad, downing a reconnaissance helicopter. 'January [2004] had the highest rate of violence since September 2003,' said an internal security report circulated by USAID, even as US officials insisted the security situation was improving. 'The violence continues despite the expansion of the Iraqi security services and increased arrests by coalition forces in December and January.'[192] Mortar attacks doubled between December and January 2004, roadside bombings tripled, and for the first time insurgents launched planned assaults of platoon-sized Special Forces against US positions.

In the months that followed resistance groups coined Islamist titles – 'Jihadi Earthquake Brigades', 'Saladin Brigades' aspiring to recover 'the capital of the caliphate', Baghdad. Mosques doubled as forward operating bases, and muezzins as vantage points to eye the battlefield. Al-

Mutawakkilun, or those who rely on God, filmed an attempted ambush of John Abizeid, the top US general in Iraq, from a mosque overlooking the US base. Further north, Ansar al-Sunna distributed video CDs of what it claimed to be a double suicide bombing in the Kurdish capital, Irbil. Along the bottom of the screen flashed the subtitle: 'Martyrs are offered a place in paradise adorned with *houris.*' Suicide bombing, a horrendous but highly effective form of advertising, had become a local speciality, so much so that insurgents took Iraqi journalists on tours of suicide training camps. A former intelligence officer disguised as a Shia cleric took an Iraqi colleague on one such tour and, after dumping him in the boot of a car in Baghdad, released him an hour later in a crusted desert dotted with palm logs. He emerged to find a skinny youth in a small battered Corona trying to negotiate an obstacle course before ramming a metal drum with his left-hand tied to the steering wheel to thwart second thoughts. Another trainee guarding the drum dressed in a light blue shirt nervously fired blanks back at him. 'Kill him before he kills you,' shouted the instructor, a former Saddam Fedayeen officer who called himself Director 1000, but the youth succeeded only in ramming his car into a log.

Mishaps were frequent, particularly in the early stages of the campaign. On a crisp December morning, the remains of two cars littered the forecourt of the Lovers of Mustafa mosque in Hurriya, west Baghdad, which Vice-President Douri had handed over to Salafi preachers before the war. In a version of events echoed by the US military, mosque elders in starched Salafi tunics accused Shia militias of firing two rocket-propelled grenades from a school roof at the mosque. ('As the Shia do unto you, do unto them,' intoned the imam, Ahmed Dabbash.[193]) But the more credible version given by nearby residents was that the car-bombs had detonated prematurely, after dawn prayers, as two drivers prepared to embark on suicide missions. In an apparent effort to cover their tracks, the car wreckage, mangled by the force of the blast, had been towed clear of the mosque. But Salafis armed with white plastic bags scoured the mosque entrance for body parts, as masked guards with machine guns tried to disperse the crowds.

The first wave of car-bombings in August 2003 concentrated on America's perceived foreign accomplices: the Jordan Embassy, the UN headquarters, foreign aid agencies such as the Red Cross, and reconstruction companies. But Shias – chastised as America's prime local collaborators – quickly emerged as the prime and softest target. In late

August, Mohammed Baqir al-Hakim was killed in a car-bomb with 120 congregants outside the Najaf shrine following Friday prayers. The two members of the Governing Council to be assassinated – Aqila Hashemi (Tariq Aziz's former assistant) and Izzedin Salim – were also both Shia. Preachers fed the confessional contagion. Salafis renamed their main Baghdad mosque Ibn Taymiya, after their thirteenth-century mentor, who preached that believers who killed four Rafida would merit a *houri*-filled paradise, and that shrines, especially Shia ones, were a blot on Islam's unblemished monotheism and should be desecrated.[194]

Faced with Shia triumphalism, preachers struggling to retain a tradition of communal tolerance lost their flocks. In Abu Ghraib, a Baghdad satellite town with a mixed Sunni–Shia population, a local Imam, Sheikh Yasseen Zubaie, sitting cross-legged on his mud floor, grumbled that over a fifth of the town's 20,000 adult males had gravitated to Salafi mosques. To stem the exodus, Zubaie said he had toned down his own preference for civil resistance and early elections, and called for violent confrontation. Graffiti in the name of 'Mohammed's army' adorned his mosque walls, promising death to Shia spies. Shia pilgrims returning from the *hajj* to Mecca still paid courtesy calls to the Sheikh on their return, but the latter did not hide his disgust that Sunni pilgrims no longer had priority treatment. Loudspeakers at a Salafi mosque in the market opposite the Shia *husseiniya* called for the creation of Shia-free zones. Reverential images of Ali and other Shia Imams on the lampposts were either torn down or defaced. Coalition troops from Estonia garbed like storm-troopers sat in stationary open-topped trucks uncomprehending.

In early 2004, American military commanders captured a computer they claimed contained a 17-page letter from Zarkawi to fellow Jihadis in Afghanistan seeking approval to ignite a sectarian war against 'a religion that does not meet with Islam', whose followers 'were the bridge over which Islam's enemies pass'. With twenty-first-century tools, he suggested, the Salafis could complete the eighteenth-century mission of their founder Ibn Abdel Wahhab, who launched raids on Shia shrines intent on eradicating the sect. One month later on Ashoura, the holiest day of the Shia calendar, and the first after the liberation from Saddam, Abu Taysir, a pilgrim standing near the golden doors of Baghdad's Kathimiya sepulchre, heard a voice shout: 'You are polytheists and you worship Hussein son of Ali like a God.' Over 150 were killed in the blast of nails packed round explosive that followed – there, and simultaneously inside Imam Hussein's shrine in Karbala – on the bloodiest day of American rule. The forecourt tiles, already stained by the first public processions of scalp-slashing for 25 years, were drowned in blood. Carts, which seconds earlier had been piled with sweetmeats, morphed into ambulances. And on the day Iraqis had turned out in their millions to celebrate their new ritual freedom, the heavy teak-doors of their places of worship banged shut and clerics laid barbed-wire barricades to keep back their flock. At the nearby Kathimiya Hospital, the dead overflowed from the morgue onto the grass, heads covered from the sun with cardboard boxes. Tormented relations moved from fly-coated cadaver to cadaver lifting the flaps. 'It's not worth the price,' screamed a daughter sifting through the jumble of bodies. Against such atrocity, attacks on Shia markets, clerics and vendors seemed commonplace, and no longer made headlines.

Shiites were not the only victims of the Jihadi assault. Months before the car-bombing and shelling of five churches in July 2004, Christian children found leaflets pinned to school gates, warning non-Muslim Arabs to convert or die. In Jihadi eyes there was a host of evidence to prove Christians collaborated with their crusading coreligionists. Vicars allowed US army soldiers into their congregations, and accepted donations from western churches. Western missionaries – some doubling as CPA officials – had also proved as quick to rush into Iraq's vacuum as their Muslim counterparts, and gained access to Iraq's postal system to flood Baghdadis with evangelical literature. Christian professions, most particularly liquor traders, but also the owners of beauty parlours and barbers offering western-style haircuts, were conduits of western influence. Christian women trucked in daily to clean US bases were beheaded by the busload, but the violence tapped into a wave of recrimination. 'Sometimes we can't even buy our bread locally,' said Father Sorijan of a monastery in southern Baghdad hitherto patronised by Uday Hussein. 'They tell us to go and get it from *khawalna*, our cousins, the Americans.'[195]

The simultaneous attacks on five Christian shrines in August 2004 left only ten dead, a relatively modest toll for Iraq. But the plumes of smoke spiralling into the sky above Baghdad's bombed Christian shrines hung like a question-mark over the viability of the survival of one of the world's ancient Christian communities, comprising Chaldeans, Syriacs and Assyrians. As he swept up the stained glass inside the former reception hall of St Peter's seminary in the southern Baghdad suburb of Doura, caretaker Yohanna Shaya shook with anger, less at the attack than the young onlookers who had shouted at bleeding congregants that Christians had got what they deserved. 'The educated said the bombing was *haram*, or against Islam, and came to help, but the unemployed youth just drove past, jeering and tooting their horns,' he said. His three eldest children were already in Holland. 'I feel I've become a stranger in my own country.'

Spiritual leaders, including the Shia's Grand Ayatollah Ali Sistani, denounced the bombings, and politicians sent police cars to park in church courtyards. Even the self-styled political wing of the Sunni resistance, the Association of Muslim Scholars, blamed the attack on 'foreigners [attempting] to make our people quarrel with each other'. But the US invasion had overturned an ecumenical world 16 centuries in the making in which a Chaldean Catholic – Tariq Aziz – was deputy prime minister and Easter services were broadcast on national television. In its place, it had unleashed a Salafi reckoning that was turning Iraq into another Saudi Arabia cleansed of idol worship. Fearful of further attacks, Christian shopkeepers removed their church calendars, and secretaries tucked their crucifixes under their tops. Some donned veils; others recalled the fate of the Jews, the collapse of whose 2,500-year-old community 50 years earlier had also been precipitated by bombs in their places of worship and much official hand-wringing. With preferential access to western visas, the 800,000-strong communities of Assyrians, Chaldeans, Armenians and Syriac Christians weighed the option of joining the 2 million Iraqi Christians already residing abroad.

As Napoleon at the outset of the modern era, the neo-conservatives had gone to war dedicated to building Iraq as the standard bearer of modernist Islam and the antithesis of Salafist Saudi Arabia. Instead, in less than a year, Iraq was transformed from an officially secular state into what Francois Heisbour, of the Foundation for Strategic Research in Paris, called 'a Jihad factory' for regional action. An Iraq-based group, the Abu-Hafs al-Masri Brigades, bombed two synagogues in Istanbul during Ramadan in 2003, and a cell in Falluja led by another Afghan veteran, Abu Salama al-Hijiazi, claimed responsibility for the raid on a housing complex for foreigners in Riyadh in May 2004, killing 18 people. By the summer of 2005, insurgents were firing at Kuwaiti and Saudi border posts. Anguished pro-western Arab regimes, emerging drained from suppressing uprisings in the 1990s led by Jihadi *Afghaniyyin* who had defeated the Soviet superpower in Afghanistan, warned of a second Jihadi blowback from *al-mujahidin al-Iraqiyyin*, and braced for round two.

CHAPTER 11

The Sunni Arab Emirates

Falluja made an unlikely base to realise Sheikh Sumaidy's ideal of a separatist Sunni emirate. Under Saddam, the city had earned a reputation as a domestic tourist resort for sanctions-besieged Iraqis on the banks of the Euphrates, and a nearby safe haven when the West bombed Baghdad. Coupled with tourism, it owed its relative prosperity to the smuggler traffic that plied across the baked-cake earth of the desert wastes that linked it to Jordan and Saudi Arabia. But its independent income had also bred an independent spirit that had made it a traditional thorn in the side of regimes. Its tribesmen were almost the only Iraqi Sunnis to join Shias in the 1920 revolt against the British. Two decades later, the town had backed the military coup of Rashid Ali, who led an aborted assault on the nearby British military base of Habbaniya. Fallujans had also defied Saddam, refusing to chant the requisite cheers when his motorcade passed by. Rather than risk a showdown, Saddam chose an alternative route.

Two weeks after taking Baghdad, US forces ambled into Falluja all but unopposed, and turned a school into their base. A week later, Fallujans gathered outside the gates to demand their property back. Unnerved by the burgeoning crowd and untrained in peace-keeping, the commander ordered his men to open fire. Seventeen Iraqis were killed in the subsequent salvo, some in their homes across the square. Military claims that Iraqis had fired first were belied by the absence of bullet-marks on the school façade. US forces never apologised. Their commanders, they said, had responded with 'precision fire'.

Falluja's fate as the rebel epicentre was sealed. The following Friday, US tanks lumbered into position outside the town's largest mosques, prompting further demonstrations. The town's Salafis and Sufis – who traced their differences back to Hallaj, a ninth-century mystic crucified in Baghdad for the heretical claim pronounced in the midst of a trance that he was the truth – forgot their differences. Wily Baathist generals, Muslim Brotherhood preachers and itinerant Jihadis trickling into town made common cause, and though they lacked formal chain of command, recognised a charismatic Sufi master, Ibrahim al-Jannabi, as the most prominent spiritual leader. Modern entertainment in his terrain was banned, cinemas torched, and boutiques peddling pop cassettes trashed. Shia taxi-drivers were beheaded as spies. And Jannabi's mosque, Saad bin Abi Wakkas, became the insurgency's nerve centre.

By February 2004, insurgents had succeeded in overrunning the town's police station, outgunning its Iraqi officers, not least because their American overseers – fearing disloyalty – had limited ammunition to ten bullets a gun. Bereft of a permanent coalition presence, the town became a rebel encampment for increasingly frequent attacks on nearby Baghdad. In March alone, 15 foreign contractors serving the US occupation were killed in a series of road-side bombings, drive-by shootings and ambushes. And to mark America's first anniversary in Iraq, rebels captured four US mercenaries by misdirecting them into the town centre. Forced out of their vehicle after a mob had set it alight, the four were caught, lynched, dragged like Hector by vehicles through Falluja's dusty streets and, to the whoops of a crowd delighting in the ritual humiliation of a superpower, strung headless from the steel frame of the town's main bridge. Bremer was enraged, not least because the four guards belonged to the same company, Blackwater, that provided his personal detail. Contrasting with the forbearance of Iraq's Shia leaders, whose constituents had been slaughtered in far greater numbers, he ordered America back to war in Iraq.

After laying siege to the town, tanks and heavy artillery pounded suspected rebel positions. A minaret used by snipers was toppled and houses on the frontline crushed in their dozens. After five weeks of fighting, 1,000 were dead and the bodies were so numerous the local football ground was converted into a graveyard. But drawing on prepositioned arms caches buried in the city cemetery, the insurgents survived. A former Republican Guard general smuggled an anti-aircraft gun from Byelorussia into the city,[196] forcing marines to ground their helicopter gunships and bomb from warplanes 40,000 feet high. Unwittingly,

American commanders adopted tactics first employed by the British 80 years earlier, using air-power to punch their rule on the ground.

Nationwide, the siege divided Iraqis along sectarian lines. Many cried crocodile tears: however punishing the cordon around Falluja, it silenced Baghdad's dawn chorus of car-bombings in the capital. But Sunnis more than others were affected by Falluja's families, who arrived at the homes of Baghdad relatives carrying terrifying tales of destruction. America's attack on Falluja was the tipping point at which Iraq's Sunnis came off the fence and joined the insurgent camp.

Not that all Falluja's arrivistes were well received, even in religious communities. At a wedding I attended at the ramshackle Sufi *takiya*, or lodge, of Hassan the Flying Man, a fourteenth-century mystic famed for flying from Baghdad to Turkey, one such Fallujan interrupted festivities. With a perfunctory nod at the groom, the uninvited guest garbed in a golden tunic and towering white headdress launched into a sermon appealing for reinforcements for his hometown of Falluja. 'American might is turning Falluja into a mass grave,' cried the preacher, Mohammed Eissawi, a Sufi master from Falluja. 'Why are you abandoning the city of two hundred mosques and a hundred Sufi lodges? Rice sacks and prayers are not gift enough. You must give yourselves.' Perhaps for dramatic effect he stood in the open doorway so that the sunlight cast him in a halo and the wedding guests in his shadow.

His rhetoric to the confused and the apathetic shook Sunnis from a creed of torpor and acceptance that, with odd exceptions, had been the norm since the Ottomans made Sunni Islam the state religion and demanded the faithful submit to its authority. Beneath the *takiya*'s ancient cupola, tucked within the small lattice of alleyways of old Baghdad that had somehow survived Saddam's brutal modernisation, political change lost its meaning. Sunni warrior-preachers had rarely been so rousing since the war-cry of thirteenth-century Iraqi scholar Ibn al-Jawzi dammed Baghdadis for accepting the Mongol siege of Baghdad: 'Woe unto you! You continue eating, drinking and enjoying the pleasures of life while your brothers are engulfed in fire, walking through flames, and sleeping on embers?' Essawi quoted from his sermon. 'O people: the call of jihad has been made, and the gates of heaven have been opened. Unless you choose to be the knights of the war, then make way for the women to wage this war, and go to your braziers and kohl jars, you women but with turbans and beards.'

The *takiya*'s traditionalists were no match for such dramatics. Huddled in the gloom of the wooden shack, the wedding guests shifted uneasily, embarrassed at their earlier festivity. Ribs of lamb hovered in mid-air. The master of both the ceremonies and the *takiya*, Sheikh Mohammed Abu Khomra, rocked his bulk on the plinth of his crossed legs, keeping an increasingly stony silence. Only after Eissawi had left, with the melodramatic flick of his tunic, did Abu Khomra seek to regain his authority. 'The higher jihad,' he cautioned, 'is a personal struggle of faith. Now is the moment for patience and self-discipline not hot-heads,' he pleaded. 'The worthy Jihad of Sufism is jihad *al-nafs* [the spiritual struggle against the ego].'

Even here, though, times were changing. Abu Khomra's congregation was thinning. Ever fewer craftsmen, clerks and cleaners came to his *takiya* to cure their insomnia with a brush of his staff, their impotency with his herbs, or their children's colic with his spittle. Because of America's curfews, he had changed his meeting times from Thursday evenings to Friday mornings, and perhaps in the rawness of daylight, the rhythmic deep throat howling of God's name – Allah, Allah, Allah – interspersed with heavy breathing lost its magic. Perhaps also the use of hashish, wine and mild head-banging to induce a state of oneness or ecstasy with God seemed the epitome of hedonism that had roused the wrath of Ibn al-Jawzi and his current acolytes.

From his new home in Baghdad, Eissawi the Fallujan acquired a preaching stipend at the largest and oldest mosque in the neighbourhood, the Gailani, tasked with awakening the masses. This mosque was also the resting-place of the thirteenth-century founder of Iraq's most popular and most sober Sufi brotherhood, the Qadiriya, but its Sufi masters had long since revised their mission to cleanse the collective not the individual soul of its foreign impurities. From North Africa in the nineteenth century to occupied Chechnya in the twenty-first, the movement had been at the forefront of resistance against colonial rule. 'Sufism,' rejoiced Abdelwahhab al-Toma, a wizened Sufi sheikh who shared Eissawi's office at the Gailani mosque, 'is again busy with Jihad.'[197]

Brutish marble renovations that Saddam had not had time to complete well matched the message from the Gailani's loudspeakers, their decibel level thwarting Abu Khomra's attempt to incant above the fray. By the time Eissawi had begun his sermon commending the abduction of foreign hostages, only a frail, possibly deaf woman remained in the *takiya*, bent hunch-back as she stopped to collect the waters that had flooded the crypt and supposedly had curative powers. Around the alleyways, Eissawi's message intruded. Flyers stuck on walls tracked the latest victories against 'Satan's forces' at Falluja's gates – heralding the downing of one tank, six helicopters, 120 juggernauts and many infidel prisoners. In the markets, peddlers hawked DVDs of Salah al-Jannabi, a local poet who sang paeans to Falluja's fighters to the drumbeat of Sufi chants. 'We fought like a lion attacked in his lair and made the Americans scarper like rats,' he chanted. Spliced into the footage of exploding American tanks were grainy reels from 1920s Libya, when the Sufi brotherhood of the Sanussids battled Italian Fascists.

Even Abu Khomra's own family were breaking ranks. His cousin, Sheikh al-Qummer, who ran another Rafaiya shrine just north of Baghdad's arms market, turned his lodge into a shelter for Fallujan families. Following a dawn raid by US forces and the detention of four of his guests, including a 70-year-old man, the sheikh gently declared that Sufis should now defend themselves. 'Sufis were the link between the British and the Iraqis,' protested Sheikh Qummer, furious at the breach of his hospitality. Whereas the British had chosen a master Qadiri Sufi to be Iraq's first prime minister, 'America has made us into rebels. It will backfire.'[198]

Not all decisions to side with the insurgents were so freely made. Sunni Arabs who found work with the Coalition increasingly abandoned their posts. Surgeons at Falluja General treating Ahmed Shaaban, a policeman who survived the February attack on Falluja station, remained faithful to their Hippocratic Oath but warned him that it might prove more difficult to heal him a second time. Those who remained at their posts spent more time safeguarding themselves than the local population. Behind cordons of concrete and razor wire, the few police at Baghdad's police station of Yarmouk, a Sunni neighbourhood in west Baghdad, sloughed off the US-issue uniforms and opted for less conspicuous civilian garb more in keeping with their nominal role. 'How can I arrest an Iraqi whose brother has been killed or whose house has been bulldozed by the occupier?' asked one of its officers. US forces were asked to stay away. 'Deploying an American soldier next to a police station is like putting a light next to a petrol pump.'

As the ranks of insurgents multiplied, so did the rate of attack on US forces. Those besieging Falluja were attacked from the rear, and their supply routes from Amman all but cut. The highway from Amman to Baghdad, which skirted Falluja, was carpeted in ammo-casings, interspersed with the burning hulks of tanker-trucks, billowing petrol fumes which gelled with the desert dust to blacken the sun. Fearful that the insurrection was widening support for the rebels, US commanders in Falluja sued for a truce. Protesting that foreign Jihadis were 'irredeemable', they negotiated a ceasefire with high-ranking military and civilian officials from the former regime together with local Muslim Brotherhood leaders. US forces withdrew to the highway, where soldiers incredulously stood waving at the same human traffic which for the previous six weeks they had bombed.

Inside 'Iraq's first liberated city', tribal leaders feasted in celebration at their victory against the world's mightiest army, praising God for divine intervention. Revellers who had survived three weeks of bombardment swore of mythical doves that flew over US forces dropping grenades, and giant tarantulas that forced the Americans to beat a retreat. 'The angels fought with the people,' said Jawad, a colonel in the former Iraqi army. His more sober uncle, Qais Nazzal, one of Falluja's two industrialists, was only mildly less euphoric despite the 14 missiles that had ploughed into his house like slugs through a leaf. 'With God's blessing we forced them back and stopped them entering the city. The mightiest army in the world ran from the city like rats.' In his Friday sermon, the preacher at the mosque of the Bu Eissas, Falluja's largest tribe, likened the ceasefire to the early Muslim community's eviction of the Roman army from Syria. None spoke of the dead.

By agreement with the Americans, 1,200 Iraqis returned to the streets of Falluja sporting their Saddam-era uniforms of olive-green fatigues and berets. At their helm marched General Jassim Mehmedi al-Salah, a tubby commander of the 38th Infantry Division, who stood accused of involvement in the suppression of the 1991 Shia uprising. For many Fallujans, the restoration of even this segment of the Iraq army signalled that the tide was turning on Shia supremacy. In the days that followed, Bremer unnerved his Shia allies by publicly tempering deBaathification. Thousands of suspected Baathists would get back their government jobs, he declared, and for good measure he issued warrants for the arrest of several of the key architects of the Iraqi deBaathification Commission. In addition, US forces released hundreds of prisoners, including leading Fallujans such as Barakat Saadoun, the Bu Eissa chieftain, after suing for terms inside Abu Ghraib jail.[199]

Following his release, Saadoun held a tribal convocation ahead of Friday prayers and called for restraint. 'Now is the time for diplomacy,' Barakat, a soft-spoken ginger-head, told the tribal elders gathered in a vast octagonal hall that adjoined his mansion. Velvet drapes cascaded down from the centre of the ceiling to an opulent black marble floor invoking a Sultan's medieval tent. Barakat unveiled the terms of the road map he had negotiated with the Coalition in Abu Ghraib. The Americans, he told them, were ready to integrate Falluja back into the mainstream. Compensation would be paid to residents for war damage, and the city rebuilt. Nationwide, he claimed, the US was ready to steady the sectarian balance when it appointed a technocratic government in June to replace the Governing Council. 'If Fallujans do not participate in the new government, we will fail,' he warned. Two elderly Shias of the Bu Eissa tribe who had travelled from Karbala listened intently.

Once again the conciliatory tones fell wide of his battle-hardened audience. Having warded off the Americans by force, his tribesmen were in no mood for a peace which allowed them back. Nazzal, the industrialist, took to the floor of the Bu Eissa's tribal senate. He was a tall, imposing man in his sixties who gasped for air in mid-flow (the result of an only partially successful throat operation in Britain). Fallujans, he told his fellow tribesmen, should not sup with the devil, should refuse to coordinate their security arrangements with the Americans and should reject a US demand for a handover of *mujahideen* from abroad. 'The Americans brought soldiers from all over the world to attack us. If my cousin from Saudi Arabia or Syria comes to help free me how can I call him a criminal?' The convocation was followed by a lavish feast of lamb borne on vast trays carried by servants who entered like pallbearers. As they dispersed for Friday prayers, tribesmen muttered that Barakat had been broken by seven months in Abu Ghraib jail, two of them in solitary confinement.

If Barakat had hoped the feast might soothe the murmurings of dissent, he was disappointed. Meal and prayers over, they quickly departed for a second feast chez General Salah, the merry Republican Guard commander of the revamped Falluja Brigade, who declared the lifting of America's siege to be the start of the rollback of foreign conquest. 'We hope it will be a model for all Iraq,' said General Salah. 'That would be excellent.'[200] Far from mollifying the insurgency, Falluja's salvation had emboldened it.

With the lifting of the US cordon, rebels rapidly dispersed across central Iraq and over the subsequent months attempted a series of copycat rebellions along the Euphrates and Tigris valley towns. Hitherto independent cells increased their coordination, highlighted by the growing number of simultaneous attacks sometimes hundreds of miles apart,[201] and their tactics. A Republican Guard general from Baghdad took me to meet his counterparts in Samarra, and with an air of elegant self-assurance over tea and water-melon discussed the urgency of importing remote-control car door locks (used to detonate roadside bombs) from Syria. Their range of 500 metres was said to be three times those sold in Baghdad.

What united the Falluja industrialist, the Baghdad general and his Samarian counterpart was their common membership of a highly-educated but usurped elite. Their homes were decorated with mock gold-leaf Louis XIV sofas, stuffed falcons and corner cabinets carved of mahogany, and all the men stood a head taller than the average Iraqi. They had received military training in America and Russia, and had fond memories of their visits. The general from Samarra had a penchant for Mark Twain. The Baghdad general had tried, but failed, after the war to get a job in the new Iraq Army. And Nazzal had made repeated business trips to the USA. 'Americans are the best people in the world; they are generous and like to help,' he said. But Shias were his factory labourers and cannon-fodder, not rulers, destined to take not give orders. All bore the wounded pride of their fall, disdainful that Washington had so shamelessly upset the time-honoured status quo of a Sunni elite.

Nazzal had not abandoned the hope that America might reconsider. On a tour of his factory, the Shawahiq Steel Company, on the outskirts of Falluja, he gave the sales patter of a $2 million expansion plan for which he hoped to secure US investment. In other times, it would have been an attractive prospect. Beyond his factory gates lay acre upon acre of military scrap, piled five metres high with the wrecks of tanks and discarded fighter jet engines by the dozen. Converting swords into ploughshares, he said, netted as much as $6,000 per tonne on costs of some $50. At considerable risk, he had kept his foundry functioning throughout the siege, while workers brought insurgents hiding in the scrap food and water. Had the Americans come in a spirit of cooperation – as doctors not occupying soldiers – they would have received similar treatment, quipped Nazzal.

Islamist narratives had made far fewer inroads up the Tigris than the Euphrates river. Samarra, a half-hour's drive from Saddam's birthplace, was populated with majors Bremer had forcibly dismissed, and who in retirement continued to sport thick-set moustaches, Soviet fur hats, and revanchist cold-war language to boot. Unlike elsewhere in Iraq, its inhabitants felt no compunction to change their Baath-era names. A

US-appointed secretary at the town council was called Saddam. 'We want an organised united Iraqi army, not a separate militia in every town,' said Saddam Hassan, whose main function was processing CVs submitted by Samarra's decommissioned officers in anticipation that the army might be recalled.

Even so, the Council's remit extended little further than the street in which it was situated. Its US-appointed mayor, Sheikh Adnan Maher, was a lumbering former army officer and relative of the provincial governor. He smelt of booze, and had a reputation for corruption acquired after a $24 million US grant for communications failed to restore the telephone lines. Paramilitary forces who hid their identities behind balaclavas guarded his office, his home and the bridge over the Tigris that connected the two, and boosted their income by trading in their US-supplied weapons under a US-run buy-back programme and obtaining replacements. The rest of the town was in the hands of insurgents, loyal to the refined general who served melons. An undefined no man's land prevailed in between where US-backed militias and insurgents did battle and used TNT to flatten each others residencies. 'Their homes get attacked and they still come to work,' marvelled Captain Rodriguez, the most senior US soldier in the region, at checkpoints whose business was interrupted by mortars. Whatever they were doing in Iraq, they said, it certainly was not building democracy.[202]

A month later the Iraqi general and his men captured Samarra, liberating their second town from Americans. Kitted in the red boots and the same olive-green uniforms of Saddam's Republican Guard, his men saluted before firing their missiles at the last US foothold in town. A car-bomb, no doubt detonated with the aid of a Syrian car-lock, broke through the defences of the whitewashed complex. And before US helicopters had completed the evacuation of the remaining US and Kurdish *peshmergas* forces, looters and rebels entered the last base, pillaging televisions and satellite receivers. The first act of the incoming Iraqi administration was to ban the wearing of jeans.

America's footprint was rapidly receding. Following the fall of Samarra, several town centres along the Euphrates were abandoned without a fight, as troops retreated inside their remote bases. Whole population clusters of western Iraq – inhabiting the three large provinces of Nineweh, Anbar and Tikrit – fell from coalition control. By late 2004 almost every hamlet along the 200 miles of unfenced border with Syria was in rebel hands, with repeated fighting around Tel Afar – the sole buffer between Iraq and the

Kurds of Syria. In the towns they controlled, insurgents were quick to establish a parallel administration, offering their services – most critically medical care and hospital treatment – but also price-fixing; imposing, for instance, a 25 per cent cut in the price of meat. Insurgents declared mini-emirates in al-Qaim, on the Syrian border, and Haditha, north-west of Falluja. In Baqouba, a mixed Sunni and Shia town east of Baghdad, scores of rebels paraded through the city centre in black bandannas inscribed with Zarkawi's name.

By the eve of the handover to an interim government, rebels had also secured a time-share hold over Ramadi, the provincial capital of Iraq's largest province, Anbar. At 1.30 p.m., following the closure of government offices, the police abandoned their posts like clockwork, whereupon a Nissan pick-up fortified with a megaphone toured the city proclaiming the changing guard: 'Shut your shops. The fighting will begin after 14:00. Stay safe.' Fifteen minutes later a 20-vehicle rebel convoy armed with rocket-propelled grenades emerged from the side-streets to take control of the town centre.

Hailing from a Euphrates town, Ramadi's militiamen were young, masked, and garbed in *dishdashas* – white ankle-length tunics. They stayed until daybreak, and in their 16 hours of control sought not just to regain territory, but to apply the Sharia. The city's cinema was devastated in a salvo of rocket-propelled grenades, and a liquor stall converted into a boutique selling religious cassettes, after its proprietor was shot in the head. They had scant opposition. Sensibly, American regulars only patrolled the town when the police manned their posts. And the city's security chief, too, professed a studied if trained neutrality. 'I am neither with the resistance nor with the Americans,' said Colonel Khamis Jassim, commander of the city's National Guard, whose 4,000 men received their salaries and munitions via the Americans. 'I protect the city against the looters and criminals.'[203]

By the end of the summer, Iraq appeared more divided than ever into a western half of Sunni Arabs sharing tribal and religious ties with neighbouring Arab states, and an eastern half whose foreign support came from a curious cocktail of America and Iran. Much of the violence took place along the seam-line that divided the two – brutal sectarian wars of control extending from Mosul in the north through Samarra and Falluja to Latifiya and Mahmudiya in the south, with the most brutal fighting in the mixed capital of Baghdad. And yet for all their success in regaining territory, the policy of establishing emirates was essentially one of retreat. While US troops abandoned the north and south to the Kurds and the Shias respectively, Sunnis still had to fight for their territory. Exhausted by conflict, tens of thousands retreated abroad. For the first time in their modern history, Sunni Arabs sought a safe haven in neighbouring states. The fate Sunni Arabs had inflicted on hundreds of thousands of Jews, Persians, Christians and finally in the 1990s Arab Shias was ultimately rebounding on them.

In Amman, the Sunni émigrés recreated their lost Baghdad. They settled in the plushest neighbourhoods and hosted the plushest soirees. King Abdullah played host to the ex-president's daughter, Raghad Hussein, who responded with a party in the country's largest hotel.[204] Amman's 300,000 largely Shia and impoverished Iraqis who had fled the Baath in the 1990s feared their persecutors had come back to haunt them. But Jordan, which had long learnt how to derive economic benefit from the plight of refugees, revelled in the influx. Real estate prices soared, as Iraqis overtook Palestinians as the leading procurers of luxury apartments, drawing comparisons with the construction boom that had followed the Palestinian exodus from Kuwait in 1990.[205] Waiters, restaurateurs and prostitutes kept the surfeit of affluent but unemployed doctors, journalists and academics occupied. And Amman's private universities found a 400-man pool of cheap but highly experienced professors, amongst them Iraq's former ambassador to Jordan, Sabah Yassin. But for all their highlife, few forgot that they had switched places with the Amman-based Shia opposition who had rushed to Baghdad with the US invasion, and now presided over the country in their stead.

CHAPTER 12

The Local Hero and the Fighting Arm of Hizbollah

Sitting comfortably in a red-cushioned armchair, Ahmed Shaybani had converted the cloisters of Najaf's Imam Ali shrine, the holiest place in Shia Islam, into his command-and-control centre. Every 20 minutes, a telephone perched on the glass table rang with the latest field reports from across Iraq's seven southern provinces, which in a balmy April week the Mahdi Army had captured. 'Praise Be to God, five armoured coalition cars in Najaf, seven in Basra, and twelve in Nasiriya lie mortared and wrecked,' said the voice down the line. 'With the faith of God,' the trainee cleric and at 34 the youngest of Muqtada Sadr's three senior advisors, replied.

Perhaps the greatest prize of the week's fighting was the curiously peaceful shrine itself. From the first days of America's suzerainty, it had been the battlefield in a tripartite struggle for control waged between the US; their homebound cabal of Iraqi exiles, Sistani and the gentrified Hauza; and the young activist clerics supporting the puffy-faced protestant, Muqtada. And yet, somehow, the tranquillity of the cloistered forecourt that led to the gold-domed sepulchre transcended the turbulence at the gates. Aside from Shaybani's guards and pallbearers bearing cadavers, the shrine, which normally heaved with pilgrims, was left to the pigeons.

In the vacuous carpeted vestibule behind the shrine where Shaybani held court, his fighters insisted they were protecting the shrine. The wizened curators – quaintly garbed in tunics and red fezzes, and unarmed Sistani followers to a man – were more circumspect. 'Militants gathered at the gates with mortars and threatened to blow down the teak doors unless we handed over the keys,' apologised Ahmed, the bare-footed shoe attendant. 'So we gave them the keys.' Outside, Sadr's militiamen brandishing

Kalashnikovs careened round the compound in looted police cars, defending their prize.

The conquest of the Najaf shrine was the culmination of a generational struggle between the conservative clerical establishment and the activist strain led by a succession of Sadrs. The most ardent derided Sistani as a doddery ecclesiastic who had abandoned his local flock to consort with the exiled robber barons the American administration imported after the war. Their grievances not only tallied with their Sunni counterparts, but in some ways were more pronounced. After decades of hardship and deprivation, they had again been disenfranchised as the Americans parcelled out their sinecures amongst the well-heeled Shia they had fostered in exile.

It is difficult to over-estimate the chasm that divided the exiles from their coreligionists of Iraq's sanctioned generation. Trapped in poverty and too poor to escape, the bulk of the population instead found a safe haven in God. In contrast to the boom years of the 1970s when high oil-prices helped an average 2 million Iraqis visit Europe each summer, sanctions, war and impoverishment had denied their children such opportunities. 'The furthest the elite of today have been is Amman,' Saad Jawad, a politics professor at Baghdad University, lamented. In the pressure-cooker, a host of millennial cults bubbled beneath the surface before the invasion, and exploded above it after. Led for the most part by middle-to-low-ranking clerics aged in their twenties and thirties, Iraq's Shia monks of liberation theology all claimed to act in the name of the Arab mentor of political Shiism, Mohammed Baqir al-Sadr.

Long-suppressed local clerics sought to challenge the religious as well as the political order. Some seemed charlatans. Mahmoud Hassouni, a 37-year-old cleric, declared himself Wali al-Faqih, or Ruler Priest, and issued fatwas sanctioning looting in the name of the Hauza. He lured unemployed Iraqi men to sign up for a semester of studies with the promise of monthly stipends of 10,000 dinars ($7), only to recoup the funds by charging them 10,000 dinars for photocopies of his fatwas. Others came from dynasties with a tradition of revolt dating back to the British. Mohammed al-Mahdi al-Khalisi hurried back from 20 years of British exile to sound the trumpet of revolt, and inspire a host of frenetic radicals: 'Now that the idol [the statue of Iraqi president Saddam Hussein] has been pulled down, the occupation troops should leave our country. I urge all Iraqis to stand shoulder to shoulder to foil malicious plots weaved by Washington and London and prevent occupation troops from looting the fruits of such sacrifices.'

But none had Muqtada Sadr's credentials. Though pimply, podgy, sweaty and distinctly uncharismatic, the 28-year-old novice was the scion of probably the most important Shia house in the Arab world. His dynasty of *mujtahids*, or religious scholars, dated back to the sixteenth century, when the Safavid Shah Ismail declared Shiism Persia's official religion, and went head-hunting for missionaries in the undulating hills of South Lebanon. Thereafter the Sadrs had international reach. The British rulers of Iraq considered them one of the two most important clerical families in the country. And in 1948, the Hashemite monarchy rewarded them for their loyalty to the Arab cause by appointing Muqtada's great-great-grandfather, Sayid Muhammad al-Sadr, prime minister. After Iraq's 1958 revolution, three scions of the House of Sadr propagated an Arab Shia revival, a role for which all paid with their lives. In Lebanon, Musa al-Sadr moulded the downtrodden Shia majority into a political force, before he disappeared on a visit to Libya in 1978. Simultaneously, in Iraq, a great-uncle, Mohammed Baqir al-Sadr (known to Iraqis as Sadr I), rose to prominence as the Marx of Shia Islam, penning the manifesto of Shia political activism and giving it political form as the Dawa movement, for which Saddam Hussein had him killed in 1980. Sadr II, Muqtada Sadr's father, took up the baton, only to be gunned down in Najaf together with Muqtada's two eldest brothers. In short, few men can have felt the weight of history as much as Muqtada.

Conscious that his own studies were insufficient, but reluctant to bow to the greater authority of Grand Ayatollah Sistani, Muqtada rode to prominence on the coat-tails of his father's legend. He insisted on adhering to his father's precepts in defiance of Shia tradition, which frowned on emulation of a dead *mujtahid*. In the process, he prolonged the feud that had erupted between Sadr senior and Sistani for leadership of the Hauza after the death of their teacher, Ayatollah Khoi. Saddam stoked the battle for succession, portraying the rivalry as a struggle between the Arabs under Sadr against the Persians led by Sistani. Sistani was kept under house arrest and his writings censored, while Sadr was released from ten years in prison and his fatwas liberally circulated in the bazaars. Exploiting his greater margin of freedom, Sadr delivered the *khutba*, or sermon, at Friday prayers, relaunched a long-banned newspaper, refurbished libraries ravaged during the suppression of the Intifada in 1991 and opened a Shia tribunal adjudicating civil cases. In a nod to Saddam, Sadr emphasised his rejection of Iranian leadership of a single Shia Internationale, insisting that each *wilaya*, or district, should have its own *faqih*, or jurist.

But as Sadr's influence waxed, the regime grew increasingly nervous of his network. In 1997, before a congregation of 2,000, he proclaimed himself *wali amr al-muslimeen*, or Muslim commander, laying down the gauntlet to Iran's Supreme Leader Ayatollah Ali Khamenei, but also – which worried the Baath – to Saddam. His claim to speak for both houses of Islam only stoked their fears. 'There is neither Sunna and nor Shia – Yes to Islamic unity,' he proclaimed, and called on Shias to attend Sunni mosques. Far from an innocent call to religious harmony, the regime sensed a sectarian challenge. Sunni mosques were swamped with Shia congregations, in a powerful demonstration of Shia demographic power. Finally, in his open-air mass Friday prayers, Sadr dispensed with the Sunni custom of beseeching God to protect the head of state. He named himself the Wali al-Faqih, declared Baathism a sin, and publicly called on Saddam Hussein to repent. Sadr knew the punishment. He donned a white funeral shroud for the final sermon before his assassination in February 1999.

Though the assassination was the work of Baath party death squads, Sistani ducked the charge levelled both by regime apparatchiks and al-Sadr's more volatile followers of complicity. After his death, Sadr's followers taunted the Ayatollah for locking his door in the face of a spate of assassinations and for keeping mum in the face of repression, asking why he feared God. And as soon as the Americans lifted the Baath yoke from Najaf, the Sadaris took their revenge. No sooner had Saddam's Fedayeen fled Imam Ali's shrine than Sadr's underground militia moved in, killing rival claimants. Amongst them was a pro-American cleric, Abdelmajid al-Khoi, and the shrine's gate-keeper, Haider Kalidar (literally, keeper of the keys), both stabbed to death in the forecourt to cries of 'Long live Muqtada'; the militia then charged 70 yards down the adjacent Prophet Street to a side-alley, where they laid siege to Sistani's house. Amid the ensuing uproar, their resolve temporarily wavered. Sweating profusely in an interview on al-Jazeera television, Muqtada insisted he had come to shield not slaughter the defenceless cleric.

At first the rebellion seemed easily suppressed. Sistani used the gravitas of the clerical Curia coupled with a US security umbrella to humiliate the trainee cleric. Sadr's teacher, Ayatollah Ishaq Fayadh – a close acolyte of his father's – dismissed him from his classes. Sistani too refused him an audience. 'I went to meet with Sayyid al-Sistani, but I could not meet him. He only meets people who are of the same level,' squirmed the novice. More painful still, Sistani cast him out from the Najaf shrine, depriving him of his share of alms. With the exception of an occasional vespers in Imam Ali's forecourt, Sadr was ostracised to the dusty complex of a half-ruined mosque ten miles away at Kufa, a place, the genteel Ayatollahs no doubt noted, where God had also cast the serpent after it had beguiled Eve.[206] Even Imam Ali had shrunk from a burial there, shooting an arrow as far away as he could to determine the site of his grave, and in the process depriving Kufa of its shrine status, and thus its proprietor of the income accruing from selling Ali's *baraka*, or blessings. Rubbing salt in the wounds, the Ayatollahs appointed Sadr's rival, SCIRI leader Mohammed Baqir al-Hakim, recently arrived from Iran, as the leader of Friday prayers.

Sadr was incensed. Despite his lack of years and scholarly rank, the numerous martyrdoms visited on his family gave him legitimacy few others could match. Booted to Kufa's crumbling vaults, he lambasted the Ayatollahs as impostors – on the grounds of their Persian origin, their flight into exile under Saddam, their class and above all their alliance with the USA. 'Hakim represents the outside not the inside,' said Khalid al-Qathami, the Sadari leader in Karbala, a rare forty-something in the ranks of the young radicals. 'People will not support him.'[207] Much as his father did, Muqtada couched his sermons in Arab nationalist not sectarian terms. Skirting over Sadr's own Persian and Lebanese origins, Sadr's propagandists appealed to Iraqis to free the Arab Hauza from foreign occupation. Sistani was lampooned for his thick Persian accent (reason enough, said Sadaris, to exclude him from interference in Iraq affairs) and called on to leave Iraq. Hakim was pilloried as an Iranian agent.[208] The Iranian consulate in Basra, a stronghold of the Hakims, was torched.

As well as the xenophobia, Sadr drew on the class consciousness of his indigenous proletariat following. He contrasted his own activist legacy as a Sadri champion of the dispossessed with that of the Hakim dynasty, rooted in the landed gentry and mercantile and moneyed classes who had bought their way out of Saddam's Iraq. While for the Hakims religion was an apolitical affair preserving the establishment,[209] for the Sadrs it was a revolutionary creed, steeped in anti-Americanism.[210] Muqtada's father was versed in Marx's Paris Commune, and had penned a Shia commentary on the French Revolutionary *Rights of Man*. Finally, the two houses adopted radically differing approaches to the USA. First Bremer and then President George Bush feted Hakim, and invested his brother, Abdulaziz, as one of the Council's nine rotating presidents. Sadr, who had initially signalled his interest in cooperating with the Council, was barred, and subsequently hunted as an outlaw. Spurning Garner's early attempts to co-opt the House of Sadr, Bremer derided them. With typical sledgehammer diplomacy aimed at neutering Sadr's power-base, he detained Sadr's aides, including Muiyid Khazraji, Sadr's affable representative in West Baghdad, who in the early days of the invasion had signed an agreement with US commanders providing US financial support for his management of two 'pilot' secondary schools in return for his acceptance of a US military presence on the streets of Baghdad.[211]

The chasm between the two houses was highlighted during the victory parade that Hakim staged through southern Iraq on his return. Travelling in the American sports-utility vehicles beloved by the Bremer court, Hakim's convoy sped through Iraq oblivious to the impoverished surroundings. In Karbala, his posters were ripped from the shrine walls as local dignitaries stayed away. A scheduled visit to Baghdad was cancelled. While the Hakims struggled to attract the crowds, Sadr's sermons in Kufa, by contrast, drew devotees in their thousands, bussed in from Baghdad's slums.

When, in August 2003, a car-bomb obliterated all of Hakim but his pen, watch and wedding ring, Najaf's bazaar buzzed with rumours that Sadr was to blame. Though his complicity was unlikely, the killing of Khoi suggests that Sadr lacked neither motive nor resolve in his struggle for control of the Hauza. As with all car-bombs, Bremer's administration never made public – and probably never concluded – their investigations. In an attempt to scotch the allegations, Sadaris attended Hakim's funeral in their hundreds of thousands, though many seemed less minded to praise Hakim than to bury him. The crowds hummed to anti-American chants, prompting Hakim's loyalists to accuse the Sadaris of hijacking the funeral for their political gain. The crowds were so tightly packed that the truck bearing the coffin poignantly failed to reach the shrine for the traditional last perambulations.

Sadr's recourse to people power embarrassed the superpower committed to restoring power to the people. In the face of protests at the gates of Bremer's enclave demanding Khazraji's release, the Coalition erected billboards coated with the Orwellian banner 'Democracy = Responsibility'. Sadr's cohorts responded by copying Sadr's father with huge open-air prayer rallies, at which the congregation chanted 'No to America, No to Israel, No to Tyranny'; 'Out of Saddam's jails, into America's'; and, for good measure, 'Troops out, Hauza rule'. Preachers declared a boycott of American (and Israeli) produce, and unveiled their eschatological vision of a state led by Muqtada, whom they proclaimed their *qa'id*, or leader, the same title adopted by Saddam, as well as *wali amr al-muslimeen* – commander of the Muslims – a Qur'anic title he inherited from his father. In November 2003, on the birthday of Mohammed al-Mahdi – the twelfth Imam, who had disappeared in the ninth century and who Shias believed would return as the Messiah – Muqtada circulated an edict calling for mass demonstrations to inaugurate an alternative government 'of freedom and democracy'. But his ambition had overreached itself. Sadr's call failed to win endorsement from Sistani, and without it Iraqis were unprepared to take to the streets and ditch the new American order. 'It will take time to announce the names of his ministers,' said Sadr's representative, Khalid al-Qathmi, when the demonstrations failed to materialise.[212]

Unable to beat Sistani, Muqtada next pretended to act in his name. He affirmed Sistani's spiritual authority, but said that since he was not Iraqi, he had no remit over Iraq's temporal affairs. Postponing the formation of a government, he focussed on the formation of a people's army, dubbed the Mahdi Army, whose soldiers wore black shirts, evoking the colour of the eschatological twefth Imam. In his sermons, Sadr exalted the 1920 revolt Shia Ayatollahs had launched against British rule. Whereas Sistani was loath to repeat a failure that had cost 12,000 Iraqi lives and a thousand British, and consigned the Shias to underdogs in Iraq's hierarchy for the subsequent 80 years, Sadr portrayed his call to arms as an existential struggle with tyranny.

Over the next three years, Sadr built the Mahdi Army into a 60,000-strong force.[213] The foot-soldiers were Shia conscripts drawn from the ranks of the army Bremer disbanded; officers were more commonly from Uday Hussein's Fedayeen Saddam, a largely Shia paramilitary force. Middle-class girls who flocked to his sermons also took up Sadr's cry, offering their lives for the cause. An outwardly secular secretary at the US base in Najaf introduced herself as Shams al-Hurriya, or Liberty's Sun, before donning a *chador* and leading me through Najaf's alleys to the ruins of Khan Sheylan, an Ottoman fortress overshadowing Najaf's central market where the British had stashed suspects during the 1920 revolt. 'We want a Hauza state independent of US control,' she told me on the ramparts. 'If we don't get it, we will explode ourselves.'

To finance the Mahdi army, Muqtada's loyalists set up checkpoints and Sharia courts imposing tolls and fines. Ex-army explosive operatives trained recruits, who were paid handsomely in looted cars for their services.[214] Others raided hotels, and increasingly well-endowed shrines. In October,

Mahdi militiamen seized the treasury at Imam Hussein's shrine in Karbala, in violation of an agreement with Sistani's representative to share the premises.

Muqtada was not merely operating above the law; he was defining it. A parallel state emerged replete with courts, police and militia. In the neighbourhoods that slipped under his authority, his clerics replaced Baath and coalition law with Islamic law, revived his father's system of 'Sharia courts', akin to Iran's post-revolution Komitehs, and organised a clerical police force to enforce its judgments. From Baghdad to Basra, violators were detained and flogged. A local Shia journalist, whose reports for al-Jazeera television from Najaf were deemed unfavourable, was strung to prison bars, robbed of his money, beaten in the genitals, and delivered in agony back to his office the following day. In Diwaniya, a sleepy riverside town 60 kilometres east of Najaf, masked God-squads paraded the streets with Kalashnikovs hunting for sinners to fill the prison erected in the basement of the old Baath headquarters. The back of an itinerant welder, Hamid Alwan, was scarred with the marks of 80 lashes imposed by a cleric for smelling of gin. 'Every ten lashes they would give me a glass of water,' he said gratefully.

The character of southern Iraq was changing. Gangs of knee-cappers scoured Shia towns for liquor merchants, and spray-painted barbers' shopfronts with the words 'Death to the Shavers of Beards'. CD stores peddling western music had their windows smashed and their owners were forced to trade clerical recordings instead. Shops draped black flags over their awnings and stuck Imam Ali posters to their windows, like amulets, to protect them from Sadr's morality police on the prowl for the porn videos hidden beneath piles of religious sermons. Girls in trousers and cowboy boots were hauled to court. And a local cleric in Basra, Abd-al-Sattar al-Bahadili, instructed his followers to 'kidnap British female soldiers' and bring them to him in bondage. For each slave-girl, he promised a $170 reward.[215]

A more accessible prey was the *ghajar*, or gypsy communities, long associated with two of the most heinous sins in the Sadr catechism: Baathism and debauchery. For generations, Iraqi punters – from oil workers to Uday Hussein – had spent Friday afternoons intoxicated by their heady liquors and their pulsating 'dagger' dances – a routine in which girls thrust clenched fists at their pelvises. After the invasion, many found work and a safe haven in the Emirates, recording videos that in Iraq's new internet age became instant hits. 'Orange, Orange – why are you torturing me so?' sung Ala Saad, as he described peeling a girl like a fruit. (One viewing was interrupted by Ahlam, our office cook, with the words 'He who can't eat meat slurps soup'.)

The pluckiest continued their trade in Iraq. Down a dirt track on the banks of Diyala river south of Baghdad, the Sheikh of Nahawan, a tribal leader too fond of his gypsies to let them go, introduced me to Ohud and Itab, two buxom 'sisters' clad in black. Before introductions, a hand was fumbling in my pocket and a toe caressing my heel. 'I'm looking for money,' confessed Itab, as she adjusted her bra strap. The family-run business was conducted in the darkened living room. Itab's shirtless brother, Saad, turned the TV to an Arabic pop channel, and a ring of young children danced in the centre. From his pushchair a toddler waved his arms and chewed a cigarette Ohud had stuck in his mouth like a lollipop. Monitoring events in the corner, her father, Abu Saad, bemoaned the loss of revenue since Sadr's vigilantes had chased away his clientele, stolen their cars and increased the price of beer fourfold. 'Is this democracy?' he asked. 'We want to dance and drink, not pray.'

It was a risky business. In March 2004, in a midnight raid in Diwaniya, 130 kilometres south of Baghdad, the Mahdi Army – armed with pickaxes, sledgehammers and rocket-propelled grenades – demolished an entire gypsy village of 300 homes, a school and a mosque. 'It was a well of debauchery, drunkenness and mafia, and they were kidnapping and selling girls,' apologised Yahya Shubari, the ginger-haired 30-year-old commander-cleric leading 800 of Sadr's militiamen.[216] Opting for quiet (and appeasement), the local Spanish garrison kept its distance during six hours of shelling on the grounds of sensitivities to local mores. As scavengers rummaged in the ruins of their former homes, local media were advised not to report the village's destruction for fear of inciting unrest. The Sadr militia were an effective complement to the police assisting a crackdown on drugs, observed Major Carlos Herradon. US instructions to raid Sadr's courts and free its prisoners, he said, were 'provocative'. The Americans fumed. 'Effectively he [Sadr] is attempting to establish his authority in place of the legitimate authority. We will not tolerate this,' said Bremer.

By the eve of the first anniversary of the invasion, both sides were prepared for a showdown. In March 2003, the Mahdi Army declared Sadr City 'a US-free zone'; its US-appointed mayor of Sadr City was shot dead together with the head of the women's association paid by a USAID contractor. Graffiti spray-painted in Arabic on slum walls proclaimed: 'We will kill all the dogs and dollar-slaves who work with the Americans.' Bremer responded by ordering the Mahdi Army to disarm and had US tanks posted outside Sadr's home in Kufa. Simultaneously, British troops in Basra opened fire on a Sadr splinter group, Tha'r Allah (God's Revenge), who had defied eviction orders to vacate disused government offices. And in Baghdad, the gates of Sadr's inflammatory newspaper, *Hauza*, were padlocked.

Outraged at the infringement of free speech, Sadr's blackshirts took to the streets of Baghdad. Waving black flags, tens of thousands spilled out of Sadr City and staged prayer ceremonies beneath the tank turrets guarding the gates of the Green Zone, vowing to 'die rather than see the Mahdi's Army dissolved'.[217] From his pulpit in Kufa, Muqtada proclaimed 'the Revolution of Imam Mahdi'. Dressed in a white funeral shroud, just as his father had done on the eve of his assassination, he called on followers to prepare for martyrdom as 'the striking hand of Hizbollah': 'Be on the utmost readiness, and strike them [coalition forces] where you meet them. I say that they are here to stay and will occupy us for many years and as such compromise will no longer work.' The call to emulate Hizbollah was highly significant. A force, hitherto notable for its anti-Iranian diatribes, increasingly modelled itself on the strategies and principles of the Arab world's most pro-Iranian force. Sadr, himself, spent increasingly prolonged periods in Iran's holy city of Qom, supposedly on study retreats, while his Mahdi Army increased its dependence on its eastern neighbour for arms, training and finance. While the rank-and-file remained vitriolic in their regard for Iran, Sadr's detractors accused him of a volte face, slipping ever further into the Iranian camp, and becoming less the fighting arm than the cannon-fodder of an expansionist aspiring hegemon gaining ever more regional ground. Within hours, Bremer declared Sadr had 'crossed the line' and would 'not be tolerated'.[218] Based on a hitherto undisclosed arrest warrant issued by the coalition's court, the Central Criminal Court, he ordered Muqtada's arrest on the charge of murdering Khoi a year earlier. Sadr responded by accusing Bremer – plausibly – of manipulating the justice system. 'I have the honour to be termed an outlaw by a court of the occupation,' he retorted. That night, US forces seized Muqtada's assistant, Mustafa Yaqoubi.

The Revolution was unleashed the following day. Kut was the first to fall to the Mahdi Army, as it swept south from Baghdad's slums, overrunning government buildings, hospitals, police stations and even Coalition bases – which helped replenish munitions. Within a week, Sadr's forces controlled seven southern provinces, as clashes continued from Basra to Kirkuk. Ukrainian forces were sent packing from Kut and Italians from Nasiriya, in part because their rules of engagement provided for humanitarian not combat operations. In clashes at the gates of the Najaf base, 20 Muqtada loyalists and four Nicaraguans were killed, one reportedly after he was forced to swallow a live grenade. In Baghdad's Firdous Square, where one year previously US soldiers had yanked down Saddam Hussein's statue in the iconic scene of liberation, thousands of demonstrators marked the first post-Saddam anniversary by erecting portraits of Muqtada on the plinth. It was, said a US army spokesman, 'the largest firefight' since President Bush had declared an end to hostilities.

As in Falluja, the new Iraqi army – on which America had frittered billions – melted away with the first shots. 'Their militiamen say it's dangerous for us, so we're leaving the scene,' apologised a policeman who jumped into his car as soon as he spotted a Mahdi vanguard approach a Baghdad intersection. Policemen gingerly returning to their posts vowed to work for Muqtada not the occupation. 'We are brothers in the fight against terrorists and invaders,' said Sergeant Fouad Ibrahim at his station in Sadr City, before a blackshirt silenced him for speaking without Sadr's authorisation. In Diwaniya, the police flew Mahdi flags from their car aerials to spare them from attack. And in Basra, the police chief who happened to be the interior minister's brother handed over the Governorate to the militia. 'If you can't even convince your own brother to fight for you, who can you convince?' Bremer was said to have told Interior Minister Badran, shortly before sacking him.

Not only had Bremer's authority been supplanted, but so too had Sistani's. A gaggle of Mahdi guards guarded his alleyway behind metal barricades, effectively keeping the hapless Ayatollah under house arrest 'for his own protection'. Meekly, Sistani sneaked out a statement condemning 'the violation of public and private property', but in the face of the offensive his call for a peaceful transition to a democratic sovereign Iraq was almost inaudible. ('Sistani who?' quipped a Reuters colleague.) Along the Baghdad–Najaf highway vast billboards heralded Muqtada as Iraq's new leader. Icons of the Sadr dynasty festooned the colonnades of Najaf's bazaars. And Shaybani and his Mahdi cohorts evicted Sistani's orderlies from the Najaf shrine, and reigned supreme.

Sadr's front was all the more threatening for the signs of Sunni and Shia cooperation that accompanied it. Coinciding with the siege of Falluja, demonstrators marched in Mosul to express solidarity with Sadr, and graffiti decorated the walls of Ramadi hailing his 'valiant uprising'. Sadr reciprocated by condemning the US assault on Falluja, and observing the Muslim calendar as defined by Saudi Arabia not Iran. There was evidence, too, of Sunni logistical support. A delegation from Falluja headed to Najaf to rescue 15 bodies killed in a US counter-attack before they were buried in the Shia cemetery.

Fortunately for the Americans, they could rely on their Iraqi appointees to thwart a united revolt. Shia leaders in the Governing Council appealed for an American counter-attack to 'liberate' the Imam Ali shrine from Sadr's clutches. 'They [the Americans] must go in hard,' said an aide to al-Dawa leader and future prime minister Ibrahim al-Jaafari. Najaf, he added, was not Mecca.[219] Merchants in the Najaf bazaar furious at the loss of the pilgrimage trade and nervous clerics loyal to Sistani added their voices for US intervention, and the prosecution of Muqtada.[220] 'Can Muqtada cut our foreign debt?' chided a member of Najaf's chamber of commerce. And, in Baghdad, the Governing Council and 150 Shia notables publicly called on the Mahdi Army to withdraw from the Najaf shrine and the government offices they had captured. 'The people of Najaf regard Sadr as having taken them hostage,' said SCIRI's deputy leader, Adel Abdel Mahdi.

After almost a month of deliberation, General Ricardo Sanchez, the top US general in Iraq, turned *eradicateur* and launched Operation Resolute Sword 'to destroy Mr Sadr'. 'We're a conquering army,' explained a US colonel primed to attack. By day dozens of Abrams tanks parked lazily in the boulevards training their guns on barefoot children who were hurling stones and abuse, sporadically revving their engines to scare them away. Other than the tanks, the children and the perennial goats scrimmaging through the garbage, the normally teeming streets were empty, bringing a sense of serenity to the war. By night they staged 'thunder runs' through Baghdad's Shia slums. 'Say hiya to Allah for me,' shouted a gunner from Oregon, re-enacting the night's action, as he blitzed the phantoms lurking behind the columns of his palace base accompanied by gargling noises replicating the gunfire. The killing was as easy as playing a video game. 'I have the combat power to go any place I want to go. I mean, I just do,'[221] said General Marty Dempsey, the commander of the 1st Armored Division, who had the pinched intensity of a hyena and was charged with crushing the revolt.

In the face of overwhelming odds, Sadr's forces displayed often extraordinary bravery. They refrained from both the mass killings of civilians that characterised Sunni insurgents, and the beheading of hostages. On the rare occasion when a foreigner was kidnapped, they were released unharmed. Chased from their encampments and their offices across the south, they retreated to the sanctuaries of Karbala, Najaf and Kufa, and there they remained in an uneasy standoff until, in August 2004, US forces debated whether the challenge posed by Sadr outweighed an expected global outcry if their infidel forces violated the Shia holy places.

Barricaded with his blackshirts inside his fortress-like Kufa complex with its crenellated ramparts, Muqtada himself receded into semi-occultation. Under his command, the one-time springboard for the Arab conquest of Persia revived its legacy as the 'martyr city', and haven of messianic dissent for the likes of the Kharijites and Qarmithians (who spawned the Assassins). 'I would expect him to create some cataclysmic event in Shia Islam,' said General Dempsey, who argued, like British commanders in Basra, that mediation might secure their withdrawal.[222] In a series of negotiations with Sadr 'stakeholders', he proposed a 'political outcome' in which Muqtada would be spared prosecution and his 'lieutenants' would be integrated as paid recruits into the new Iraqi army. 'In the end,' he said, 'it all comes down to money.' But after three months of negotiations, the Americans despaired of luring Sadr from his shrines. In August 2004, the Iraqi government approved a US deployment at the gates to Najaf's shrine. The city's cemetery, the Valley of Peace and preferred resting place of Shias worldwide, became the apocalyptic backdrop for Sadr's warriors to engage with Washington's armies. The five square miles of cemetery, the largest on earth, was at least well-situated for burying the slain.

Initially, it seemed another instalment of the fighting that flared in March. But with the Shia establishment formally arrayed against him, it was now Sadr rather than Sistani who was under siege. Leaving the Americans to raid the shrines, Sistani flew to London on the pretext of attending a check-up for a heart condition. A fortnight later with the fighting in its final stages, he returned and graciously granted Sadr the audience the latter had long sought. The two men agreed that Sadr would hand back the keys of the shrine in return for the place in mainstream politics that Bremer had denied Sadr at the outset. The deal was signed with their respective seals. After 15 months of fighting and the loss of thousands of followers, Muqtada had salvaged the family honour.

Muqtada kept to his word. Despite a raid in late September 2004 – when US forces laid siege to his Najaf office less than 200 metres from the shrine and captured Shaybani, the one-time custodian of the shrine – Sadr's followers vacated the shrines and entered the political process, first as members of the post-Bremer National Assembly, and later as elected members of parliament. The Mahdi Army continued to deploy its morality police, burn American and Israeli flags and demand the withdrawal of US troops, but Sadr's support was crucial to underpinning Shia support for a political process that would have likely collapsed sooner without him. Few believed that he had been neutered and even fewer that he no longer aspired to be *qa'id*, but increasingly he acted from within the political system as well as without. His ability to connect with local grassroots made him a valuable ally for Shia exiles in search of a constituency, while his resistance earned him plaudits from some Sunni politicians. Variously casting himself as mediator in the sectarian killings and Shia protector, his followers insisted he remained Iraq's future religious and political panacea. Given his youth, it was not an unlikely scenario.

Over the following year, Sadr continued to operate under Sistani's nominal wing. He patched up his differences with SCIRI to campaign in both January 2005 and December 2005 on a joint electoral list known as the United Iraqi Alliance, and accepted that Abdel Aziz al-Hakim, Mohammed Hakim's brother and his replacement as SCIRI leader, should have first place. And yet in the provinces they fought on ever more violently for the Shia mantle and control of the oil-rich south. In the October 2005 constitutional referendum, Sadr joined Sunni voices in championing a united Iraq against Hakim's vision of a federal Shia super-state. And in the SCIRI-run provinces of Samawa and Basra, Sadaris orchestrated protests against dire local services. Increasingly amalgamated into Iraq's security apparatus, the Badr Brigades could only defend their positions with Coalition support, sometimes spectacularly as in Diwaniya in August 2006.[223] As Sadr's star waxed and SCIRI's waned, Sadr repeatedly launched offensives, striking ever deeper into southern Iraq – overrunning, for instance, the Amara base as the British evacuated in August 2006. Politically, Sadr reaped growing dividends. In the December 2005 election, Sadr's coalition in the Alliance won 35 per cent of the votes, substantially ahead of SCIRI's 20 per cent, propelling him into position as kingmaker. By the summer of 2006, Sadr's movement had become the most pivotal force in Iraq.

CHAPTER 13

Regime-Change and the Baathist Interregnum

The three towering heads of Saddam Hussein that had once presided over the Republican Palace lay strewn in a forgotten corner of the Highlander Forward Operating Base in west Baghdad.[224] Pending a decision from the Smithsonian Museum on whether to offer them a new home, the self-styled 'custodian of the heads' – appropriately, a California hairdresser on reserve duty – amused himself by 'tanking up, taking aim and pissing' at the bronze busts. 'I find the heads good target practice for both shooting and hairdressing,' said the petite 50-year-old, Mike Kelly.

Lost as to what to do with the latter-day Ozymandias, Washington struggled all the more over what to do with his country. After a year of smashing eggs under Bremer, a growing chorus of voices in Iraq and Washington counselled the time had come to put humpty-dumpty together again. Saddam's toppled heads might still lie discarded in a Baghdad military base, but the body of his regime was about to be resurrected.

There were good reasons why. Within a year of the invasion, Iraq's resistance was sufficiently powerful to wrest – albeit temporarily – 11 provinces from Bremer's control, a rollback comparable to the 1991 Intifada that threatened to unseat Saddam. The offensives to recover the two small towns of Najaf and Falluja cost 135 American soldiers, more than were killed in the initial conquest of Iraq. Even the capital was slipping from America's grasp. Beyond the perimeter fence of the Green Zone, Mahdi Army blackshirts patrolled the streets. And the brief nine-kilometre highway linking the US civil headquarters in Baghdad's Green Zone to its military headquarters at Baghdad airport – the most strategic stretch of road in Iraq – was also its most dangerous. In March 2004, US forces lost control of the highway from Jordan, endangering its food chain (as the food was entirely imported from abroad). Catering staff, again all imported to safeguard against poisoning by the natives, fled under a barrage of mortar attacks. The military stacked canteen shelves with bibles with camouflaged covers in an attempt to disguise the shortage of supplies for an army which more than most marched on its stomach.

With its footprint in Iraq receding, America's coalition proved increasingly unwilling. Ukrainians fled their positions in April 2004, and in their wake troops from the Philippines, Spain, the Dominican Republic, Honduras, Singapore, Thailand and Nicaragua all scampered out of Iraq. Those few who remained for the most part began to downsize, including the USA. In Baghdad, America reduced its bases from 60 to eight, leaving just one – the Green Zone – in the city centre. And after months of fighting in Falluja and Najaf, US commanders signed agreements leaving insurgents at least temporarily in charge. Iraqis scoffed that their country had yet to fall.

The distance between the coalition and the country it went to war to free was gaping. By the end of 2006, only six of the 1,000 US officials in Baghdad had a fluent command of Arabic.[225] Fraternisation between US soldiers and Iraqi women was banned by the US military, though the rule was less than uniformly observed by the heavily perfumed female translators doing overtime with the GIs in the Green Zone's Rashid Hotel. Checkpoints manned by nervous US soldiers became the most lethal place in Iraq. On the highways, chugging tanks let civilian traffic past only when they wanted to use them as guinea-pigs to test for road-side bombs. (The tactic often paid off to brutal effect. An explosion killed the taxi-driver in front soon after a Bulgarian convoy near Karbala had stopped to make way for us.) Other tactics for avoiding ambushes included denuding the roadsides of eucalyptus trees, and driving the wrong side up highways heedless of oncoming traffic. Soldiers stared down their gun-barrels at the queues of Iraqi vehicles forming behind. 'Keep 50m or deadly force will be applied,' read the board dangling from their tank rears. Since it was visible only at 30 metres and penned only in English, Iraq's morgues were frequent recipients of those who had strayed too close.

Few such deaths made the news local bulletins, and those that did for the most part involved journalists.[226] More appeared on websites, bartered as snuff movies in exchange for free access to porn sites. Frustrated at hunting a hidden enemy, marines admitted to shooting any Iraqi – known to the GIs collectively as 'muj', short for *mujahideen* – seen handling a phone near a bomb-blast for fear it might trigger another explosion.[227] 'It gets to a point where you can't wait to see guys with guns, so you start shooting everybody... It gets to a point where you don't mind the bad stuff you do,' *The Economist* quoted a marine lieutenant.[228] On house-to-house searches they kicked in front doors and screamed in English at the women within: 'Where's your black mask, Bitch? Where's the guns?' America had overthrown one military regime and imposed another.

A sign a US commander had pinned to the gates of his Green Zone barracks in the aftermath of the invasion faded in the sun, hollow and forlorn. 'What have you today done to help Iraqis?' it read. By May 2004, the Coalition held 10,000 Iraqis in custody, many of them untraceable due to the lack of a national register. Months passed while applications for family visits were processed, and representations from lawyers were banned on the grounds Iraqis might profit from a service the military rendered for free. Compensation payments lauded in press conferences were derisory. The killing of an Iraqi, valued at $3 million by the Brookings Institute was deemed to be worth $2,500 by the US military compensation board. 'Osama the Arab', an itinerant porter, earned $1,000 after a US soldier in Sadr City 'had a negligent discharge' into his left leg.[229] Claims for torture were automatically dismissed, and were anyway hard to prove since most plaintiffs were hooded during interrogation. Iraqi human rights groups focussing on abuse under Bremer's regime rather than Saddam's were warned they could forfeit their US grants.

Nevertheless, within a month of the invasion reports of appalling conditions trickled out of detention camps. Red Cross monitors gaining access to one of several detention camps near Basra found prisoners beaten with rifle butts and made to parade with boards marked 'terrorist' strung from their necks.[230] A group of farmers had been interned en masse, said a Red Cross monitor, after US troops mistook their job description, *fellahin*, Arabic for peasant, with *fedayeen* – guerrillas. Seven thousand detainees alone were crammed into Abu Ghraib jail, 2,000 more than under Saddam Hussein. Inmates emerged bearing the scars of the tight nylon cuffs which for weeks had dug into their hands strung behind their backs. Some, with puffy eyes indicating repeated beatings, claimed to have been stripped naked of all but their ubiquitous hood. Others said they had been held in packing cases for days. Three detained Reuters journalists were subjected to sleep deprivation and stress positions, and had shoes stuffed in their mouths. For highly stressed, overworked and understaffed US troops the sadism offered a quick release. Prisoners were stripped naked and forced to perform sex acts in public. British soldiers in their Basra base went for a spin on fork-lift trucks, dangling detainees naked and blindfolded from the raised prongs by their handcuffed arms. For over a year western editors found the tales too fantastic to print.

Unsurprisingly, Iraqis were soon asking whether they would be better off without the *qurud*, or monkeys, as they called the Americans. They longed for the day when their tanks would no longer rumble through their streets leaving a trail of snapped telegraph and electricity wires in their wake. (When Ahlam, the office cook, asked a passing soldier to tie down the aerials which caught on the wires before entering the neighbourhood, he trained his tank turret on her.) Within a year, approval ratings of the US military dropped from 60 per cent in Baghdad in August 2003 to less than 15 per cent. When roadside bombs killed US troops, crowds of young men and children gathered to cheer. Coalition rescue missions were pelted with stones.

With the tide of public sentiment turning against the invaders, foreigners of all hues became targets. A remorseless spate of kidnappings – 43 in April 2004 alone – turned foreign civilians into pawns of war. By June 2005 over 300 had been killed. Aid workers gave their last reports robed in orange jumpsuits with knives to their throats. Journalists became rather than reported the story, though in London their editors were selling too many papers to do much about it. Leaflets circulated Baghdad with a number to call to inform on foreign tenants. My landlady, Um Taysir, was warned her two children might suffer unless she got rid of the foreign lodger upstairs, forcing me to relocate to across the river. As before the invasion, Russia again airlifted its nationals out of Iraq. Those left behind were imprisoned behind sandbags and tinted glass, as if under house arrest.

By the summer of 2004, most had slunk into the Green Zone or other military bases, never daring to leave its confines. Even so, the threat followed them. Four bodyguards accompanied Bremer when he went to the bathroom, even as he insisted that the mortars were merely the convulsions of a dying enemy. Coalition drills trained officials to hide under their desks in the event of incoming fire, preferably with a mattress on top. The British opened a dormitory in the Green Zone's underground car-park, dubbed the 'batcave'. But the perimeter fence was increasingly permeable. In October 2004, bomb-blasts ripped through two Green Zone cafes.

When the Green Zone was judged too dangerous, US contractors retreated to the comfort of Amman's five-star hotels. Rather than abandon lucrative contracts, they worked on endless feasibility studies. 'Lots of work can be performed in Amman,' assured a spokesman for Bechtel, which by April 2004 had relocated most of its staff on its $1.8 billion Iraqi reconstruction programme abroad.[231] After repeated delays, Baghdad Expo – hyped as the show to relaunch Iraq – launched in Turkey. As contractors abandoned their projects, the number of Iraqis employed by America's $18.6 billion reconstruction programme halved from 7,744 in March 2004 to 3,517 the following month – further undermining a scheme designed to cut Iraq's unemployment rate to 20 per cent. USAID, which had budgeted for the construction of 286 schools in 2004, completed eight. US funding was diverted to fund close protection. As western reconstruction magnates moved out, the mercenaries had moved in, creaming a large slice of Iraq's oil revenues[232] and under CPA regulations operating above Iraqi law.[233] The $184 million earmarked for clean water projects in the original reconstruction programme was reallocated to build an American embassy.

Retreating into the inner sanctum of the Green Zone, Bremer concentrated on sculpting the final touches of the legal framework of his virtual *Civitas Dei*. The more his laws multiplied, the fewer were his means for implementation. Bremer's Bill of Rights, guaranteeing freedom of belief and expression, was a white paper elephant, and his economic reform a miasma. Tom Foley, charged with sweeping privatisation, departed Baghdad in March 2004 without floating a single factory. Policies to slash subsidies, prune the bloated civil service, shut down unprofitable banks, and replace the food ration with cash vouchers – unveiled to a fanfare at the Dead Sea in the summer of 2003 – remained on the drawing board. Far from cutting expenditure, Bremer inflated the pay-roll with pay increases and higher petrol subsidies. The 30 weathermen at Baghdad's International Airport dutifully recording that Baghdad was sunny were replaced with a computer but kept their jobs. Foreigners fared far better. Shortly before leaving Iraq, Bremer doled out contracts worth billions of Iraqi oil revenues to favoured contractors, including western military companies hired to secure the country's prime strategic estate, including its major sea and airports.

America's public was losing patience. After a year of swallowing Washington's line that US soldiers were democratising and civilising Iraq's natives, the April 2004 scandal at Abu Ghraib shattered America's innocence. The scenes of US soldiers forcing hooded prisoners to stand naked on boxes with wires attached to their genitals exposed the US president's lie that 'there are no more torture chambers' in Iraq.[234] Under attack on the home-front, as well as Iraq, the administration began to rethink their strategy.

The parameters of the debate were confined, focussing on how not whether the US should be present. In essence the arguments dated back to Saddam's invasion of Kuwait when US policy-makers sparred over the merits of replacing the regime versus replacing the leader, perhaps through an elusive golden bullet. The debate raged throughout the 1990s, with the protagonists increasingly divided along institutional lines: the neo-cons in the Pentagon championing revolution versus those in the State Department and the CIA advocating a policy of realpolitik in which the personnel not the system was changed.

Consciously or not, Iraq's sects were sucked into the departmental turf war. Long-standing Sunni leaders looked to the State Department to uphold the old order, while the Shia underdogs bent on a regional sea-change gravitated to the Pentagon. In the first months following the invasion, the Pentagon, basking in its easy march to Baghdad, had the upper hand. The Pentagon's protégés on the Iraqi Governing Council outnumbered those of the State Department's by three to one, and of the 20 State Department staffers initially posted to the CPA, 16 were sent home by the Pentagon, according to insiders, on the grounds they were 'Arabists'. But as Iraq began to unravel, the State Department and CIA saw increasing opportunities to regain control, leaking a succession of reports that warned that unless demilitarisation and deBaathification were reversed America would lose Iraq. In November 2003, Deputy Secretary of State Richard Armitage travelled to Cairo, promising to restore Iraq's Sunnis to the political process. And soon after the State Department launched al-Hurra, or Freedom, in February 2004, to compete with the Pentagon's ham-fisted Iraqi Media Network, otherwise known as 'the Pentagon's *Pravda*'. The Abu Ghraib scandal enabled them to press the advantage further. Richard Jones – a career diplomat and ambassador to Kuwait – was appointed Bremer's deputy, and quickly mediated a truce in Falluja in May 2004, which put Saddam's former military brass and Sunni leader in charge – much to the discomfort of the Pentagon's Shia favourites.[235] 'This is a major change,' said Hajm Hassani, a Sunni Islamist leader with a PhD from Connecticut University, who helped negotiate the deal. 'Changing the policy is going to solve Iraq's security and diplomatic crisis.'

The decision to delegate control of Iraq to one of Saddam's Republican Guard commanders in Falluja in the wake of the failed May 2004 siege was replicated across much of Iraq. In the town of Kut, a Sadr stronghold 180 kilometres south of Baghdad, US forces replaced the police chief and his deputy with two Republican Guards. Former officers in the Republican Guard gained key police posts in Diwaniya. In the Green Zone, US officials repackaged Bremer as *conciliateur* not *eradicateur*. Bremer's spokesman, Dan Senor, announced the new Iraq Army was undergoing a rapid expansion and that deBaathification was a 'technical correction'. On 28 June 2004, two days before scuttling out of Baghdad without even a farewell address, Bremer promulgated his last decree, No. 100, rescinding his first: the creation of the deBaathification Committee.

Bremer's plans for the handover were also substantially revised. Instead of the installation of a government chosen by an indirectly elected assembly, a greying UN envoy, Lakhdar Brahimi, was parachuted in to handpick a government with the Americans.[236] Where Shias had anticipated a democracy that would propel the Shia majority to power, US officials planned an interim government micromanaged CIA-style by a US ambassador. As Bremer flew off in his helicopter for the last time, John Negroponte, a former US ambassador to Honduras who had overseen the CIA's funding of the Nicaraguan Contras, flew in as Iraq's new US ambassador. Though the title had changed, the workplace – Iraq's presidential palace – and many of the proconsul's de facto powers remained.

Anticipating their demise, the Pentagon's Shia darlings counter-attacked with accusations that the CIA's rehabilitation of Saddam's henchmen was akin to restoring the Nazis to Germany. Ahmed Chalabi refused to readmit former Baathists, and his relative, Defence Minister Ali Allawi, refused to recognise the Falluja battalion as an army unit. 'The way to deal with rebels is to arrest them. If they resist you fight back,' he snapped.[237] Brahimi, a former Algerian foreign minister, was derided as a Sunni outsider partial to his sect.[238] The newly empowered State Department responded by hounding the Chalabis and their ilk from power. Donning shaded sunglasses, CIA agents and Iraqi police launched a succession of raids on Chalabi's Baghdad headquarters in April 2004, and the following month sealed off his home, smashing his portraits in the process. Documents and computer disks, including the laptop of Defence Minister Allawi, were removed by the lorry load, along with a fleet of cars Chalabi had purloined from the Finance Ministry, allegedly for safekeeping. One by one his followers were subpoenaed by the Coalition's court, the Central Criminal Court, in what they decried as a CIA-engineered coup.[239]

In place of the fallen Chalabis, Brahimi and his posse of US officials appointed his rival, Iyad Allawi, as prime minister of Iraq's first post-war government. For over a year, the leader of the Iraqi National Accord and the most prominent of the CIA's protégés had been a lone voice on the Governing Council lambasting deBaathification and demilitarisation as the two prime causes of the insurgency. 'The party was history,' he said. 'DeBaathification brought it back to life.'[240] As chairman of the Governing Council's Security Committee, he tried to mitigate against their effects. He restored the Iraqi intelligence agency that Bremer had abolished ten months earlier, under the baton of Mohammed Shahwani, a senior army officer who had led an unsuccessful INA-sponsored coup against Saddam Hussein in 1996. And having failed to recall Iraqi soldiers and petty Baathists into the fledgling Iraqi army, he drafted them into his party instead.

Allawi's victory against Chalabi had been nearly 50 years in the offing. In many ways, they were of identical stock. Both were Shia, were sons of ministers under the monarchy, were the same age, had British passports, and had married into the same Lebanese family, making them cousins. They had shared their first experience of American tutelage in the same class at the same elite school, the Baghdad College run by Boston Jesuits, where together in Class 5 they had commemorated Petroleum Sunday in the name of 'Our Lady of Arabia for all men of the oil industry'. In school photos, Chalabi dons the pose of an immaculately dressed young aristocrat; standing above him, Allawi's beady eyes survey his fellow pupil. Even then, he was considered a bully.

They were separated by the 1958 Revolution. The urbane Chalabi fled to the United States, first to the Massachusetts Institute of Technology and then to the University of Chicago, where he fell under the influence of the America neo-con mentor Albert Wohlstetter, whose circle included students Paul Wolfowitz, Zalmay Khalilzad and Richard Perle. Armed with a circle that was subsequently to plot the conquest of Iraq, Chalabi returned to the region first as a maths lecturer at the American University in Beirut, and then in 1977 as the founder of the Petra Bank, whose regional accounts he appears to have had little compunction about sharing with the Americans.

Unlike Chalabi, who fled the republic, Allawi joined it. After completing his studies at Baghdad College, where biographers claim a priest first enticed him to the CIA, he enrolled in Baghdad University's Medical

College, where he crafted a reputation as a Baathist thug. 'The big husky man carried a gun on his belt and frequently brandished it, terrorising medical students,' wrote a fellow medical student, Dr Haifa al-Azawi.[241] On the eve of the February 1963 Baathist coup, he kidnapped the dean. 'We took Iraq's first hostages,' recalled a fellow conspirator, Adil Abdel Mahdi, another Baghdad College schoolmate who Allawi subsequently picked as his finance minister.[242] After surrendering the unfortunate dean, Allawi and Abdel Mahdi were incarcerated in the same prison cell until they were freed by the coup.[243]

Although Allawi denies personally conducting the post-coup interrogations, when the coup collapsed a few months later he and Saddam were rounded up and thrown together in jail. Allawi's family bailed him out and Saddam escaped. In the more successful Baathist coup of 1968, Allawi seized Baghdad's radio station and thereafter worked with Saddam in the Republican Palace.[244] Two years later, he won a grant from the UN's World Health Organization to study in London, then the Iraqi émigré capital. Under the cover of a conducting doctoral thesis at Guy's Hospital, he worked as the Baath's chief representative in Europe, and is remembered as the shadow at the shoulder of the Iraqi ambassador to London and by some as an assassin of dissidents.[245] 'If you're asking me if Allawi has blood on his hands from his days in London, the answer is yes, he does,' Cannisatraro is quoted as saying. 'He was a paid *mukhabarat* [intelligence] agent for the Iraqis, and he was involved in dirty stuff.'[246]

If he was not already a double-agent, Allawi quickly became one. Dagham al-Qathim, who subsequently joined Allawi's INA, claims that Allawi first sounded him out about forming an opposition in 1972. Allawi narrowly escaped assassination himself after defying Saddam's order to return to Baghdad on suspicion of conspiring with MI6 and stealing party funds. When an axe-man attacked the Allawis in bed in their London home, his injured Christian wife, Athour, asked him to choose between her and politics. A hospitalised Allawi chose the latter, and in 1987 remarried.

Once again the paths of the two former classmates overlapped. Both were in London, on the run – Chalabi from Jordan after the collapse of his Petra Bank, and Allawi from Saddam – and jostling for western and Iraqi patronage. Allawi became a magnet for disaffected Baathists, plotting to replace Saddam but preserve the regime; Chalabi attracted a more quixotic assortment of debonair monarchists and human rights activists. On the proceeds of his western backers, 'that silk-suited, Rolex-wearing guy from

London', famously described by General Anthony Zinni, the US chief of Central Command,[247] took a Mayfair apartment and a series of villas in Salahudin, a hill-top town in the Kurdish haven, from where he preached for the overthrow of the Baath. While Chalabi courted Iran and Jewish lobbies in Washington,[248] Allawi shored up his pre-war ties with other CIA favourites, including King Abdullah of Jordan. Shunning the talking-shop of Chalabi's Iraqi National Congress, Allawi found employment in London's Belgravia working for the Chevron Corporation, a US oil company which counted future US Secretary of State Condoleezza Rice amongst its directors. Flush with funds after prospecting in South Yemen,[249] he bought a £1 million town house in Kensington and established a forward base in Amman to plot his 'surgical coup'. So great was the Chalabi–Allawi rivalry that from the first each accused the other of leaking their plots to Baghdad.[250]

Despite subsequent claims of intrepid raids in the western desert, Allawi and his henchmen spent most of the 2003 invasion in their Amman apartment, watching the war on satellite television. Only the sight of Chalabi popping up in Nasiriya goaded Allawi to race to Baghdad. They arrived too late to grab the best real estate and had to console themselves with party offices in a former Baath party training college. 'Everything else had already gone and so we were lumbered with this huge dusty elephant building,' bemoaned Allawi's then deputy, Dagham al-Qathim. Under its new masters, the building lost none of its sinister pre-war air. Sentries with machine guns were posted on each flight of steps, and visitors required prior written invitations.

Whatever anxieties the Sunni satraps might have harboured about Allawi's Shia origins on his appointment as prime minister were quickly assuaged by his Arab nationalist and Baathist security credentials. His own beliefs seemed as watered down as those of Saddam's own Shia appointees, and the leaders of Jordan, Saudi Arabia and Egypt all rushed to embrace Iraq's new leader as one of their own. The Hashemite monarchy benefited in particular with the revival of the special relationship it had joined under Saddam, after Allawi agreed that 32,000 Iraqi police should be trained in Jordan at a cost of $1.2 billion.[251] As his ties with Arab regimes prospered, those with Iran – the first regional country to recognise the Governing Council – floundered. In a speech panning the handover, Iran's Supreme leader, Ayatollah Ali Khamenei, damned Allawi as an American 'lackey', who sought to 'remove the clergy from government'. For good measure, the chief of Iran's Revolutionary Guards, General Yehya Safawi, called

Allawi 'US-imposed, treacherous and perfidious'. Inside Iraq, Shias joined in the chorus of disapproval. Beneath a banner headline screaming 'the Baath returns to Iraq', the pro-Sadr paper, *Ansar al-Mahdi*, derided Allawi for having 'nothing to do with the political visions or religion of the Shia' and likened him to Saddam's information (Shia) minister, Sahaf. Allawi, who had waited a year to secure a meeting with Sistani, was treated to an encounter clerics described as 'frosty'. With the revival of Arab–Persian confrontation, Iraq was looking more and more like a typical Arab state.

In a cabinet approved by Negroponte, the government was purged of the Hauza. Shia religious parties were either booted from their ministries or relegated to minor posts.[252] In their place, Allawi appointed at least ten former students he had chaperoned as European head of the Baath party, including many who had climbed high up the party ladder under Saddam.[253] His justice minister, Malik Hassan Dohan, who had been the pre-war head of Iraq's bar association, was so much a staple of the former regime that Saddam's secretary, Abdel Hamid Mahmoud al-Tikriti, sought to appoint him his lawyer when he appeared before the Special Tribunal. Sunnis regained control of both their traditional domains (even under Saddam) of the interior and trade ministries and retained the electricity ministry, and for the first time since the war a Sunni (the Interior Minister's brother, Thair al-Naqeeb) was made government spokesman.[254] And while a Shia exile, Hazim Shaalan, retained control of the defence ministry, he did his utmost to appeal to the prejudices of the old regime by lambasting Iran as Iraq's 'enemy no. 1'.

Allawi himself did little to hide his Baathist affinities. In interviews with Arab satellite channels, he presented himself as Saddam Lite – the 'corrective' face of the Baath – and Saddam as a deviant who had sent Iraq careering off course. 'I am honoured to have confronted this deviation,' he said. 'My affiliation with the Baath Party has made me gain a great political experience.'[255] And in his swearing-in ceremony staged against a backdrop of the old Iraq flag, he promised to end the anti-Baath witch-hunt in the name of national reconciliation. Twelve thousand civil servants sacked for their Baathist membership regained their jobs in the first weeks of his premiership. 'Allawi recalled a lot of Baathists, because he's one of them,' said Baghdad University Professor Nadhmi, another of Allawi's former wards from London.[256]

The prime minister was reviving not just the old-regime personnel and rhetoric, but also its disbanded institutions. Saddam's information ministry was also brought out of mothballs, and renamed the Higher Media Commission. Its new chief, Ibrahim Jannabi, a former intelligence officer and Allawi's INA deputy, spoke encouragingly of self-censorship.[257] Within weeks satellite stations had been banned for airing interviews with regime opponents, and the independent-minded editor of the state-funded television station, *Iraqia*, was forced to resign. In his wake, the station began broadcasting confessions extracted from alleged insurgents bearing the marks of duress. And Allawi's own paper, *Baghdad*, was filled with paeans which might have made Saddam blush. 'You [Allawi] are a heaven sent gift to bring back the greenery to this paradise lost,' wrote a sycophant hoping for a government contract in an advert spanning half a page. It was just like old times.

Far from reeling in embarrassment from comparisons to a former strongman, Allawi relished the coverage. In press performances, he declared curfews and martial law in 'emergency zones' and raised the prospect of delaying elections. His justice minister brought back the death penalty, and his defence minister vowed to chop off rebel heads and hands. Allawi waited a week before denying reports that he had personally shot dead six suspects – handcuffed and blindfolded – at a Baghdad police station. To much fanfare, he recalled five of the 70 armed force divisions Iraq had maintained before the war, two more than the Coalition had agreed, and set a target for the recruitment of 230,000 security personnel, with next to no vetting.[258] Saddam's internal intelligence agency, the General Security Directorate, dissolved by Bremer, was re-established, as was a new intelligence agency under Interior Ministry control. 'Old Baathists are resuming their old jobs in intelligence,' said Adnan Karim, a former army officer who advised Allawi. State Department officials showed little discomfort at the revival of Saddam's 'apparatus of oppression'. The National Human Rights Commission stipulated in Bremer's Transitional Administrative Law was quietly shelved.[259] 'At least he's our bully,' said a State Department mandarin.[260]

In the name of a morality drive, Allawi's police had kicked the stands of the beer pedlars beneath Baghdad's Jadarriya Bridge into the Tigris. Five hundred drug-pushers and pimps were detained in a sweep of Baghdad's red-light district, the former Jewish quarter Betawaeen (so called because it was 'in between' two more reputable districts). Chiming with the former regime, Allawi's next target was Shia renegades. Within a fortnight of assuming office, he authorised the US to attack Najaf's shrine, where Sadr's forces were besieged. Sunni insurgents, by contrast, were openly courted, as plaudits for Allawi poured in from the Sunni heartlands. 'Allawi is sending a message of peace to Arab Sunni families,' crooned Mishaan al-Jibouri, a Sunni tribal leader who headed the Homeland Party. 'He's the best Shia prime minister Sunnis could have.'[261]

CHAPTER 14

The Staying Power of the Shia

For all his roar, Allawi was a paper tiger, operating amidst far weightier forces. His six-month term in office was abruptly ended in January 2005, when Iraq's electorate proved their new power by booting him from office. A threefold combination of US straitjacketing, endemic corruption and a Shia genie which once out of the bottle could not be pushed back all conspired to hamstring his attempts to co-opt the Sunnis and turned Iraq's public against him.

The first was perhaps the most obvious. Allawi's interim government was hemmed in by regulations, not least UN Security Council Resolution 1513, which required him to uphold the self-serving contracts and legislation decreed by the CPA. But even without the legal entrapments, Allawi had few tools at his disposal. While Washington commanded 150,000 men and 7,400 planes in Iraq, Allawi inherited a sole division of 8,000 men, a National Guard of 40,000 ill-trained local levies, and 16 transport helicopters. The Defence Ministry's much vaunted 'house-to-house' raid across western Iraq was hampered by its lack of a phone system and arms, since after the conquest the Coalition had pulverised its arsenal. With rebel and party militias armed with mortars, rockets and machine-guns, government forces were simply out-gunned.[262]

The country's major assets, including its 160 airfields and Saddam's palaces, remained similarly under coalition control. Proposals submitted by Iraq's president to convert the palaces into museums, hotels, a children's water-park and a seat for the National Assembly were rebuffed. And to highlight their powers, Coalition troops raided the home of the president's relatives. The Republican Palace, the presidential seat, remained in US parlance an 'embassy-annex'. A week after the 'handover of sovereignty', bare-chested mercenaries with holsters on their hips marked the 4th of July by playing drinking games in Palace gardens oblivious to the irony that they were celebrating their own Independence from a colonial Empire while robbing Iraq's. Against the backdrop of a giant video screening a fireworks display (lest the real thing be confused with incoming rockets), a couple were caught inflagrante on the roof-top of what had once been the showpiece of Iraq's power. Male and female soldiers shrieked in the swimming pools below, sporting T-shirts embossed with the logo 'Let Freedom Sting'.

US forces had little compunction about showing who was boss. In the halls of the Central Criminal Court at 10.26 a.m. on 28 June 2004, an Iraqi judge marked the appointed hour of the handover by acquitting prisoner No. 27075 of killing Coalition personnel. US forces bundled him back to Abu Ghraib jail regardless. 'He could still be a security threat,' explained an American military prosecutor, stating the Geneva Conventions for occupied territory still applied. 'We have the feeling the judges are not really putting their heart into the prosecution of crimes against Americans.' Allawi's initiatives to mobilise two additional army divisions, offer an amnesty to 'resistance fighters' and apply martial law were similarly overturned on the grounds Iraq was constrained by Bremer's Bill of Rights, and that only US-led Coalition forces had the right to adopt emergency powers. To further tighten his control, Ambassador Negroponte prepared to plant 10,000 US military advisors amongst Iraq's forces. Army training remained in the hands of a US contractor, Vinnell, and police training in those of DynCorp, further enforcing the hierarchy.[263] A year later, US Central Command deemed only one Iraqi battalion ready to operate independently of US forces. Allawi's efforts to resupply his counter-insurgency forces were similarly proscribed, on the grounds that the Saddam-era 'UN weapons embargo' still applied. So too did spending curbs to prevent rearmament, and the no-fly zone, which was simple enough given that Iraq remained without an airforce.[264] In joint missions, US soldiers drove tanks, and their Iraqi counterparts soft-skinned open-top Nissans.

Rather than engage Iraqis to defend their country, the undermanned Coalition farmed out security to foreign contractors. By late 2004, there were 20,000 mercenaries in Iraq, including 6,000 on combat duty, comprising the second largest contingent of Coalition forces in Iraq. Blackwater's fleet of fly-like Kiowa helicopters buzzed in the skies above the

Green Zone, and other US firms maintained B-2 stealth bombers and spy planes, and destroyed enemy ammunition. On the eve of the handover, intelligence gathering was farmed out to a small British company, Aegis Defence Systems, run by Lieutenant Colonel Tim Spicer, a former officer of the Scots Guards who was investigated for arms smuggling in violation of UN embargos to support mining and oil operations from Sierra Leone to Papua New Guinea.[265] The contract – worth $293 million – was described as the 'largest security contract in the private sector'.[266] South Asians were imported to perform key frontline duties. Gurkhas guarded Baghdad Airport and the Republican Palace, and Fijians the Palace in Basra. There was no status of forces agreement: as in bygone colonial times, the Americans refused to sign one.[267] Unregulated and immune from prosecution, many alienated Iraqis further by abusing their privileges. 'What right do they have to come to my country and push me around?' asked Khalid Shammari, a prominent Iraqi businessman after South African guards put a gun to his head as he entered a Baghdad hotel. Iraqi officials echoed the protests at the outsourcing. 'I don't want to see them swaggering around over-armed and behaving like private armies,' said Iraq's pre-handover defence minister Ali Allawi, shortly before he was dismissed. 'We can save our government a great deal of money defending ourselves.'

Faced with continued occupation, Sunnis went back to war lampooning Iyad Allawi as another US contractor. 'Our jihad and resistance against the foreign occupier and all the agents who collaborate with it... will continue until true sovereignty – not a deceptive smokescreen – has been achieved,' said a statement from the Islamic Resistance Front, a coalition of Islamist movements based in Mosul. After a brief interlude following Allawi's appointment, insurgent ranks surged with fresh recruits. Far from the 'few dead-enders' claimed by Defence Secretary Rumsfeld, the Coalition faced a full-scale insurrection numbering 40,000 active Sunni fighters, according to General Andrew Graham, Britain's deputy commander of Coalition Forces.[268] Iraq's intelligence chief said a further 160,000 sympathisers provided logistical support. In August 2003, 14 per cent of Sunni Arabs thought it legitimate to attack US personnel and facilities. Three years later, 70 per cent did. Attacks soared from an average of 20 per day in December 2003 to 120 a year later, and an average of a car-bomb a day. Explosions grew in sophistication. 500-pound bombs of a magnitude to destroy armoured vehicles were buried in tarmac or beneath animal carcasses.[269] And amongst the booty captured in the marines' Falluja assault in

November 2004 was an ice-cream van converted into a mobile car-bomb workshop. Attacks on power plants blackened the capital, inducing a state of siege. Officials switched off their mobiles for fear the Egyptian employees at the mobile company, Iraqna, might leak their coordinates to the insurgency. The marine assault on Falluja and the flattening of thousands of homes, while initially militarily successful, further stoked resentment. 'Saddam never destroyed Falluja. Allawi did,' said Saleem al-Imam, a one-time Allawi loyalist. 'Is that the new face of democracy?'[270] Within six weeks, rebels were reported to have regained a foothold in Falluja, and insurgents in al-Qaim and al-Haditha, two towns close to Syria, repulsed a succession of US offensives.

Bounced between the US and insurgents, the outgunned security forces acted like men on the run. As insurgents fanned north after November's Falluja assault, they stormed all Mosul's police stations, dumping around 200 dead policemen, mostly beheaded, about the city. To protect the 4,000 who survived, the city's police chief called on his men to join the rebels. 'They defected not only because they were afraid but because they feel emotionally with their people and the violence they have suffered,' said Ibrahim Jannabi, Allawi's deputy. Elsewhere in western Iraq, the provincial administration either mutinied or imploded. Anbar's governor resigned after his children were kidnapped.

The government's inability to rule coincided with a vast increase in government funds. For the first time since the UN imposed the straitjacket of its oil-for-food programme in 1996, Iraq's government controlled its own oil revenues. Freed from sanctions and flushed with income from oil prices at their highest for 20 years, Iraq's budget jumped from barely $1 billion before the war to over $16 billion in 2004. With scant scope to spend it inside Iraq, the government followed the procession of diplomats, aid agencies and businessmen to Allawi's old haunt of Amman. Amongst the fresh-cut lilies, the lobby of Jordan's Four Seasons Hotel took on the role of a state function room bustling with Iraqi politicians and officials, chaperoned by American and Jordanian bodyguards somewhat to the annoyance of disgruntled guests. 'Before the war we had single-figure occupancy. Now all our rooms are full,' said a jubilant manager at the hotel, who on a typical day in December 2004 numbered amongst her guests five Iraqi ministers, an Iraq trade bank delegation, an Iraqi construction magnate and an American contractor who had block-booked the top floor. Much as the Kuwaiti Emir during Saddam's occupation, Allawi's regime was a government in exile flush with funds waiting for America to reclaim their state.

Amman flourished under the influx. As Iraq emptied, Dyncorp moved into a wing of Amman's Sheraton Hotel, and much of the rest of the building was block-booked by USAID. House prices in the capital soared 35 per cent in the 18 months following the war. New suburbs sprouted by the season. Amman, once the most conservative capital in the Levant, joined the ranks of the libertine with its first lap-dancing bar. Clubs sweated with tattooed ex-soldiers, and prostitutes from Eastern Europe and the Philippines. Despite the anti-American diatribes bellowing from mosques in the refugee camps of East Amman, businessmen in West Amman profited from a host of unaudited deals, from the construction of electricity generators to new security firms. As under Saddam, bankrupt Iraq was again bankrolling Jordan. 'What we are seeing is the reconstruction of Jordan, not Iraq,' said a senior Iraqi finance official, fuming at the hundreds of millions of reconstruction dollars haemorrhaging into Jordan.[271]

Some corruption was to be expected, given that most ministers were living beyond their means. 'My salary as a minister is $1,200 [per month],' huffed Bakhtiar Amin, the human rights minister. 'They give us $500 for hospitality, and $2,000 for residence. I have no insurance and I'm expected to risk my life and entertain contractors earning $200,000 a month.' But the scale – far exceeding the misappropriation under Saddam – was a second factor that unseated Allawi. 'The political vacuum which followed the change of regime has created an excellent opportunity for corruption,' concluded Judge Radhi Hamza al-Radhi, the head of the state-funded Commission of Public Integrity. 'Seventy per cent of officials are involved in malpractice.' Their attitude was typified by the Electricity Minister Ayham Samarrai who, when summoned by Bremer to explain why he had exaggerated projections of power output, replied: 'What do we care? We're both going to lose our jobs anyway.'[272] Once feted by Washington as the architects of the new Iraq, exiles such as Samarrai were now parodied as thieves.[273] 'It is disappointing that we went to reform Iraq, and it's more of a shambles than when we arrived,' said Haydar al-Uzri, who after a year spent overseeing Iraq's banking sector headed home for London. 'All the people know they have a limited time-scale and are grabbing as much as they can.'[274] Iraqis called it the 'Titanic Syndrome'.

Allawi's home on the leafy slopes of the Amman suburb of Rabia became a trading office run by his long-standing secretary, Mona Alwash. And at

least six of his ministers followed suit. The Trade Ministry deposited
$400 million earmarked for food rations in two Beirut banks, bypassing
standard procedures, said the minister, in order to speed up deliveries for
Ramadan, although months after the end of the Muslim fasting month
the stock had yet to arrive.[275] Despite the close watch of many US
advisors, Defence Minister Shaalan squirrelled a further $300 million to
Beirut for undisclosed purchases. The American embassy in Baghdad, too,
was helping itself to Iraq's revenues. According to a senior Iraqi finance
official, US diplomats transferred $800 million in Iraqi oil funds to a new
fund in New York named DFI 2, to administer 'old contracts signed under
the CPA'.

Those officials left in Iraq perfected the old system of corruption, coupled
with new techniques acquired under the CPA. Ministerial heads of
department sold civil service posts.[276] 'Before me, there was another prime
minister. His name was Bremer,' explained Allawi. 'He ran this country, and
a lot of the corruption started then.... There was no auditing. Airplanes
were flying in and the money was handed out in suitcases.'[277] Ibn
Khaldoun, the North African philosopher, had noted the phenomenon
seven centuries earlier: 'The conquered always want to imitate the
conqueror in his main characteristics – in his clothing, his crafts and in all
his distinctive traits and customs.'

As under the Governing Council, nepotism in the cabinet was rife. Iraq's
Kurdish deputy president, Rowsch Shaways, eased his son, Bruska, into the
job of deputy defence minister; Thair Naqeeb, the interior minister, helped
his brother to the post of prime minister's spokesman; and the transport
minister, Louay al-Erris, promoted his brother to the comfortable sinecure
of deputy-manager of the Arab Bridge Maritime Company, a Red Sea ferry
operator. Another brother based in Amman traded licences for airplanes
seeking to land in Baghdad. At least two ministers – defence minister
Shaalan and interior minister Naqeeb – established their own government-
financed militias, the special police commando brigade and the Amarah
brigade respectively, manned by their tribesmen. 'Iraqi government has
become a family business,' said Zuheir al-Amadi, a former senior cadre of
Allawi's INA based in Amman.[278]

Few dared point the finger at Allawi. As a member of the Governing
Council, he had diplomatically distanced himself from his son-in-law, Nouri
Badran, who was forced to resign as Interior Minister when he was caught
filching government funds in Beirut. But he was less able, or willing, to

shrug off the commercial schemes of his brother, Sabah, a bygone INA fundraiser when as a UN diplomat he had lived in Riyadh. On Allawi's official missions to Arab and European capitals, Sabah could be found slumped on the sofas of five-star hotels swivelling prayer-beads and offering access to his elder brother. He denied charging for a word in his brother's ear, but did not consider it immoral: 'If you are doing a business, it is obvious you get a financial reward.'[279] His Baghdad-based office clerk, Nasser Badran, was less guarded. 'I can get you a meeting with any minister in ten minutes,' he said.[280]

Apparently to cover their tracks, Allawi's government also took steps to neuter the little outside auditing that the CPA had established on the grounds it undermined Iraq's sovereignty. The Major Crimes Office, Iraq's equivalent of the Britain's Serious Fraud Office, was assigned to Interior Ministry control. And Allawi took charge of the Supreme Oil Committee to oversee the country's prime export earner. Security fears further limited scrutiny. The Inspectorate General, a US body established to monitor reconstruction projects, shed 42 per cent of Baghdad-based workforce within six months of the handover, and limited much of their inspection to the Green Zone. Key audits, including that into Tim Spicer's Aegis Defence Systems' contract, were simply scrapped. Most of the 90 senior officials accused by the government-financed Commission of Public Integrity fled the country long before the warrants were issued. The only minister imprisoned for embezzlement escaped – twice.[281]

As the money drained from Iraq, the economy limped from crisis to crisis. Despite three years of nominal reconstruction and the boon of record oil prices, Iraq was still registering chronic shortages of cooking gas and petrol. Barely half the population had access to safe drinking water, and food rations were sporadic. According to a 2005 UN report, almost a quarter of young children were chronically malnourished. Electricity output, which electricity minister Samarrai predicted would triple to 8,000 Megawatts by the end of 2004, plummeted from 15 hours a day to two. Average household incomes had dropped from $255 before the war to $144 under Allawi.

Massive government buildings wrecked in the US invasion continued to scar the Baghdad skyline. A pro-government newspaper reporting on the reconstruction effort had to resort to printing a photo of a rusting crane at a pre-war construction site because no new ones had yet reached the capital. In the fifth year of occupation, Iraq remained a cash economy where Iraqi dinars were airlifted by the crate load around Iraq. Ministers blamed the insurgency, but their own squandering of funds was equally to blame. 'The insurgency is there, the violence is mounting. But you have all of Kurdistan relatively safe, and most of the south and centre south is relatively safe,' said Isam al-Khafaji, an Iraqi economics professor who resigned in protest from the US-led administration in Baghdad. 'Why is no reconstruction taking place in peaceful provinces?'[282] By the time of the January 2005 elections, voters who might otherwise have been enthusiastic were fuming. 'Fine, fine. Take all the towels and ashtrays you want on your way out the door,' wailed a Baghdad blogger on election eve. 'Just as long as you leave, okay?' It was no joke. According to the Public Integrity Commission, one of the transport minister's last orders was to auction 183 railway bed-sheets.

The third factor conspiring to unseat the government was rump resistance to a revival of any semblance of the former regime, particularly from the Shia south. As corruption spread, services crumbled and the US military presence grew more punishing, raw Shia politics emerged as an untested panacea. With the arteries leading out of Baghdad under rebel or bandit control and senior civil servants fearing assassination embedded behind Bremer's walls, the provinces enjoyed virtual autonomy and quickly filled the vacuum left by ineffective government. Southern governors raised their own taxes (a pilgrim's tax in Najaf and port duties in Basra) and applied their own laws. The governor of Samawa seized the local television studios to broadcast his own news. Countrywide, the authorities claimed 500 courts were functioning, but in much of Iraq, Sharia courts had become the prime instruments of justice, further splitting societies that had once embraced intermarriage with separate religious legal codes for Shias, Sunnis and Christians.

The rise of sectarian attacks – in which Shias were randomly targeted simply for being Shia – further helped forge a group identity by playing into the Shia persecution complex of ancient lore. The greater the atrocity and the more dysfunctional the society, the greater the need for the militias' protection even amongst secular Iraqis, and the greater their consequent room for manoeuvre. Despairing of Allawi's inability to rescue them from attack, Iraq's Shia electorate increasingly looked to their demographic weight and the agreed democratic timetable to restore them to power.

Finally, Iraq's Shias had the benefit of national and supra-national leaders commanding networks able to cobble the centrifugal forces and the collective identity into Iraq's single most powerful alliance. Of these the most effective was the Hauza under Ayatollah Sistani, who for over a year propounded a single message: do not divide the Shia. In the build-up to elections slated for 30 January 2005 he turned the Hauza into an election machine, his *husseiniyas* into canvassing offices, and his home into the campaign headquarters, with three arms of organisation. His political office – consisting of a six-member committee of largely western-educated advisors led by Hussein Shahristani, an atomic scientist whose brother Jawad ran Sistani's office in Qom – negotiated the order of a single Shia List, embracing 16 parties and named the United Iraqi Alliance. His treasury, under Shahristani's brother, Jawad, collected and disbursed alms of an estimated \$20 million a month, raised mainly from the Gulf. And his representatives in some 2,500 mosques and *husseiniyas* in Iraq – and hundreds more serving 4 million Shia Iraqi exiles, who were also entitled to vote – broadcast voting instructions to the faithful.

That the Shia politicians – hitherto arch rivals – fell into line owed much to the networking skills of Ahmed Chalabi. Within weeks of his fall from American grace, he had begun to assemble a 'Shia House' of the parties that Allawi and his CIA advisors had ousted from power. In opposition, pariahs new and old began to consort. By July 2004, at least half a dozen former Governing Council members had agreed on a powerful bloc, uniting the fallen angels surrounding Ahmed Chalabi, with the native Shia Washington had considered pariahs from the first, foremost amongst them Muqtada Sadr. Other members included Abdel Karim Mohammadawi, a Governing Council member and ex-bandit from the southern marshes, whom Bremer had had indicted after he voiced support for Sadr. Seeking to reap its share of the Shia *vox populi*, SCIRI joined the bandwagon, papering over its differences with Sadr.

Outwardly the aristocratic Chalabi represented all that Sadr with his lumpen-proletariat following despised. But their relatives had worked happily together under the monarchy in the days when the Chalabis were the Hauza's traditional financiers, and by casting them both into the doghouse and besieging their various headquarters America had given them common cause. For Chalabi, the benefits were marked. His pact with Sadr helped him shed his image as the effete exile with slippery lips and at last secured him the local constituency he craved. In a way few of Allawi's clique did, he went native defying threats of extradition, assassination and arrest, and remaining stubbornly outside the Green Zone. Conversely, from Chalabi, Sadr gained long-denied access to the inner sanctum of the American-made political process. At the same time, Chalabi succeeded where the Americans had failed in drawing Sadr into the democratic game. Simultaneously, he reached out to other Shia movements, particularly Dawa and SCIRI, ensuring that no major Shia force was excluded. Sistani made little effort to hide his approval for the Shia bloc. In contrast to Allawi's single visit, Chalabi was granted an audience on at least a dozen occasions.

In the early months of the occupation Sunnis as much as Shias had looked to the ballot to rid Iraq of America. 'We want elections now so we can finish with this occupation,' said Sheikh Yasin Zubaie, an elderly Sunni prayer leader of a scruffy mosque sunken in sewage in Abu Ghraib. 'We don't care whether our leader is Sunni or Shia. We just want the Americans to go.' But two years on, the formation of a single Shia bloc with only a handful of token Sunni Arabs appeared designed to wrest power for a single group, at the expense of Iraq's other composite sects. The electoral system itself further was in part to blame. Instead of a constituency system, which would have required politicians to represent a cross-section of the population in their constituencies, the Americans introduced a proportional electoral system which treated Iraq as a single electoral district, enabling politicians to address a particular sectarian or ethnic group. Iraqis were forced to vote to be Sunnis, Shiites or Kurds.

In addition, a ban on the participation of the Baath party – punctiliously enforced by a Kurdish and Shia election committee – only served to chase those Baathist movements which had tentatively tiptoed into the mainstream back underground, and deprive the political process of a key secular voice.[283] Sunni leaders and movements who had initially joined the political process, including the Iraqi Islamic Party, the only Sunni Islamist group to join the Governing Council, turned their back on the elections, openly siding with al-Qaeda in Iraq in the call for an electoral boycott. 'It's like asking Turkeys to vote for Christmas – why would you possibly take part in a process that disempowers you?' noted a political commentator in Baghdad.[284]

The election campaign laid bare Iraq's sectarian fissures as never before, embroiling every adult Iraqi in the struggle. Islamist groups from the Mujahideen Army to such secular Sunnis as Baghdad University professor Wamidh Nadhmi waged a counter-election campaign, in which Zarkawi's voice was the loudest. In a taped manifesto issued a week before the elections, he cited seven reasons why the Greek import of elections surrendered sovereignty to human hands and was thus a denial of God.

'Democracy is based on the principle that the people are the source of all authority, including the legislature,' he said. 'The legislator who must be obeyed in a democracy is man, and not Allah.'[285] Above all, he protested against the principle of majority-rule, even if the majority 'agree upon falsehood, error and heresy'. Ultimately, what Zarkawi feared most was democracy's sanction of Shia rule.

To underscore his message, he threatened to kill any infidel who dared vote, reverting as had Saddam in his last referendum to conjugal imagery. 'Black-eyed virgins,' said Zarkawi, had laid their beds in paradise to receive the grooms at the 'martyrs' wedding', or union with God. After the US military announced an election-day ban on driving to obviate car-bombs, he declared scores of volunteers were donning suicide vests. 'Take care not to go near the centres of heresy and abomination, that is, the election [booths.] He who has warned has carried out his duty; if something happens do not blame us, but yourselves.' Baathists joined in the bloodshed, killing local election monitors to scare off potential voters. The names, telephone numbers and addresses of journalists in Mosul who had registered, as required, with the election committee were pinned on mosques all over the city.

In the run-up to the vote, electoral tensions wrenched at Iraq's sectarian seams. Religious leaders on both sides flung charges of apostasy at their opponents. Sistani used the same term, 'infidels', to denounce the boycotters as Zarkawi used of voters. The media in neighbouring states joined in the fray, with Iranian papers urging Iraqis to vote, while Arab states emphasised the 'blazing path of fire', in the words of a Saudi editorial, that awaited those who dared to participate. 'One wonders if Iraqi officials, who are backing these elections, realise the danger of what could happen to their country before the hatchet falls on their heads. Those officials should work towards ending this farce called "elections", and safeguard Iraq and its people!'[286] gushed a commentary in Jordan's Dustour.

Deeply sceptical of a democratic roller-coaster set to surrender power they had won at huge financial cost to a Shia-led and possibly ecclesiastical government, America's politicians shuddered at the prospect almost as much as did Arab Sunnis. Several US officials argued that a client strongman in the shape of Allawi was preferable to the unpredictable *vox populi*. Some even echoed the increasingly desperate pleas of the prime minister's camp – not least those of his brother and spokesman sitting comfortably in their hotel armchairs – to delay elections for six months, pending the long-awaited improvement in security. Despite the looming elections, US democracy projects – including a $29 million grant from the US supplemental – were quietly shelved.

But having set the timetable, they had scant wriggle room. An insurgency in one-third of the country was better, mused Negroponte's advisors, than a rebellion embracing almost all of it. Sistani never overtly threatened violence, but the breaking of Washington's promise to stage parliamentary elections by January 2005 was an unmistakeable red line. Since no census had been compiled amid the worsening violence, Bremer's objections to using the UN food ration database as an electoral roll were quietly dropped. It was Sistani's perseverance not Washington's principle that secured Iraq its first taste of democracy.

Without Arab Sunni electoral movements to counterbalance the Shia, the United States had little option but to look to Allawi to keep the Shia from power. Spurning an offer to join the Shia List, Allawi campaigned on a nationalist anti-clerical ticket. In an attempt to rustle up the Sunni and secular Shia vote, he cast Sistani less as father of the nation than sectarian lord. His campaign team, led by the defence minister, Shaalan, mocked 'the Iranian List' headed by such 'Iranian agents' as Shahristani, whom he accused of betraying his country by selling Iraq's nuclear secrets to its 'greatest enemy'. Where the Shia List used the Hauza's machinery, Allawi with full American backing deployed the state's. In the run-up to elections, he raised salaries and pensions, and mobilised the police to coat the walls with his own image. Behind the scenes, a slick publications team, led by the former British CPA spokesman Charles Heatly, pumped out press releases and produced a campaign website sparkling in electronic shades of blue.

Desperate for a success, Washington trumpeted the electoral turnout. In defiance of warnings from UN election organiser Carina Perelli that 'mortar bombs and ballots do not marry well' and threats of a morning rush of suicide bombers, more than 8 million Iraqis, some ululating with joy, dipped their fingers in indelible purple ink at the voting booths.[287] But in their praise, Washington and London focussed almost exclusively on the event not the choice Iraqis had made.[288] America's allies were trounced. Individually, Allawi earned more seats than any other individual political party, but scored less than a third of the Shia alliance's 140 seats in a 275-seat Assembly. Sunni Arabs, with just 17 parliamentarians, were all but squeezed out of Iraq's representative body. So great was the shortfall that the role of speaker of parliament, earmarked for an Arab Sunni, in fact went to a Turkoman, Hajm al-Hassani. Two of the most prominent Sunni candidates, Adnan Pachachi and the royalist pretender Sherif Ali, both lost their tickets after failing to secure the 29,000 votes required for a single seat. The party of the incumbent president, Ghazi al-Yawar, secured five seats, a disastrous result for a leader who claimed to be the son of the sheikh of Iraq's largest tribe – the Shammar. The pull of religion had taken precedence over tribal allegiance. Shia politicians were in control.

In an attempt to forestall the inevitable, the Americans delayed the formation of an ecclesiastical government. Under the terms of the Transitional Administrative Law, parliament could choose the president but not the prime minister and his government. Three months of horse-trading followed, during which Allawi, whose party had come third, remained the incumbent. US diplomats struggled to secure him a second term, leaning on presidential favourite, Kurdish leader Jalal Talabani, to establish a secular alliance with the anti-religious Allawi and any secular renegades they could lure from the Shia List. But after years plotting together in exile, Kurdish and Shia politicians were unwilling to forgo their first taste of power. Though wrangles over the limits to Kurdish autonomy and control of Kirkuk's oil wealth remained unresolved, the northern and southern flanks of Iraq increasingly coalesced to sandwich the Sunnis. To mollify US concerns they were creating an Islamist state, Shia leaders shuttled to Washington, emphasising that only six of the Shia coalition's 228 candidates for the Assembly had been clerics. In a meeting with Rumsfeld on 12 April, the Shia List's final choice for prime minister, a besuited Ibrahim Jaafari, pointedly avoided the word 'withdrawal', conceding that the cabinet would not exercise its sovereign right to set a timetable for the departure of American forces. On 28 April, Jaafari was sworn in as Iraq's first Shia Islamist prime minister. After delivering his valedictory speech, Allawi retreated to the backbenches – a peaceful transfer of authority without precedent in Iraq's bloody history.

Washington found the incoming prime minister, Ibrahim Jaafari, hard to accept. Although Bremer had picked him as the first rotating president of his Governing Council, the bearded Shia leader was perhaps the least known of the exiles in Washington. Prior to a meeting in 2002 with US officials in the grey London suburb of Neasden, he claimed never to have met an American. Unlike his Shia rivals, he was of humble stock and had the retiring appearance of a dormouse. His rambling press conferences could cure an insomniac. And yet, amongst Iraqis, this mumbling politician without a hint of charisma was repeatedly voted the most popular and recognised member of the Governing Council.

Perhaps after 50 years of egoistical strongmen, Iraqis craved a recluse. More plausibly they were voting less for the persona than the party. Founded in 1959, Dawa, the Party of Islamic Call, was Iraq's oldest and largest Shia party, a sort of Shia Muslim Brotherhood formed to lure Shias away from leftist secular movements. After Saddam banned the movement in 1979, Jaafari fled to Tehran, spending a decade engrossed in the anti-American exuberance of Khomeini's Revolution. He was the Dawa's spokesman in 1984 when the movement orchestrated a series of suicide and car-bombings against the embassies of Iraq, France and the USA, then staunch Saddam allies, in Kuwait. When other Shia groups rushed to reap the largesse accruing from Clinton's Iraq Liberation Act 14 years later, the State Department excluded Dawa on account of its terrorist record. To distance himself from Iran, Jaafari moved to Greenford, a suburb in east London, joining a doctor's surgery. Five months before the invasion, Washington embarked on formal talks with the Dawa, but failed to ease its suspicion of US intentions. Opposed to the war, Jaafari continued to conceal the identity of Dawa's spiritual mentor, and as prime minister used his *nom de guerre* not his real name, Ibrahim al-Ushaiqer.

Though free of turbans, Jaafari assembled his cabinet in the spirit of Shia triumphalism. Although on the surface the division looked equitable,[289] with the exception of the defence minister, Saadoun Dulaimi, an academic whom the Americans had employed as their pollster, its nine Sunni Arabs held either minor or ceremonial posts. The new president was Kurdish and the prime minister Shia. Sunnis were also stripped of the interior, trade and housing ministries, and the office of the prime minister's spokesman that they had held under Allawi. Bayan Jabr Solagh, a Badr Brigade commander, became interior minister; Ibrahim Bahr al-Uloum, the son of a Shia cleric, oil minister; the estranged Ahmed Chalabi resurfaced as deputy prime minister responsible for Iraq's energy sector; and Chalabi's close relative Ali Allawi became finance minister.

In response to critics who questioned the wisdom of excluding Sunnis, officials replied that if Shias had learnt to lump Sunni supremacy over the centuries, so could Sunnis. Sunni Arab humiliation was compounded by the presence of the Kurds, particularly under President Jalal Talabani, who during years of struggle against Saddam Hussein had established close ties with Iran. Within hours of the government taking office, Mishaan Jibouri, leader of one of the few Sunni groups in parliament, appeared on al-Jazeera to denounce Jaafari for imposing 'Safavid' rule, a reference to the Persian rulers who converted Iran from Sunnism to Shiism in the sixteenth century. 'This is a sad day for us,' he said. 'Our existence in this country has not been respected and a process of serious sectarian isolation has been exercised against us.' The Assembly responded by lifting his parliamentary immunity and putting him on trial for corruption.[290] The new government had become an alliance of two empowered sects against a third disempowered one.

CHAPTER 15

The Country Once Called Iraq

Over the next year, a referendum and another election gnawed at Iraq's sectarian seams. Embarrassed by the blemish of being perceived as anti-democratic, Sunnis were cajoled to join the process, but only in opposition to the Shias – further deepening the communal divide. 'Elections will separate Iraq,' warned Mudher al-Kharbit, an Anbar businessman US forces accused of financing the resistance.[291] Asked to comment on the conduct of the December 2005 elections, 89 per cent of Shias described it as fair; 94 per cent of Arab Sunnis proclaimed it unfair.[292]

In their euphoria, Shia restraint, remarkable in the years of waiting, rapidly ebbed once they had power. They had become triumphant *eradicateurs*. 'For us in the Alliance, we think negotiations are surrender, and the Iraqi people will not accept surrender,'[293] said Shahristani, Sistani's political advisor and the new deputy speaker (he was subsequently made oil minister). The DeBaathification Council was resuscitated, and civil servants reinstated under the Allawi regime either demoted to the lower ranks or rooted out of the administration. Shahristani said it would even apply to 12 of the 17 Sunni deputies, whose Baath ties he said rendered them ineligible for Assembly posts. In its new bastion of the Interior Ministry, SCIRI oversaw the 'militia-isation' of the security forces, easing out Allawi's mainly Sunni commandos to make way for their own forces, the Badr Brigades. Hadi al-Amiri, the Badr leader, acquired an office in the Interior Ministry to reorganise its personnel into 12 commando brigades of Special Forces (some keeping their Allawi-era names, Volcano, Wolf and Hawk), operating as an autonomous body, much as the Executive Force under Hamas. Shia recruits to Jordan's police academy, diplomats noticed, surged from 60 per cent to 80 per cent of the intake, cementing a sectarian hold on the security forces that not even Saddam had dared. Kurds made up most of the rest. SCIRI's hold on security was further fortified by its sweep of eight of the 11 southern governorates in the January 2005 provincial elections. In August 2005, Badr paramilitaries also captured Baghdad by physically evicting its US-appointed mayor. While Shias dominated the 188,000-strong police force, Kurdish militias under close US supervision tightened their clutch on the 138,000-man army. [294]

The anti-insurgent counter-attack began on May Day, four days after Jaafari was sworn into office. In a raid on 11 Sunni mosques in Baghdad, the security forces arrested 30 Sunni imams and preachers, including a professor of Islamic Law from Baghdad University. Many of their cadavers were later found on the roadsides. Simultaneously, Kurdish and Shia security forces were deployed within or against Sunni areas, especially Mosul, where the local police force had acquired a reputation for mutiny. Mirroring the summer 2004 raids against Chalabi's offices, the security forces repeatedly stormed Allawi's headquarters, as well as those of the National Dialogue Council, an umbrella association of 31 Sunni groups, whose secretary general, Fakhri al-Qaisi, the mild-mannered Salafi dentist, had signalled his willingness to parley with Iraq's government. Sitting amid his ransacked furniture and purloined files, an unusually rattled Qaisi dismissed the government as a sham. 'I think it's a scheme to wipe us out, destroy us,' he said. 'Their slogans about democracy are all lies.'[295]

In the following months, reprisals against Sunni targets increased in magnitude and barbarity. Each Interior Ministry battalion reportedly acquired its own secret prison.[296] The Wolf Brigade, in particular, acquired a reputation as a death squad. In an offensive on suspected insurgents in Baghdad, dubbed Operation Lightning, nine Sunni construction workers were shut in a closed metal container and left to perish in the brutal summer heat. Adopting the tactics of Sunni insurgents, Interior Ministry units manned flying checkpoints in Baghdad neighbourhoods and surrounding villages to sift out Sunnis from Shiites, often for elimination. Police cars were used during the daylight abduction of the Higher Education Ministry employees in November 2006.

Other ministries, similarly, became fiefdoms or forward positions for militias, using their budgets to bankroll their members. The most important part of the application process for the civil service was the *tazkiya*, or attestation of good conduct: the interior ministry required such a document from SCIRI; the oil ministry from the Fadhila party;[297] and those of Agriculture, Transportation and Health from the Sadr movement, which as the largest party in the Alliance (after the December 2005 elections) had a key stake in government. Sadr's mullahs again took command of hospitals as in the aftermath of the war, purging senior Sunni doctors or pharmacists, sometimes through hit-squads who trained their guns on doctors as they interrogated patients. Included in the political alliance, Sadr circumvented a de facto US-ban on his participation in the security forces, by manning the Facilities Protection Service guarding his three ministries. Government departments channelled services to their own constituency. Civil servants in Sunni provinces went unpaid, often on the dubious grounds that the security vacuum made them inaccessible. And Allawi's commitment to compensate the Falluja victims in the November 2004 US military assault was forgotten: alone of the government ministries, the Sunni-led Industry Ministry undertook Falluja's reconstruction. Even rubbish collection and provision of electricity were organised on sectarian lines.[298] Dependent on the movements who backed them as prime ministers, Jaffari and his successor, Nouri al-Maliki, provided no central non-partisan correction. 'We are not really in government,' said Tariq al-Hashimi, leader of the Islamic Party, and one of Iraq's two vice-presidents. 'Maliki and his coalition never gave us any real role in the government, and our ministers' actions are therefore paralysed.'[299]

In foreign policy, Iraq again turned from West to East. After Jordanians in Salt staged a memorial for one of their sons who killed 135 Shia police in a Hilla suicide-bombing, Iraq recalled its ambassador from Amman, and Shia protestors overran the Jordanian embassy in Baghdad. A burgeoning of ties with Iran swiftly followed, facilitated by the long-standing relationships government ministers – Kurds as well as Shia – had cultivated as opposition movements.[300] On a visit to Tehran in July, Defence Minister Saadoun Dulaimi signed an agreement for Iran to train and supply Iraq's armed forces, prompting US anguish that Tehran was aspiring to replace its Coalition. Two weeks later, following a formal apology by Iraq for the eight-year Iran–Iraq war, in which half a million people were killed, Jaafari led the biggest Iraqi delegation to Iran for 40 years. In addition to agreements to share intelligence, the two sides discussed railway links, direct flights to Iraq's pilgrimage cities and a pipeline connecting Iraq's oil infrastructure to Iran's. 'We're a role-model of unity for the region,' said Iran's vice-president, Mohsen Mehralizadeh, on receiving Jaafari. To further boost the relationship, Iran pumped funding into southern Iraq, much as it had done in those parts of Lebanon under Hizbollah's control. 'Southern Iraq now reminds me a lot of the situation in southern Lebanon fifteen years ago,' said a veteran Middle East analyst. 'Iranian influence is everywhere.'[301] Pictures of Khomeini were even draped over government buildings.

Instead of Iraq serving as a US springboard against Iran, the country was rapidly devolving into a theatre to contain the US not Iran. A Najaf Ayatollah, backed by Sadr and possibly also supported by Sistani, orchestrated a petition that quickly collected names demanding Jaafari set a timetable for a complete exit. Jaafari, himself, no longer baulked from the word 'timetable', and publicly called for the reduction of the American presence in the Kurdish north and Shia south. As Coalition forces gradually withdrew from the south, Shia forces tightened their hold, particularly in towns close to the Iranian border. 'We can begin with the process of withdrawing multinational forces from cities as a first step that encourages setting a timetable for the withdrawal process,'[302] said Jaafari, who backed Badr leader Amiri's opposition to the deployment of Australian troops in his stronghold of Samawah. Whole ministries – particularly the three headed by Sadr's supporters – were declared America free-zones. As Washington had feared, democracy was giving rise to demands for America to begin its exodus and its replacement with a Shia hegemon straddling both banks of the oil-rich northern Gulf.

The containment of Shia revanchism rapidly became a focal point of American policy. In May 2005, Secretary of State Condoleezza Rice flew to Baghdad to urge Jaafari to seek a political not military solution. 'If there is to be a united Iraq in the future, then Sunnis have to be included in the processes going forward,' she said in a rare US admission that Iraq was in danger of partition. At the same time, the Pentagon's band of revolutionaries who had espoused the meek Shia's inheritance of the world, or at least of Iraq's bit of it, were eased into retirement in favour of 'imperial realists'. By early 2005, Feith had resigned as Undersecretary of Defence 'for personal and family reasons'; Richard Perle had left the Defence Policy Board, the body advising the Pentagon on Iraq policy, and Wolfowitz moved to the World Bank. Donald Rumsfeld finally resigned after the Republicans were defeated in Congressional elections in November 2006.[303] The incoming US ambassadors – first Negroponte and then Afghan-born Zalmay Khalilzad – devoted their energies to wooing Sunni representatives, organising a series of meetings with Islamist and Baathist rebels, at times using a farmhouse owned by Allawi's disgraced electricity minister, Ayham Samarrai, some 50 miles north of Baghdad.[304] The *mukhabarat* formed under Allawi was ringfenced from the effects of the deBaathification programme, reportedly capping a Shia quota at 12 per cent, and SCIRI denied access to its archives.

US intervention did notch some successes. The largest Sunni groups agreed to participate in future polls as a first step back to the political process. The Association of Muslim Scholars even issued a fatwa calling on Sunnis to serve in Iraq's nascent security forces. Shia politicians, too, responded with conciliatory noises. They agreed to draft 'non-collaborating Sunnis' into the parliamentary committee drafting the constitution, only two of whose 55 members had hitherto been Sunnis. But for the most part, the concessions appeared half-hearted and token.[305] Three weeks before the deadline for completing the draft constitution, the Sunni participants withdrew after one of their members was shot dead as he emerged from a Baghdad restaurant. Shia politicians seized the initiative to reconfigure the state regardless. Even their partners, the Kurds, protested that the Shia majority were riding roughshod over their demands for autonomy and secularism, and threatened a boycott.

In the pendulum of America's shifting support from one sect to the other, Iraqis felt they were the victims of that well-established tradition of divide and rule. Iraq, it seemed, was the missing link in the Anglo-American band of sectarian partition in Asia from India to Palestine. Washington's closest allies in Iraq to which it entrusted the security forces – the Kurds and SCIRI – were the two forces most ardently pushing for federalism, while its most intransigent enemies – the Sunnis and Sadaris – were both committed to a united Iraq. Whether deliberate or not, America's political process was precipitating the dismembering of Iraq.

Washington may also have looked to federalism as the best means to safeguard an oasis of stability for future bases. Or – particularly at a local level – it might have hoped that by stoking sectarian fears it could secure local alliances.[306] But if so, it was sorely mistaken. Alongside the sectarian conflict, the Bush administration continued to bleed lives, dollars and votes. By the end of 2006, a 22-year-old Texan had become the 3,000th American soldier to be killed in Iraq – exceeding the total lives lost on 11 September 2001. Though US forces were better protected and increasingly confined to their bases, the death toll had climbed steadily, from an average of one per day in the first six months, to three per day in the last.[307] The war in expenditure, though not in lives, cost more than the Vietnam War. By

December 2006, weekly war costs had doubled from $1 billion to $2 billion, totalling $400 billion since the invasion. The Baker–Hamilton report estimated final costs at $4 trillion. For the investment of a sum many times that of Iraq's annual GNP, and considerably more than New York City's annual budget, Washington had bought untold global distrust and damaged American prestige. Finally, the Bush administration was haemorrhaging votes – losing control of both Houses of Congress in the November 2006 mid-term elections. Never can so much money have been spent for such a hideous return.

Iraqis were bleeding far faster. By the end of 2006, estimates of the monthly toll began at 3,000 a month. Between 2 and 5 per cent of Iraq's 27 million people were believed to have been killed, wounded or uprooted.[308] Estimates for the total dead ranged between 40,000 and 655,000, or an average of 500 per day.[309] (US-led forces were the biggest killers of Iraqis. Insurgents accounted for less than 10 per cent.) Amid the reign of terror, an average of 100,000 people a month fled the country a month, or over 2 million by the end of 2006, a middle-class brain drain that further damaged the country's long-term possibilities of recovery and ability to operate what remained of its civil service, and reinforced the leverage of Iraqi warlords, tribal sheiks and sectarian parties.[310] Many eked out a living in neighbouring capitals on tourist visas; some turned to prostitution to survive. Inside Iraq, there were almost as many displaced, often from hitherto religiously mixed areas of Iraq, in a population movement that saw Sunnis head one way, Shias another.[311] And the country was a wreck. Washington spent only 3 per cent of its funding in Iraq on reconstruction (by November 2006, the US had spent $16 billion on reconstruction and about $400 billion on its military). In 2007 the administration proposed reducing aid to Iraq to $750 million.

Except for massacres of over a hundred, most western news editors found killing and maiming less than compelling: the gouged-out eyes of slaughtered Iraqi hostages who had failed to pay their ransoms; the discarded cadavers, their hands still tied with a bullet or drill-hole through the brain; the mortar attacks on cafes frequented by Shia militiamen; the random bombs left in vegetable carts in religiously mixed neighbourhoods; the bombing of buses laden with Iranian pilgrims; the grenade attacks on the Najaf road when funeral corteges passed from Baghdad; and an exploding fuel truck aimed at the children swarming round a US soldier distributing sweets in Baghdad. All blended into a death cult too commonplace to make headlines.

America was also losing the will and ability to reverse the killing fields. After Jaafari's succession, Washington dropped its demand of defeating insurgents as a condition for troop withdrawal, differentiating between its war on al-Qaeda and defeat of the other resistance groups in Iraq. To safeguard its own, Central Command increasingly attacked from the air rather than risk ground forces.[312] Shortly before his resignation, Rumsfeld proposed a drawback from 55 bases in Iraq to five by July 2007, and the repositioning of much of its army and armaments to the country's peripheries – Kurdistan and Kuwait.[313] The December 2006 Iraq Study Group report chaired by two American patricians James Baker and Lee Hamilton went further, calling for 'all combat brigades not necessary for force protection [to] be out of Iraq... by the first quarter of 2008', safely in time for the November 2008 presidential elections.

Even without a timetable, a less-ordered pullback was in motion. Under Shia attack, the British retreated from Camp Abu Naji near Amara to Basra on August 2006 on a day's notice, abandoning hundreds of thousands of dollars of equipment to the Mahdi Army.[314] Soon after, Chief of the General Staff Sir Richard Dannatt said British forces were 'exacerbating the security problems' and should 'get out some time soon'.[315] US Marines touted the withdrawal of their 30,000 troops from the Sunni stronghold of Anbar to Baghdad. In an attempt to hold back the tide, US forces surrounded al-Dora, a mainly Sunni enclave in southern Baghdad, with a wall. Swathes of territory were being ceded in a country that no longer existed in a coherent form, leaving Iran the most prominent dominant foreign player.

The Americans could point to a successful completion of their electoral programme for legislative and general elections, largely to timetable. But so they could in South Vietnam seven years before their South Asia retreat. Behind the electoral façade, central government in Iraq was disintegrating even faster. The number of people who ruled Iraq over the first three years of the US invasion exceeded the number who had ruled it in 60 years. Many of the institutions were stillborn. The Assembly failed to meet for entire months because with so many Iraqi politicians out of the country – often in London – it could not attain a quorum. And in the Sunni provinces 'nearly all government institutions from the village to provincial levels have disintegrated or have been thoroughly corrupted and infiltrated by al-Qaeda in Iraq', reported a marine officer.[316] Even when the prime minister gave orders, he had scant chance of them being obeyed. The security forces no longer fought for Iraq, but for their sect or militia. Once a force for unity, they had become an agent for – as well as a microcosm of – the decomposition of the state. Struggling to maintain the political system, al-Maliki became a near puppet of the militias, co-opting them as private security armies to defend oil installations and government buildings in a short-term bid for survival.

Indeed, the approaching demise of America only spurred the sects to commit ever greater excesses in the struggle for succession. The triangle of death south of Baghdad expanded to include much of the centre, a strategy Zarkawi declared was part of a plan for taking Baghdad. The capital was a city of nervous wrecks. By the summer of 2006, between two and ten suicide bombings a day struck Baghdad, many targeting the security forces' recruitment centres. 'Whenever a National Guard batch finishes its training and leaves camp, they [Sunni rebels] follow it and kill and butcher every one of them,' said Ali al-Adib, a Dawa leader. Rumours of a suicide bomber loose in the crowds of pilgrims on the bridge linking the two shrines of Sunni and Shia Iraq precipitated a hysterical stampede, in which close to 1,000 people were killed, the single worst casualty rate of the post-occupation era.

Each new death triggered fresh howls for revenge, drowning out the often duplicitous calls for restraint. In the single deadliest assault since the invasion, car-bombs and missiles interrupted a memorial in Sadr City to commemorate the killing of Muqtada's father, Mohammed Sadiq al-Sadr, killing over 200 in November 2006. That in turn triggered a barrage of mortars on the Baghdad shrine of Abu Hanifa, the eighth-century founder of the largest four schools of Sunni Islam. Days later gunmen stormed the Higher Education ministry, a traditional Sunni domain. Sunni gunmen responded by taking hostage civil servants in the Sadr-run Health ministry en masse. Attacks on Shia shrines, a Salafi practice for centuries, became de rigeur, propelling as intended the internecine bloodletting to new heights. In February 2006, six weeks after fresh elections confirmed Shia control of Iraq, bombers in the heavily Sunni town of Samarra blew the gold-plated top off the al-Askariya shrine – where two Shia Imams, Ali al-Hadi and al-Hassan al-Askari were buried – and ignited what Iraqis said would not happen: a civil war. Sectarian violence between Sunnis and Shias increased twelve-fold. Attacks that had numbered 250 per day in 2005 were topping 1,100 a year later.[317]

The prospects that Sunnis might regain Iraq – even in the event of a US withdrawal – were remote. Where insurgents could muster perhaps 50,000 paramilitaries, the Kurdish and Shia militias comprising the security forces could muster five times that number. At least four of Iraq's cities had over a million-strong population, most with their own armed population ready to fight outside rule. But nor could a dysfunctional failing state crush a multitude of non-state actors and guerrilla movements. A hideous stalemate prevailed.

Nor could Iraq's violence be easily defused. As the US invasion entered its fifth year, the conflict had acquired a self-sustaining dynamic of its own. The atrocities gave the militias a *raison d'être* as protector of the faithful in an absent state, driving even secular Iraqis to seek succour in their domains. Fear of the other became, in the words of International Crisis Group, 'the militias' most valuable asset'.[318] Operating in place of the central authority, the militias established their own internal economy, system of taxation and provision of services, such as cooking gas, and welfare. As the pipelines slipped out of government control, militias battled for control of key arteries, draining Iraq of an estimated 200,000 to 500,000 barrels of oil per day.[319] In addition to more nefarious activities, such as hostage-taking or the selling of the cadavers of those they had slaughtered back to their families, the Mahdi Army ran entire networks of petrol stations. Militias also raised their own business taxes, often disguised as religious tithes, or protection-racketing, for instance by guarding pipelines or traffic of goods through the Anbar province or the Um al-Qasr docks.

Sistani protested from the sidelines, but after riding to power on his bandwagon the militias were now in control. Like Gandhi, he had sought to keep his country united and safeguard 'the nation's unity', while simultaneously ensuring the Shia majority assumed their share of power. In the wake of the Samarra bombing, his appeal for tolerance and restraint were out of sync with the times, and militia leaders no longer wanted to hear his homilies against reprisals. 'Sistani is sleeping,' read the slogan daubed on a Baghdad school wall.[320] Now he was something of a tragic figure, and increasingly a spent force, the flow of politicians to his door slowed to a trickle.

As the militias' domain expanded, public neutral space and common ground shrank. Civilians abandoned the streets, even when the state lifted the curfew. Fridges once piled high on the pavements were locked indoors, schools closed, and the few functioning banks and courts suspended operations. The Palestine Hotel, once packed with carpet-baggers and journalists, and engineers, was empty.

Measures once intended to draw a line under the past only deepened the divide. Saddam's trial had been carefully orchestrated by the Coalition to recall past horrors and justify their overthrow of his rule. Microphones were switched off, and translations interrupted when the transmission wavered from the script. But instead of turning a page, the 18 months of his show-trial reopened a Pandora's Box of old wounds. Sunni Arabs interpreted Saddam's frequent appearances before the Tribunal as if they were in a collective dock. 'He's our president, and those who have orchestrated this show-trial are Iranian traitors,' said one of four intelligence officers watching the first televised courtroom drama in Baghdad's Sunni suburb of Athamiya in July 2004. Chewing on chicken legs, they mocked that the only charge for which Saddam should be held to account was deserting the battlefield in the midst of the invasion. Over the bridge separating old Sunni and Shia Baghdad, pedlars plying the pilgrims heading for the Kathimiya shrine also demanded an end to the trial. 'Why are they giving him the rights he refused others, and not killing him outright?' asked Raid Khudair, as he fanned his sweetmeats dripping away in the heat. 'Why are we giving him a podium to poison Iraq?'

Saddam was probably aware of the impact his execution might have on the few remaining sinews of Iraq's unity. His last testament was tailored to absolve himself of responsibility for Iraq's sectarian rift. 'The enemies of your country, the invaders and the Persians, found that your unity stands as a barrier between them and your enslavement. They planted and grounded their hateful old and new wedge between you,' wrote Saddam.[321] Even he may have been surprised how amply the Coalition and Iraq's new government proved his point. On 30 December 2006, the day Sunnis – though not Shias – marked the festival of Eid al-Adha, the Feast of the Sacrifice, US forces handed Saddam over to his Iraqi executioners. The festival, which commemorated Abraham's willingness to sacrifice his son to God, was a traditional day of forgiveness, on which even Saddam was wont to pardon prisoners. In the new Iraq, it morphed into a day of vengeance. As lambs across the Muslim world were led to the slaughter, Saddam, wearing his trademark black trench-coat, was led to the gallows by Badr Brigade guards in black face masks. To his last, he was taunted by an assembled crowd of witnesses. Some praised the House of the Prophet for deliverance, others chanted paeans to the Mahdi. The mockery of Sunni tradition was compounded by the image of the trap door opening under Saddam as he cried the word Mohammed. His death on the holiest day of the Sunni calendar was celebrated with shut-downs in Sunni quarters from Kerala to Casablanca and dancing in Shia ones from Karbala to Kabul, emphasising how polarised Iraq had spurred the Muslim world to become.[322] President Mubarak called him a martyr.[323] 'They stole our Eid from us,' said a Sunni merchant in Bahrain. 'Now it will be remembered as the day when they executed Saddam.'

As Iraq atomised into its constituent parts, Sunnis, Shias and Kurds adopted separate heroes and villains, separate television stations, separate legal systems and, when the schools were open, separate curricula. A separate Kurdish airline took to the skies. Kurdish parliamentarians dropped the word 'Iraq' when swearing their oath of loyalty in the regional Kurdish Assembly, and the Kurdish not the Iraqi flag flew from its roof. In one of its first acts of legislation, the Assembly banned deployment of 50,000 *peshmergas* outside the region and non-Kurds within it without its express approval. Perhaps in response to Kurdish separatism, southern Shias began to echo their calls with an eye on full control of the oilfields that pumped most of Iraq's oil exports. Chalabi was one of the first senior Shia politicians to express Shia federalism, and after winning control of eight of 11 provinces in the January 2005 local elections, SCIRI took up the cry. 'Federalism has to be in all of Iraq,' said Badr leader al-Amiri, launching the bid for a nine-state oil-rich confederacy.[324]

Both Kurds and Shias sought to enshrine their desire for autonomy in the constitution, preparing a blueprint that rather than providing the glue to hold the country together hastened not just the devolution of Iraq, but its dissolution. Approved by referendum in October 2006, its far-flung federalism sanctioned a Kurdish autonomy in the north, and the creation of a super-Shia region in the south in which oil revenues would be carved out amongst the sects.[325] The DeBaathification Council was one of the few national institutions it preserved, further stripping Sunnis of their power and pushing them into the arms of the resistance.[326]

Ironically, the Sunnis were also tempted to vote for the first time because of a clause in Bremer's Transitional Administrative Law, which, drawn up on the insistence of the Kurds, gave any three provinces the right to veto the constitution. Realising their clout and backed by neighbouring Arab states that feared the encroaching tentacles of Iran in a partitioned Iraq, imams in the three Sunni provinces of Anbar, Salahudin and Nineweh preached for congregants to register at electoral centres. In Ramadi, the capital of Anbar, thousands took to the streets after insubordinate Jihadis threatened to kill voters.[327] Instead of attacking the polling stations, most insurgent groups protected them.

Though they insisted they steadfastly opposed the federal constitution, their entry accelerated the sectarian divide. With Sunnis voting for Sunnis, the non-confessional vote collapsed. Allawi's party shed almost 40 per cent of his vote a year earlier. Other non-confessional leaders – such as Ghassan Attiya's tribal party – failed to secure a seat. So too did Chalabi, with his Sunni deputy. Sectarian identification hitherto taboo became a badge, and intermarriage – hitherto an Iraqi trait – best avoided, not least because at weddings the guests turned on each other. Government offices and even foreign press bureaux became infected with sectarian rivalries, and language more sanctimonious. Sunnis adopted the Jihadi moniker for Shia, *Rawafid*, or rejectionists of the Sunni Caliphal line of the four righteous Caliphs, and the Shia the ancient moniker for Sunnis, *Nawasib*, usurpers of the rightful line of the Imamate succession.

While paying lip-service to a united Iraq, Sunnis were actively carving out sectarian cantons. In an internet statement in October 2006, al-Qaeda in Iraq declared an independent Islamic state comprising all Sunni Arab provinces, led by Abu Omar al-Baghdadi.[328] In pursuit of their pure new order, Jihadis accelerated the rate of killing of Shias and Kurds on the edges of the ethereal Sunni emirate, be they teachers, bakers or simple day labourers. Under siege from Shia militias, Sunnis moved out of areas particularly in and around Baghdad where they found themselves in a minority, in an act of communal cleansing that wrenched heterogeneous towns and communities apart. The pluralistic capital, Baghdad – which before the war had been the largest Arab Sunni, Shia and Kurdish city – was increasingly split in two: a Sunni Karkh on the west bank of the Tigris, and a Shia Rusafa on the east. The roads filled with heavily laden cars taking Kurds and Sunnis north and Shias south. Sunni taxi-drivers steered clear of Shia suburbs, for fear of ID checks by Shia police. Real estate prices in Baghdad plummeted, while those in the ethnic or sectarian heartlands climbed.

Large enclaves remained inside Baghdad's sectarian zones, most strikingly Kathimiya – the traditional Shia shrine district on the west bank – and the Adhamiya, a district home to key Sunni shrines in the east.[329] The ranks of the displaced provided an ample pool of fresh recruits – armed with useful local knowledge and a burning resentment – for reprisals. To protect themselves by day, Sunnis in mixed areas erected Imam Ali posters and stacked up on Mahdi Army literature as amulets. By night they organised vigilante groups to man barricades of palm-tree trunks and trash cans against Shiite-led commando raids, sending out alerts by flashlights, mosque loudspeakers and cellphones when strangers approached. Although a surge of US forces in 2007 appeared to temper the rate of the sectarian killing, the damage had already been done. Seeking security Iraqis had retreated into their sect, in the process redrawing the country's demographic map.

SECTION 4

THE REGIONAL WARS OF RELIGION

CHAPTER 16

The Reawakening of Arab Shiism

Cross-legged on cushions, a fresh intake of Qur'anic novices at a gleaming Shia seminary in south Lebanon gazed past their lecturer through the netting shading the French windows to the hills rolling south to Israel. The contrast with the Hauza in Najaf could not have been more striking. In place of parched flatlands, Lebanon's colleges were set in the greenery of rich undulating fields; palms morphed into pines, Iraq's mules into Mercedes, and tumbledown seminaries into mansions sporting arched marble balconies, crazy-paving driveways, underground car-parks, and carpets as soft as mattresses. Funded from remittances sent by Lebanon's Shia exiles diamond-hunting in West Africa or building cars in Detroit, student stipends at this country-club Hauza were three times those of Najaf. Yet for all the contrast between Lebanon's opulence and Iraqi atrophy, the seminary looked to Najaf for spiritual leadership. It named itself after Iraq's holy city – the Najaf College for Islamic Studies – and in empathy fed its 70 seminarians a diet of *timan wa qima* – Iraqi gruel.

Najaf was regaining its status not just in sedate modern seminaries, but in the tumble of Middle East politics. For over a century its Curia had been in decline, and by the mid-1990s all but certified dead by western academics. 'The first Gulf war, which enabled Iraq to put an end to Najaf and Karbala's de facto extraterritoriality, marked the end of a certain Shiism,' wrote Olivier Roy, perhaps the premier scholar of political Islam.[330] Less than a decade later, Najaf resurfaced as the centrepiece of Shia refulgence in the Arab world. Delegates from across the Arab world as well as Baghdad sought the blessing and advice of its *marjaiya*, or source of spiritual Shia leadership. Western leaders prefaced their references to Ayatollah Sistani, an unknown before the invasion, with the epithet of 'Supreme'.

The reasons for the regional resurrection of Iraq's Curia have less to do with a physical revival – although from its decrepit base there was some of that – than its role as a source of emulation for Shias. Within months, the Hauza's liberation had become a model for Shias across the Arab world, whose downtrodden status so closely corresponded with that of pre-war Iraq's. Shias long accustomed to considering themselves a suppressed minority suddenly saw the possibility of emancipation through membership of an empowered club. With the addition of oil-rich Iraq and Iran, Shias in the Gulf were an overwhelming majority. In Bahrain, they formed 60 to 70 per cent of the population, and elsewhere sizeable minorities: 42 per cent in Yemen, 35 per cent in Kuwait, 15 per cent in the United Arab Emirates and 11 per cent in Saudi Arabia. Zoom out, and Shias comprised 140 million people, or about half the population in the arc stretching from the eastern Mediterranean through Iran and Azerbaijan to the borders of Afghanistan. In Lebanon they were the largest single confessional group, officially estimated at 38 per cent, and there were substantial constituencies in Syria, Turkey, Pakistan, India, Sri Lanka, Myanmar, and East and South Africa. If Iraq's Shias could shrug off Saddam, the most brutal of Arab dictators, what more could they achieve with the effete corrupt royals in neighbouring states?

Such democratic aspirations were buttressed by a religious tradition that was by no means obvious at first sight. Shias after all venerated an Imamate dynasty as divinely appointed and infallible and as such vested with absolute executive, legislative and judicial authority. The early Sunni community, by contrast, elected its leader, or Caliph, through a *shura*, or consultative council, and subjected his rule to a law derived by human – albeit clerical – effort. But with the disappearance of the twelfth and last Shia Imam in the ninth century, the rival conceptions of power had all but switched. Bereft of their Imam, Shia clerics agreed that the temporal authority left behind was illegitimate but argued over what alternative system of government, or *wilaya*, would conform to God's will.[331] In the latter half of the twentieth century, two broad schools emerged from Iran. Khomeini's theory of the *wilayat al-faqih*, or sovereignty of the religious jurisprudent, was realised in Iran. But Iraq clung to Mohammed Baqir al-Sadr's rival theory of *wilayat al-umma*, or popular sovereignty, in which the people as the vice-regents of God held legislative and executive power:

Islamic theory rejects monarchy as well as the various forms of dictatorial government; it also rejects aristocratic regimes and proposes a form of government, which contains all the positive aspects of the democratic system.[332]

The two contrary political theories do much to explain the different courses adopted by the Iranian and Iraqi revolutions. Khomeini elevated himself to supreme leader basking in a messianic aura which promised that with the return of the Imam, the meek would inherit the earth. Najaf's clerics, by contrast, stuck religiously to the democratic principle. Ayatollah Sistani precluded clerics from holding political office, and recognised the *vox populi* as a legitimate source of legislation and thus of the divine will.[333] He trumpeted elections as the Islamic means to end occupation, and voting as a religious duty. He was democracy's best salesman in the Middle East.

The Ayatollah's mantra of 'one man, one vote' galvanised Shias from Iraq to the oilfields of Saudi Arabia. Shia demonstrations modelled on those in Iraq erupted in quick succession in Lebanon, Bahrain and Yemen, all demanding elections which might end their second-class status. Even Iran, long the beneficiary of Najaf's decline, seemed to fall prey to the Sistani effect.[334] Iranian reformists such as Grand Ayatollah Yousef Sanei openly considered seeking asylum in Najaf, and Khomeini's own maverick grandson, Hussein Khomeini, briefly took up residence there, giving interviews calling for America to do to Iran what it had done in Iraq.[335] In 2005, Iran and Iraq both staged multi-party elections. In each case the victors – prime minister Ibrahim Jaafari and president Mahmoud Ahmedinajad – were besuited politicians, not turbanned clerics. Non-Shia Islamists also fell sway to the message. Hamas, a Sunni Palestinian protest movement, jettisoned their boycott of the political process and was rewarded with an electoral victory in January 2006. Wherever democracy was allowed to run its course, Islamist politicians rose to power.

Hizbollah also followed suit. For over a decade, its leaders had accepted the unwritten agreement whereby it kept its militia as a resistance in return for accepting a smaller stake in the country's confessional system than was owed the country's largest sect. By 2005, however, that formula was facing considerable pressure. Israel's withdrawal from southern Lebanon in May 2000 had deprived the rebel movement of its justification, but not the threat it posed northern Israel, or potentially other Lebanese sects. In 2004, the UN Security Council passed Resolution 1559 calling for Hizbollah's disarmament. While rejecting the resolution, Hizbollah began preparing for its transition into national politics, adopting Sistani's model for capturing power.

Following the assassination of Lebanese prime minister and Sunni leader Rafiq al-Hariri, Hizbollah's leader Hassan Nasrallah staged the largest rally in the country's 25-year-old history of Shia activism, with an eye on filling the vacuum. On 8 March 2005, hundreds of thousands of Lebanon's Shias took to the streets of downtown Beirut chanting for Imam Ali and their democratic due in the country's electoral system.[336] There were no guns, no militia flags, and no segregation between men and women. Instead, Nasrallah presided as father of the nation, inviting Christian and Druze clients to the podium while his followers waved Lebanese flags. In the wake of Hariri's death, he had become Lebanon's most powerful figure. After years of political isolation, Nasrallah was seeking not just integration within but domination of Lebanon's mainstream body-politic. Following elections in May 2005, Hizbollah entered government for the first time, and egged on by Sistani's representatives in Lebanon agreed to discuss integrating its militia into Lebanon's army, given international security guarantees. For a time, it seemed Hizbollah had accepted Sistani's democratic rules of the game.[315]

The cry for elections was also raised in Gulf states, several of which accorded Shia even fewer legal rights than Saddam-era Iraq. On the island of Bahrain, Shias comprised some two-thirds of the electorate but were treated as second-class citizens by an Arabian tribe, the al-Khalifa, which had conquered the archipelago in the eighteenth century.[338] Most were restricted to residence in the ramshackle villages on the far side of the island, a form of apartheid, and excluded from bastions of power, including the security forces. Public gatherings, including Ashoura processions, were brutally crushed, often by migrant riot police recruited from friendly Sunni states such as Jordan and Pakistan. Shia rallies in support of Iraq and Sistani-intended were repressed with rubber bullets and tear-gas.

But Iraq's clarion call for Shia representation was too inviting to be suppressed by Bahrain's bully boys. In March 2005, 50,000 protestors took to the streets demanding the king make parliament sovereign. 'I think that Iraq could represent a democratic model for the Arab-Muslim world which has experienced futile and utopic conflicts for 14 centuries,'[339] Ali Salman – a prominent Shia leader – told the crowd as the security forces prepared to charge. Initially, King Hamad ibn Isa al-Khalifa stood his ground. He refused to accept a petition demanding constitutional reforms, and instructed his intelligence agents to round up the organisers and ban Shia websites. But the protests continued, and each daybreak revealed a new crop of spray-painted slogans crying for change. Fresh elections were endorsed for November 2006, whose results were almost as resounding as in Iraq. Despite gerrymandering, Shia opposition candidates won 16 of the 17 seats they contested, or 40 per cent of the total.

In neighbouring Saudi Arabia, the Shia minority was on the move. More than any other Arab state, the kingdom had suppressed its 1.6 million Shias, comprising some 10 per cent of the population and concentrated in the Eastern Province atop the world's largest oilfields.[340] Wahhabi clerics, who traditionally deemed Shias heretics and closet polytheists conspiring with Muslim enemies, presided over the legislature, and monopolised the judiciary. As in Bahrain, Shia residence rights were limited to particular zones, and they were denied access to the security forces. The Saudi embassy in Washington remained free of Shia, and Saudi schools – a traditional Wahhabi domain – continued to teach that Shia Islam was a Jewish heresy, and its practitioners a fifth column. Again, the precedent of Najaf's Ayatollahs prompted Shias to organise a petition. Within days of the fall of Saddam, 450 Saudi Shias penned a tractate to King Abdullah – entitled 'Partners in the Homeland' – demanding an end to religious discrimination and the establishment of a Shia religious authority to regulate their internal affairs. A month later, Abdullah agreed to meet them, and regained the initiative by unveiling a programme for municipal elections, the first of any kind in the kingdom. There were numerous restrictions. Half the seats on the council were appointed and both women and political parties were banned,[341] but again following Sistani's lead, Shia leaders opted for political participation not boycott. In campaigning for the spring 2005 polls, clerics cited Sistani's fatwa declaring voting a religious duty. Candidates played down calls for autonomy, and played up demands for equal rights to local civil service posts, hitherto staffed by Salafis parachuted in from Wahhabi strongholds.

The results were impressive. While Sunni Saudis trickled to the polls, the Shia flowed. In the town of Qatif – where the bulk of Sistani's adherents lived – almost four-fifths of registered voters cast their vote, the highest turnout countrywide, compared to less than a third in Riyadh. Where Shias had hitherto organised underground, they campaigned publicly. A relaxation of state restrictions quickly followed. The Hauza established an unofficial training college for Shia clerics, Saudi Shias were permitted to mark Ashoura with hitherto banned processions, and clerics in Qatif launched their own website[342] and even found outlets for their writings in the state-monitored press.[343] As a sign of the glasnost, Jaffar al-Shaib, a veteran campaigner for Shia rights, won a seat. 'We were a sect with no voice. We got our voice heard,' said Sheikh Hassan al-Safar, Sistani's representative in the Eastern Province and the long-time leader of the Saudi Shia Islamist movement.

Briefly, it seemed as if Iraq had ushered a lasting age of democratic Islamism into the Arab world. Yet in few – and arguably none – of the elections did increased representation translate into a commensurate increase in power. Washington continued to occupy Iraq and arm-twist its government, and sanctioned the Hamas government that won Palestinian elections. In Lebanon, the ruling elites clung to the distribution of political posts on a confessional basis, capping the political clout of Shias despite their electoral success. And Arab autocrats sought to fob off demands for political reform with a hangover from the colonial era, by instituting talking-shop assemblies not sharing power.

The failures of the reform movement were seized upon by activists who, following the lead of Sistani's Shia opponents in Iraq, argued that only a more radical programme, including the 'defence of beliefs with their blood', would realise meaningful change. An Ayatollah who had once formed the backbone of Bahrain's Shia opposition movement, the Islamic Front for the Liberation of Bahrain, resurfaced in Karbala, calling for Iraq's Shias to lead the way in liberating Shias region-wide. 'We thought the Bedouin on Camels,' said Iraq's interior minister, Bayan Jabr Solagh, referring to Saudi Arabia, 'should be paying more attention to the rights of the Shia, who are considered third-class citizens, and the Ismailis, who are considered fourth-class.' In a milieu where loyalty to the sect was fast outstripping that owed to the state, a host of overlapping transnational networks of Shia revivalists sprouted across the region, constructing a common mutually reinforcing discourse challenging the co-opted pragmatists. Iran – itself led by Ahmedinajad, a millennialist who like Bush claimed to communicate with the divine[344] – stoked the radicalism. As with Hizbollah's Lebanon in the 1980s, its Revolutionary Guards found a foothold in the Mahdi movement by offering support. After his first visit to Iran, Muqtada Sadr proclaimed his fighters to be the Iraqi arm of Lebanon's Hizbollah. Hizbollah returned the compliment by offering his party's military assistance to Iraqi Shia insurgents during the siege of Najaf in May 2004, an offer in turn reciprocated by Sadr in the midst of the summer 2006 Lebanon war with Israel, during a demonstration in which the Mahdi army carried Hizbollah flags. Regardless of actual military cooperation, the symbolic political capital of one reinforced that of the other, without any requisite transfer of people or arms. The impression of a tactical region-wide Shia pact had been sown.

The reach of revolutionary Shiism percolated to the peripheries of the Arab world. Of all large Arab states, Yemen's sectarian composition most closely resembles that of Iraq. Two out of five Yemenis are Zaydi Shias who have traditionally subscribed to the doctrine of *khuruj*, or separation from the sinful state.[345] There, too, they lived as a suspected fifth column, hankering after a Shia supremacy, which was wrenched from them in 1962 when Republicans staged a military coup ending 11 centuries of Imamate rule.[346] The Imam himself fled to London, but the clerics who maintained his theocracy retreated to Yemen's mountainous extremes close to the Saudi border. In the ancient walled town of Saada, they propagated the last flickerings of Zaydi teachings under the watchful eye of the state authorities, who imported an odd mixture of Baathists and Jihadi veterans of the Afghan war to control them in an early instance of the fabled 'marriage of convenience'. Its cafes bustled with moustachioed Iraqi intelligence agents, operating under the guise of teachers and engineers, who were joined by a fresh influx of Baathist émigrés after the US invasion. Simultaneously, President Saleh encouraged Wahhabi missionaries and graduates of the Afghan Jihad to relocate to the desert oasis of Damaj, a few miles to the north. Beneath its deceptively simple mud houses, the newcomers built a vast concrete bunker containing prayer halls and dormitories with the semblance of an underground car park. By the late 1990s, Damaj and its charismatic sheikh, Moukbil al-Wadai (subsequently identified by the Americans as Bin Laden's representative in Yemen),[347] were attracting a veritable United Nations of Salafi acolytes, some praying with Kalashnikovs at their sides. In the waning heat of late afternoon, students from as far afield as Leicester and Lahore surfaced from their troglodyte world to play cricket on the hard-baked sands. Algerians, fresh from the Afghan Jihad, went shooting doves, and Californians played volleyball.[348]

And yet inspired by Iraq's Shia liberation, Yemen's Zaydi leaders dared to challenge this powerful alliance. One year after Iraq's conquest, a young Najafi-trained cleric from Saada called Hussein Badr al-Din al-Huthi raised the cry to restore the Imamate. Taking flight to the same mountainous redoubt of Um Issa where the Imamate had made its last stand, Huthi declared himself the new Imam and called his followers – the Faithful Youth – to challenge the regime of President Saleh, the longest-reigning Arab ruler bar Qaddaffi. 'He [Huthi] stormed into mosques, raised the flag of Hizbollah instead of the national flag and collected money from people forcefully,' said President Salah, after dispatching his troops to lay siege. Hundreds were killed in the onslaught, including two months into the siege Huthi himself. In a statement, Ayatollah Sistani condemned 'the repressive persecution of the Zaydi sect', and accused Saleh of 'waging a kind of a war' against Yemen's Shias, in a campaign his advisors likened to the persecutions of Saddam. Urged by Iraq's Shia, Huthi's martyrdom only stoked the zeal of his survivors. After two months of inconclusive negotiations, Huthi's elderly father retreated from the capital to the hills above Saada to again rouse the faithful.

If Iraq and Yemen had shown the way, Lebanon was the turning point in fortunes of the revolutionary path. In the spring of 2006, Nasrallah joined Lebanon's other confessional leaders in a national dialogue designed to coin a new compact for the country after Syria's withdrawal. On the table was the prospect of decommissioning Lebanon's weapons in return for replacing Lebanon's communal arrangement with a democratic system of one person, one vote.[349] Whether Nasrallah recoiled first is unclear. Hizbollah flinched from disarmament, just as other communal leaders flinched from a political system that led to Shia predominance, and perhaps an Islamic state under Nasrallah, the anointed representative of Iran's Ayatollahs. After flirting with Sistani's methods, Nasrallah rejected reform for resistance with a verve that surprised even his Iranian patrons. Barred from being Lebanon's prime political force, he reverted to being its prime military one. 'Sistani's a pacifist who should have resisted the American occupation long ago,' declared a news editor at Hizbollah's Manar TV.[350] 'Now is the moment for action.'

Bolstered by arms from Syria and Iran in July 2006, Nasrallah felt sufficiently confident to launch a cross-border raid on an Israeli patrol, triggering an Israeli riposte that left 1,500 Lebanese civilians dead, hundreds of thousands homeless, but Hizbollah still standing as a force that had challenged the region's most powerful military in what was one of Israel's longest wars.

Though by exposing a key component of Iranian deterrence, the confrontation came too soon for the liking of Hizbollah and its patron, Iran;

it betrayed the punch that Iran's regional satellites were preparing to muster. Medium-range missiles struck Israel's third largest city, Haifa, and an Israeli battleship at sea; and electronic intelligence penetrated Israel's mobile network. What arsenal Israel destroyed was quickly rebuilt, as was the real estate with the support of an annual Iranian stipend of $200 million. Portraits of Khamenei the height of buildings cast their shadows over a capital in which Sistani's image was absent. In contrast to the extensive offices of Iran's Ayatollah's, Sistani's representative shut himself in a squat windowless first-floor flat above a gun-shop, where a woman in crisp black body coverings peddled balaclavas, rifles and framed portraits of Iranian mullahs.

Nasrallah's populism, however, stretched beyond the confines of his sect. His symbolic success at halting the onward march of Americana electrified the Sunni as well as Shia Arab world, restoring the *karama*, or dignity, and reversing the humiliating countdown of the Iraq invasion. In the cafes of Cairo and Amman, shopkeepers, farmers and workers gazed at television reports, sipped their tea, and silently mouthed the numbers to themselves: 'seven', 'nineteen', 'thirty-three'. Even on the 34th and final day, Hizbollah managed to fire hundreds of rockets deep into Israel. And unlike Saddam's army, no Hizbollah soldier surrendered. In the aftermath, the confessional schism carved through the Muslim *umma* appeared to subside. Outpourings of newspaper columns, cartoons, blogs and public poetry readings transformed Nasrallah into a folk hero. Egypt's press called him a neo-Nasser, and vendors in Lebanon's Sunni stronghold of Tripoli peddled tapes of his speeches. 'We do not share Hizbollah's ideas. But we share their pain,' a barrel-boy was quoted as saying.[351] Yusuf Qaradawi, leader of the often staid Muslim Brotherhood, declared it incumbent (*wajib*) on all Muslims to support Hizbollah.[352] Even Bin Laden's mentor and right-hand man, Ayman al-Zawahiri, felt compelled to call for a pact with 'Lebanon's disinherited', and praised their resistance despite 'the treachery' of Arab governments.[353]

Indeed, in the wake of Zarkawi's death, the sectarian censure appeared to subside. Prominent Salafis in Saudi Arabia, including the former firebrand Salman al-Auda, joined 15 Shia intellectuals to petition for constitutional reforms, including demands for a constitutional monarchy, an elected parliament, respect for human rights, and an end to anti-Shia discrimination.[354] Shia revolutionaries, from the Sadaris in Iraq to Lebanon's Hizbollah, similarly shunned sectarianism discourse, addressing a Muslim rather than confessional audience. On a tour of the Emirates, Iran's top national security official, Ali Larijani, urged the Arab world to join Tehran in a regional security alliance and evict the US military from their regional bases.[355] Ahmedinejad also kept out of the sectarian fray, seeking to bridge the Sunni–Shia divide by spotlighting a common enemy with his anti-Israeli and anti-American diatribes. At the victory parade in Beirut on 22 September 2006, Nasrallah took the rhetoric one stage further, adding the Arab world's appeasing rulers to his target list:

> The problem is that when one [a monarch] is torn between two choices and is asked to choose between his people and his throne, he chooses his throne. When he is asked to choose between Jerusalem and his throne, he chooses his throne. When he is asked to choose between the dignity of his homeland and his throne, he chooses his throne.

In his speech, Nasrallah carefully avoided sectarian terms dividing the region not between Sunnis and Shias but between the haves and the have-nots, the disenfranchised masses from the moneyed few, the liberation theologians against the tired orthodox, the radicals and the reformers, the non-state actors from the helmsmen of state, the Islamists from the 'Westoxicators', and the followers of *tariq al-muqawwama* (the way of resistance) from those of *tariq al-musawwama* (the culture of compromise). The radical wings of Sunni and Shia Islam had found common cause in their revolutionary bid to overthrow the old reactionary order.

Amid the euphoria surrounding Nasrallah's vision, Sunni sympathisers adopted much of his worldview. The Hizbollah effect swept poor quarters of Arab cities, providing a groundswell of support for Shia groups to tap, sometimes through Shia conversion – or *Tashia*. Iran secured a growing toehold in Syria by funding schools, offering stipends at Shia religious colleges and funding translation agencies that encouraged the trend. And a Sunni organisation, the Committee of the Ulemas of Damascus, protested that Shias were violating the ban on religious education in primary schools. Shia majorities formed in Damascus' suburb of Sayda Zeinab and in Hatla, near the Iraqi border. Smaller, more clandestine Shia gatherings occurred in Amman and Cairo, spawned initially by exiles, under the cover of *umsiyas*, or cultural soirées.

Movements as well as individuals also seemed to fall under the thrall of the Shia. Ousted from power in Iraq, Sunni guerrilla groups adopted the discourse of victimisation, the theology of suffering and the salvation myth of the meek inheriting the earth, which were all hallmarks of Shia Islam. Rebel groups forsook Sunni orthodoxy requiring subservience to Muslim rulers, however corrupt, for a creed that was similarly millennial: the toppling of tyranny.[356] As the Ayatollahs, the means could be democratic: Salafi firebrands, such as Saffar al-Hawali, swept inner-city seats in Saudi Arabia's 2005 municipal polls by endorsing a 'Golden List' of candidates Sistani-style, and by campaigning through text messages and sermons in internet chat-rooms to ensure that, after Shias, Salafis were the kingdom's most active voters. But the methods could also be those of the self-sacrificial cult, more traditionally associated with the Shia rite of martyrdom. From their Afghan hideouts in Tora Bora, Jihadi Salafists were held in as much shock and awe as twelfth-century Ismaili Assassins in their mountain redoubt of Alamut. In effect, Salafis appeared to be deviating from their role-models, the *sahaba*, or Prophet's Companions, none of whom were suicide bombers, opting instead for the Salafi anathema of a *bida'*, or innovation, drawn from contemporary Shiism. While decrying many Shia rites – particularly shrine worship – in pursuit of regime-change, the Salafis were revamping Sunni Islam in Shia hues.

In addition to individuals and movements, states were also lured to Hizbollah's success. Cornered by western as well as Arab regimes, Syrian and Palestinian leaders beat fresh paths to Tehran and Beirut. The Alawite regime that had tried unsuccessfully to regain the Israeli-occupied Golan Heights through diplomatic means for over 30 years increasingly asked whether Hizbollah's doctrine of *muqawwama*, or resistance, which had ousted Israel from South Lebanon, might yield better results. In an interview following the Lebanon war, President Bashar al-Assad pointedly referred to 'other options'[357] if Israel rejected his offer of peace. Singing from Nasrallah's hymn sheet, Assad denigrated 'Arab leaders' as 'half-men adopting half-positions' during the Lebanon War. At the same time he bolstered his alliance with Iran, signing a pact which gave Iranian forces a foothold. Syria also became a favoured destination for other regional radicals, including Muqtada Sadr as well as many Sunni Jihadis heading to Iraq's front. In contrast to the first years of his rule, when he reached out to the Sunni fold – coordinating closely with Saudi Arabia, signing a series of lucrative economic agreements with Saddam Hussein, and promoting his marriage to a Sunni Syrian as a metaphor for the unity of Syria's Sunni and non-Sunni halves – Assad was ever more wed to the Shia world.

Domestically, Bashar retreated deeper within his sect. He surrounded himself with his Alawite family and friends, including his brother-in-law, Asaf Shawkat, who ran military intelligence, and his brother, Maher al-Assad, who ran the presidential guard. He cleared the decks of his father's old guard of Sunni loyalists,[358] including the secular Sunni mercantile class, which had lost their foremost representative, former prime minister Hariri. How far Assad was influenced by his own sectarian origins rather than circumstance is much debated. The secretive and dissimulative Alawites originated as an offshoot of Shia Islam and share with the Shia mainstream a veneration for Imam Ali (indeed, they consider him God Incarnate and at *quddass*, or mass, transubstantiate bread and wine into his body and blood). Repeatedly during periods of crisis, the Assads turned to the Shia world for succour. When the Sunni Muslim Brotherhood claimed that the Alawites were non-Muslims and thus constitutionally barred from presidency, the Alawites sought and obtained fatwas from Shia clerics in Lebanon and Iran recognising that they were Shia Muslims.[359] And when the Sunni majority rebelled against 'the heretics' in the early 1980s, the Assads allied with Khomeini's Revolution – the only Arab leaders to do so. Tens of thousands of Sunnis were killed and whole city quarters flattened in the suppression that followed. And although Syria initially intervened in Lebanon on behalf of the Maronite Christians against the Sunni Palestinians, by the mid-1980s it was protecting the Shia. Lebanon's Shia returned the favour after Syrian forces were chased from Lebanon by a combined alliance of Sunnis and western powers. Before a vast crowd in Beirut, Nasrallah promised 'Assad's Syria' his morale and military support against attempts to topple his rule.

Despite its internal imbroglio, Iraq was serving as the crucible for a Shia Arab awakening and shift of Middle East power. Four years after Iraq's invasion, its own confessional upheaval was sending shockwaves to the four corners of the Arab world, threatening to redraw the geo-political map of the Middle East that colonial powers had carved out of the wreckage of the Ottoman Empire. Shia revivalists in Lebanon, Bahrain and Yemen were all seeking to replicate Iraq and uproot the foundations of an order held in place for nearly 100 years by a mixture of foreign occupation, outside meddling, brutal dictatorships and minority rule. From the Caspian Sea to the Mediterranean, non-state Sunni actors, too, were succumbing to the discourse and methods, if not the creed of an emergent Shia Internationale. While US forces had opened the door, the winds of change were blowing through the region not from Washington but Najaf.

The Two Stripes of the Arab World: Shia Protestantism and the Sunni Counter-Reformation

Where Shias celebrated a renaissance, Sunni Arab leaders perceived a Shia horde eroding a time-honoured Sunni primacy over the Arab heartland. In the course of two generations, they had lost first Syria and then Iraq, and seemed on the verge of losing Lebanon – creating a 1,600-kilometre-long heterodox driveway from Iran to the Mediterranean. Elsewhere, Shia Islam had pushed its contours 1,000 kilometres westwards to the Jordan border, and was making inroads elsewhere in what appeared a slow game of chess, in which one by one Shias captured the pieces. From its garb to its policies, Iraq's new elite had refashioned itself in the image of its eastern neighbour with the Hauza in the ascendant. In the words of a Sistani acolyte, 'we didn't politicise religion, we religionised politics'. To cap the seminal shift in the balance of power, Iran seemed intent on acquiring the first Shia bomb, casting the region under a nuclear umbrella which would see its friends emboldened and opponents at its mercy.

Worldwide, Sunni Arabs could still take umbrage from the fact that they enjoyed an overwhelming 85 per cent majority of Muslims. More worrying was that this majority was concentrated far away in South Asia, Indonesia and North Africa. Closer to home the balance was less comforting. From Iran to the Levant, Shias constituted half the population. Exacerbating the erosion of Sunni Arab power, America's elevation of the Kurds threatened to carve a non-Arab bridgehead linking Iran to the Syrian border. As for the region's mineral wealth, three Shia governments – Iran, Iraq and Azerbaijan – owned as much of the world's oil reserves as Sunni Arab states. And even those fields that the Sunni world did control were largely inhabited by Shias.

From their televised pulpits, preachers warned of a second age of colonialism designed to eliminate Sunni rule from the Fertile Crescent: the first had bequeathed the western half to Jewish, Christian and latterly Alawite rulers; 80 years on, the second would hand the eastern half to the Shias. It was as if, said one commentator, the new mandatory power had written a Balfour Declaration for the Shia and the Kurds. All that was missing was the half-hearted apology to the Sunnis 'that nothing shall be done which may prejudice the civil and religious rights of existing' non-Shia and non-Kurdish communities in Iraq.

Their anxieties were compounded by the fragility of the old Arab order. A crisis of legitimacy and confidence beset many regimes, which the mass support for Hizbollah's methods had only stoked further. There were direct military threats as well. Far from being a sponge for the region's Jihadis, Iraq as Afghanistan before it had become a net exporter of battle-hardened zealots, exporting new guerrilla techniques from roadside bombs to rocket attacks.[360] In early signs of a blowback, a series of suicide bombings ricocheted through the Sunni capitals of Amman, Doha and Riyadh, targeting westerners employed by the Coalition. The opposition was nebulous and multifaceted. Using the tools of the interactive information age, a heady brew of transnational ideologies and networks was challenging the foundations of their Sunni regimes, united if not in their creeds at least in their demand not for reform but Reformation. Much as the age of printing in Europe had enabled fifteenth-century Christians to challenge their orthodoxy through unmediated access to the sacred texts, the new technologies were subjecting the Sunni Church not merely to protest, but to Protestantism.

The great rulers of the Muslim world had defused tensions amongst their many sects with a policy of inclusiveness and pluralism that prioritised ecumenical stability over doctrine. The Ottoman Sultans decorated their mosques with the names of the first three Shia Imams as well as the four righteous Sunni Caliphs, and they together with Moghul emperors in India patronised large numbers of Persian-speaking Shia scholars at their courts. Under their rule, the Sunni–Shia fault line from Beirut to Bombay lay largely dormant, even during the simmering struggle against the Safavids. With rare exception, it was only when European colonial powers sponsored opposition movements based on ethnic or sectarian identify that confessional tensions between Muslims surfaced.

Initially, Arab leaders, led by the kingpin of Arab Sunni sentiment, Saudi Arabia, seemed to opt for a similar flexibility. Following the collapse of the

Soviet Union and the effective handover of Saudi leadership in 1995 from King Fahd ('the panther') to King Abdullah ('the servant of God'), Riyadh abandoned the anti-Shia rhetoric designed to contain the Iranian and Communist revolutions in the 1980s, and set about healing the schism. In December 1997, Abdullah flew to Tehran for the first talks between the leaders of the Shia and Sunni powers since the overthrow of the Shah. A few days later, he and Iran's equally reform-minded president, Mohammed Khatami, opened the summit of the Organisation of Islamic Conference, the umbrella body of Muslim states, in Tehran. Given that all but four of the OIC's 56 members were Sunni-majority states (Iran, Azerbaijan, Bahrain and Iraq were the exceptions), the summit was a remarkable testament of Muslim reconciliation. In the wake of the 11th September attacks, he strove to reverse course from Wahhabi dogma – the kingdom's ruling creed – even more vigorously. He met with the Sunni and Shia signatories of a petition demanding constitutional reforms and promised that within 20 years the kingdom would be a democracy. Restrictions on Shia religious activity were eased, with Shias and Sunnis granted limited, but equal, electoral rights.[361]

Such gradual measures were no match for the forces spilling from Iraq to lap at Sunni rule. Increasingly, they looked back with nostalgia at the iron fist of Saddam, bemoaning the loss of their former bulwark against Shia ascendancy. His hanging evoked an outpouring of mourning from Sunni autocrats, fearful no doubt of a similar fate. President Mubarak declared him a martyr. Libya's leader, Muammar Qaddaffi, ordered his statue be erected alongside Omar Mukhtar, the Sunni progenitor of the Libyan state. There was even praise from a Kuwaiti sheikh. Their conclusions were similarly sung in unison: only by donning Saddam's armour as Sunni defenders of the faith could they hope to contain the contagion.

A counter-reformation swung into action with a three-pronged campaign fought on local, regional and international fronts. To re-establish domestic control, Arab rulers erected a series of physical and psychological walls, aimed at separating their subjects from the Protestants. Using the mosques and the media to instil the sectarian paradigm, King Abdullah of Jordan was the first leader to scaremonger with the image of a Shia arc encircling Sunni Arabs.[362] Arab leaders soon joined the chorus. In a satellite television interview, President Mubarak of Egypt warned that 'Shias are mostly always loyal to Iran not to the country where they live', generically stripping Shias of their Arab identity.[363] Kuwait, which again felt vulnerable to an Iraqi push south, this time instigated by Shia militias, castigated the

Iraqi government for taking what its foreign minister called 'this dangerous and detestable road' to Shia sectarianism.[364] Further banging the drums of bigotry, Bahrain's state-controlled press denigrated Iraq's Shia-led government as American lackeys and Sistani as 'an American general'.[365] Sunni suicide bombings – provided they remained within Iraq's boundaries – were hailed as legitimate acts of resistance, even when they killed Shia civilians.

Nor did they shy from social engineering, deploying their police and immigration authorities to contain the demographic surge in Shiism spread by the influx from Iraq.[366] Egypt launched a much-publicised witch-hunt for closet Shias involved in missionary work.[367] Jordan deported Shiites who made the pilgrimage to a Shia shine, and rejected demands to build a mosque on the grounds it might stoke a revolution. Some advocated more extreme measures, including the 'quarantining' or expulsion of their Shia population. In Bahrain, a government minister coined a five-year plan to alter the island's confessional composition, which included broadening the scheme to naturalise foreign Sunnis, and payment of a stipend to poor Shiites who converted to Sunnism.[368]

Yemen's methods were perhaps the most persuasive. Ahead of his assault, President Saleh allied himself with the Muslim Brotherhood, whose leader Sheikh Abdullah al-Ahmar had like himself been born a Zaydi, albeit a lay one not a *sayid*, or descendent of the Prophet's family. Though this slight of birth proscribed him from holding power under Imamate tradition, he summoned Yemen's clergy and bullied them into blessing him. He then proceeded to nationalise the country's 25,000 religious schools, launching the campaign with Shia *madrasas*, which he had padlocked. After facing resistance under Huthi, helicopters and tanks were dispatched to strafe Shia redoubts in the highlands. Eye-witnesses penetrating a cordon imposed around Saada spoke of charred rebel carcasses tied Hector-style to official vehicles and dragged through the dust. In a rare statement, the authorities said over 500 were killed in Saada alone.

Though often with less brutality, Sunni leaders across the Arab world were stamping out internal dissent. The security systems they had begun to relax were resurrected, and democratic privileges withdrawn. Jordan's monarch waxed lyrical in support of the electoral boycott declared by Iraq's Sunnis, highlighting the dangers of an unharnessed popular vote. In Saudi Arabia, King Abdullah also back-pedalled on his reform programme, arresting reformers who suggested his Consultative Council be elected.

Elections to a Consultative Council in Qatar were repeatedly postponed in violation of the country's constitution. Bahrain's king promulgated an amended constitution that spared him accountability and ensured the appointment of his relatives to senior cabinet posts. Elections were also grossly gerrymandered to ensure that parliament kept its Sunni majority.[369] In Egypt, Mubarak arrested his strongest rival, Ayman al-Nour, after authorising a contested presidential election in 2005, and harassed the media trying to report on his campaign. Municipal elections were postponed and rent-a-mobs hired to baton-charge voters outside polling stations in pro-Muslim-Brotherhood constituencies during parliamentary elections. Judges who questioned the polls' integrity became the subject of criminal probes. By the end of 2005, the Arab reform movement had been smothered. At the 2006 Arab League summit, the Arab reform programme launched in Tunis in 2004 passed unmentioned. Instead, leaders focussed on distributing the fruits of their monopoly on power, conveniently facilitated by soaring oil prices that swelled government coffers.

Having shored up the home ground, the defenders of the faith went on the offensive. In the four of the 21 Arab states without Sunni leaders, they cultivated the local Sunni population as a forward defence against the Shia tide. 'Major Saudi tribal confederations, which have extremely close historical and communal ties with their counterparts in Iraq, are demanding action. They are supported by a new generation of Saudi royals in strategic government positions who are eager to see the kingdom play a more muscular role in the region,' wrote an advisor at the kingdom's embassy in Washington.[370] Pitting Sunni against Shia, intelligence agents drew on old Iraqi structures, including ex-*mukhabarat*, to fortify Sunni ranks against Iran-backed militias. In Saudi mosques, preachers delivered lachrymose sermons appealing for fresh recruits for Jihad, likening America's occupation of Iraq to Russia's in Afghanistan. Of the 1,200 foreign fighters Syria claimed to have caught crossing into Iraq, 85 per cent allegedly came from the kingdom.[371] Arab leaders continued to mouth platitudes about the unity of Iraq, but as Shia rule grew more entrenched, they largely worked to subvert it. Secular strongmen, foremost of whom was Iyad Allawi, were courted in the hope they might launch a coup against the ruling Shia Islamists.[372] Requests for forgiveness of Saddam-era debt were declined and standard letters of goodwill that greeted incoming governments never sent. Riyadh even considered flooding the oil markets to reduce the oil price and cripple the Iranian economy.

As so often in the past, Lebanon reverted to the role of proxy in the regional arm-wrestling, with Sunni powers backing the Sunni prime minister, and Shia ones Hizbollah. To thwart Nasrallah's efforts to fill the vacuum left by Hariri's killing,[373] Saudi Arabia rushed financial and diplomatic support to bolster his heirs, underpinning the Cedars of Lebanon revolution when Sunni, Christian and Druze leaders took to the streets en masse to counter Shia support for Syria. Hanging from cranes or filing past his dove-laden coffin, male and female demonstrators – some baring not just their heads but their tattooed midriffs – demanded the disarmament of Hizbollah, and the withdrawal of its ally, Syria. Within two months Syria's 30,000 troops were out of Lebanon, its client intelligence agents defrocked, and murals of Assad the length of buildings whitewashed. Sunni leaders continued their pursuit. President Assad was required to submit himself for questioning by the UN Commission investigating Hariri's killing. The regime's most senior Sunni offiical, Abdel Halim Khaddam, was persuaded to defect and denounce the Assad regime from Saudi-owned satellite stations. Syria's Muslim Brotherhood in exile was granted considerable airtime. The prospect that, as the largest sect, Sunnis might regain control of Syria, in partial compensation for the loss of Iraq, was repeatedly raised.

With the Assads recoiling in Syria, Arab rulers mobilised to defang Hizbollah. When Israeli prime minister Ehud Olmert launched a pre-emptive strike to eliminate the Shia militia after a July 2006 cross-border raid, the autocrats could scarcely conceal their delight. The Saudi press accused Nasrallah of 'recklessness and adverturism', and did nothing diplomatically to frustrate Israel's mission.[374] But their plans went awry. Having banked on a rapid Israeli victory, Hizbollah held on, and, worse, their subjects rallied with, not against, the Shia movement. Inside Lebanon, the war propelled confessional tensions to new highs. Sunnis and Christians remonstrated at the destruction wrecked by Hizbollah's war of choice and fumed at the loss of summer tourism. Salafi websites further stirred up resentment with old fatwas declaring the Shias as heretics. For their part, Shias chided Lebanon's confessions for abandoning Hizbollah to fight Israel alone. Some seeking refuge in the capital tore down the pictures of Hariri inside houses of Sunnis who welcomed them. 'They think they can invade my city,' said Mona Jawadi, a post-graduate at the American University in Beirut, fuming at the scuffed-shoe movement of Lebanon's dispossessed into Beirut's chic city centre.[375] When the anti-Shia insurgent leader Musab

Zarkawi was killed, Sunni Lebanese in Tripoli staged memorials, while Shia in the Shia south distributed sweets.

In the brief respite that followed, Shia and Sunni powers rebuilt their forces. Sunni powers welcomed the deployment of international forces in place of Hizbollah, and Qatar even joined them. Hizbollah sought to capitalise on its political capital by launching a bid for power. After prime minister Siniora refused Nasrallah's demand for a government of national unity in which he had a veto, all five Shia ministers withdrew from the cabinet. Hizbollah's supporters struck camp outside the government offices, the Grand Serail, a siege Nasrallah vowed to continue until Siniora – trapped inside – was toppled.[376] To further puncture their confidence, one of Siniora's loyal ministers, Pierre Gemayel, was shot dead in November 2006. With his government on the brink of collapse, Sunni leaders rallied to his rescue. King Abdullah personally telephoned each minister to promise support. Arab League chairman Amr Moussa and Turkish prime minister Recep Tayyip Erdogan arrived to offer their services.[377] The struggle for Lebanon was degenerating into a zero-sum game that threatened to hurtle the country back to civil war. 'This country cannot survive a victor and a vanquished mentality,' warned a former Lebanese prime minister, Salim Hoss.[378]

With their counter-reformation facing at best a stalemate and at worst a routing, the Sunni defenders of the faith searched for foreign assistance to restore their primacy. European states, who as colonial rulers were the architects of the old order, proved willing partners but their power was limited. The United States – which had coined the neo-con vision of regime change, democracy and the empowerment of the region's Shia as the panacea to a Sunni mindset responsible for the 11th September attacks – required more convincing.

Had Iraq not been such a mess and Iran such a threat, Arab endeavours to win the support of the global hegemon in their struggle against the regional one might well have failed. But by mid-2005, Washington was clasping for old sureties in a neighbourhood that increasingly resembled a no-go zone. The Islamic Republic's nuclear programme seemed unstoppable, and Shia refulgence had proved to be no friend of the Americans. In the Lebanon war and elsewhere, Sunni Arab leaders and Washington both shared a common threat. With Hizbollah's supporters poised to storm the serail, vice-president Richard Cheney flew to Riyadh to hear from King Abdullah that, as a Saudi advisor explained, 'the Saudi leadership will not and cannot allow Iran, through Syria and Hizbollah, to bring down the Lebanese government and overtake the levers of power in Beirut'.[379]

Almost overnight, Washington rehabilitated its regional foster children from their post-9/11 pariahdom, and signalled that bygones were bygones by attaching the epithet 'moderate' to their names. Shias and others who championed democracy were once again condemned to be the region's radicals. In return, the region's leaders offered their territory as bases and ports for the US to station its forces, including its fifth fleet, and even considered allowing Israel – which shared the same enemies – to join their alliance. A spate of reports surfaced of meetings between Israel's prime minister Olmert and high-placed Saudis. Not for the first time, Washington was backing both sides of the Sunni–Shia schism – not least in providing the close protection detail for the Iraqi prime minister – in what detractors perceived as a grand regional plan of divide and rule.

In their struggle for territorial control, both the Sunni and Shia camps nurtured rival proxies, even where no sectarian differences existed. In Palestine, two rival Palestinian movements grappled for regional influence almost precisely replicating the alliances they had formed in the Lebanon War. In one corner, the US, Israel and the Sunni patricians backed Palestinian president and Fatah leader Mahmoud Abbas. In the other, the forces of the Shia crescent – Iran, Syria, Hizbollah – and much of popular Arab opinion backed the Hamas movement, which won Palestinian Authority elections in January 2006. With Palestine's budget almost entirely dependent on outside sources, the forces holding its people together were weaker than those wrenching them apart. Western and Arab League donors cut off funding to Hamas, while doling out aid to President Abbas. With its traditional avenues cut, Hamas turned to Iran. 'We are standing by the Islamic Republic of Iran, and with this country we will resist American and Zionist pressures,'[380] said prime minister Ismail Haniya on a visit in November 2006 to Tehran, by then one of his few remaining bankrollers.

Facing a stalemate, the US-led alliance opted for a military solution, approving the supply of fresh arms, training and finance for Abbas. Hamas' backers did the same. By the summer of 2006, they were assassinating each other's cadres, and declaring each other's forces illegal. In rallies, demonstrators of Abbas' Fatah movement mocked Hamas loyalists as *rawafid*, or rejectionists, deliberately adopting the term 'Salafis', used to denigrate Shia. Others derided them as *falayk Hamas* – the Hamas Brigades –

after the Iranian-trained Badr Brigades, who Fatah scoffed had also killed Palestinians. Haniya responded by donning Saudi dress, as if to prove his Sunni credentials. The regional struggle as much as despair on the ground was fuelling tensions, relegating Palestinians to the status of proxies in the struggle between Iran and its satellites versus the US and its. In terms of the showdown between the forces of Shia and Sunni Islam, Palestine – in that sense at least – really did lie at the core of the conflict for the Middle East.

Five years after its Iraq invasion, Washington faced the ignominy of having realised an infinitely bloodier Middle East. Iraqis, with few exceptions, rued the day the Anglo-American armies arrived on their land. What was supposed to be a mission to replace a dictatorship with a liberal-leaning and secular democracy had instead morphed into an existential battle for identity, power and legitimacy that affected not only Iraq, but the entire tottering state system in the Middle East. Iraq was partitioned de facto in a civil war that was bleeding over its borders. Following Iraq's footsteps, Lebanon and Palestine both stood on the brink of disintegration into communal acrimonious mini-states dependent on more powerful patrons, or worse – full-scale atomisation. With the Arab world splintered into its confessional shades, the battlelines were drawn for a regional conflict of possibly nuclear proportions. While battles still raged amongst their proxies, Arab Sunni leaders weighed their options on building a Sunni bomb to offset a Shia one. The worldview and beliefs of Sunnis and Shias alike had grown darkly apocalyptic. The time of the Shia that promised so much at the outset had degenerated into a sadly bloody affair.

Shiites in Selected Countries

Percentage of population that is Shiite (estimated)

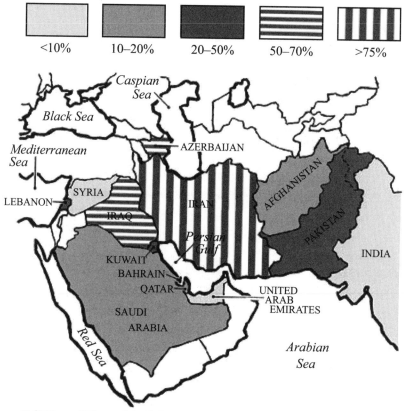

<10% 10–20% 20–50% 50–70% >75%

From Vali Nasr, 'When the Shiites Rise', *Foreign Affairs*, July/August 2006

Muslim Population by State and Sect

Data is estimated as of mid-2005 for countries with the largest Muslim population, representing about 92% of the total world Muslim population.

Country	Population	Muslim (%)	Muslim	Shia to Muslim (%)	Shia Population	Sunni to Muslim (%)	Sunni Population
Saudi Arabia	24,600,000	100%	24,600,000	11%	2,460,000	89%	22,140,000
Turkey	72,900,000	99%	72,750,000	20%	14,550,000	80%	58,200,000
Algeria	32,800,000	99%	32,472,000	<1%	3,280	100%	32,796,720
Morocco	30,700,000	99%	30,393,000	<1%	607,860	100%	29,785,140
Afghanistan	29,900,000	99%	29,601,000	18%	5,328,180	82%	24,272,820
Yemen	20,700,000	99%	20,680,000	42%	8,685,600	55%	11,994,400
Somalia	8,600,000	99%	8,600,000	<1%	86,000	100%	8,514,000
Mauritania	3,100,000	99%	3,100,000	1%	31,000	99%	3,069,000
Kuwait	2,600,000	100%	2,600,000	36%	910,000	64%	1,690,000
Oman	2,400,000	99%	2,376,000	5%	118,800	55%	1,306,800
Bahrain	700,000	99%	700,000	70%	490,000	30%	210,000
Maldives	300,000	99%	300,000	5%	15,000	95%	285,000
Western Sahara	300,000	99%	300,000	3%	9,000	97%	291,000
Iran	69,500,000	98%	68,805,000	85%	61,924,500	15%	6,880,500
Tunisia	10,000,000	99%	9,800,000	<1%	196,000	100%	9,604,000
Comoros	700,000	98%	686,000	1%	6,860	99%	679,140
Pakistan	165,803,560	98%	160,829,450	20%	33,160,712	80%	127,668,738
Iraq	28,800,000	97%	27,936,000	65%	18,158,400	35%	9,777,600
Niger	14,000,000	97%	13,580,000	<1%	407,400	100%	13,172,600
Libya	5,800,000	97%	5,626,000	<1%	56,260	100%	5,569,740

Country	Population	Muslim (%)	Muslim	Shia to Muslim (%)	Shia Population	Sunni to Muslim (%)	Sunni Population
Azerbaijan	8,587,000	88%	8,329,390	80%	7,329,863	20%	999,526
UAE	4,600,000	83%	4,416,000	15%	662,400	85%	3,753,600
Gambia	1,600,000	95%	1,520,000	1%	30,400	99%	1,489,600
Qatar	800,000	95%	760,000	10%	76,000	90%	684,000
Egypt	74,000,000	94%	69,560,000	<1%	695,600	100%	68,864,400
Senegal	11,700,000	94%	10,998,000	2%	549,900	98%	10,448,100
Jordan	5,800,000	94%	5,452,000	<1%	109,040	100%	5,342,960
Djibouti	800,000	94%	752,000	<1%	7,520	100%	744,480
Syria	18,400,000	90%	16,560,000	15%	2,484,000	85%	14,076,000
Tajikistan	6,800,000	90%	6,120,000	5%	306,000	95%	5,814,000
Turkmenistan	5,200,000	89%	4,628,000	4%	185,120	96%	4,442,880
Indonesia	221,900,000	88%	195,272,000	1%	1,952,720	99%	193,319,280
Bangladesh	147,365,000	88%	129,681,509	5%	6,484,075	95%	123,197,434
Uzbekistan	26,400,000	88%	23,232,000	6%	1,393,920	94%	21,838,080
Guinea	9,500,000	85%	8,075,000	1%	242,250	99%	7,832,750
Kyrgyzstan	5,200,000	75%	3,900,000	3%	117,000	97%	3,783,000
Sudan	40,200,000	73%	29,346,000	1%	586,920	99%	28,759,080
Bosnia & Herzegovina	4,500,000	60%	2,700,000	2%	189,000	98%	2,511,000
Ivory Coast	18,200,000	60%	10,920,000	1%	436,800	99%	10,483,200
Lebanon	3,800,000	63%	2,104,310	53%	1,200,000	47%	850,000
Nigeria	131,500,000	47%	65,750,000	5%	3,287,500	95%	62,462,500
Tanzania	36,500,000	50%	18,250,000	6%	1,095,000	94%	17,155,000
Burkina Faso	13,900,000	50%	6,950,000	1%	208,500	99%	6,741,500
Eritrea	4,700,000	50%	2,350,000	1%	23,500	99%	2,326,500
Kazakhstan	15,100,000	47%	7,097,000	5%	354,850	95%	6,742,150
Ghana	22,000,000	20%	9,900,000	13%	1,118,000	87%	8,712,000

Country							
Ethiopia	75,067,000	41%	24,471,842	1%	387,000	100%	23,135,000
Macedonia	2,000,000	32%	630,000	1%	6,300	99%	623,700
Kenya	33,800,000	24%	8,000,000	7%	560,000	93%	7,440,000
Benin	8,400,000	20%	1,680,000	1%	50,400	99%	1,629,600
Russia	143,000,000	13%	15,250,000	8%	1,212,000	92%	13,488,000
Serbia/Montenegro & Kosovo	10,700,000	19%	2,030,000	15%	304,500	85%	1,725,500
Uganda	26,900,000	16%	4,304,000	7%	301,280	93%	4,002,720
Israel & Occupied Territories	10,800,000	46%	5,000,000	2%	21,760	98%	1,066,240
India	1,103,060,000	14%	154,500,000	10%	30,900,000	90%	123,600,000
Malaysia	23,000,000	61%	14,030,000	2%	280,600	98%	13,749,400
Bulgaria	7,700,000	12%	890,000	10%	89,000	90%	801,000
France	60,700,000	8.5%	5,980,000	6%	358,800	94%	5,621,200
Albania	3,200,000	63%	2,120,000	25%	540,000	75%	1,580,000
Mongolia	2,600,000	6%	160,000	5%	8,000	95%	152,000
Germany	82,500,000	4%	3,060,000	10%	306,000	90%	2,754,000
China	1,303,700,000	3%	39,111,000	8%	3,128,880	92%	35,982,120
United Kingdom	59,668,000	3%	1,600,000	10%	160,000	90%	1,440,000
United States	296,500,000	2%	6,960,000	15%	2,300,000	85%	4,640,000
South Africa	46,900,000	2%	938,000	10%	93,800	90%	844,200
Canada	32,200,000	2%	620,000	10%	62,000	90%	558,000
Brazil	184,200,000	1%	921,000	30%	276,300	70%	644,700
Argentina	38,600,000	1%	500,000	10%	50,000	90%	450,000
Australia	20,400,000	1%	280,000	10%	28,000	90%	252,000
Italy	58,700,000	<1%	50,000	5%	2,500	95%	47,500
TOTAL	**4,997,550,560**	**29%**	**1,453,443,501**	**15%**	**219,757,850**	**85%**	**1,227,507,098**

Source: Wikipedia http://en.wikipedia.org/wiki/Demographics_of_Islam. Percentage figures are accurate up to 0 decimal places.

Bibliography

Abdul Majid Saman, *Les années Saddam* (Librairie Artheme Fayard, 2004)

Abdul-Jabar, Faleh (ed.), *Ayatollah, Sufis and Ideologues: State, Religion and Social Movements in Iraq* (Saqi Books, 2002)

Abdul-Jabar, Faleh and Dawod Hosham (eds), *Tribes and Power: Nationalism and Ethnicity in the Middle East* (Saqi Books, 2003)

Aburish, Said, *Saddam Hussein: The Politics of Revenge* (Bloomsbury, 2000)

Ajami, Fouad, *The Vanished Imam: Musa al-Sadr and the Shia of Lebanon* (Ithaca, NY: Cornell University Press, 1986)

Ali, Tariq, *The Clash of Fundamentalisms* (London: Verso, 2002)

Ali, Tariq, *Bush in Babylon: The Recolonisation of Iraq* (London: Verso, 2003)

Allen, Charles, *God's Terrorists, the Wahhabi Cult and the Hidden Roots of Modern Jihad* (Little, Brown, 2006)

Anderson, Jon Lee, *The Fall of Baghdad* (Penguin, 2004)

Anderson, Jon Lee, 'A man of the shadows', *New Yorker* (24 January 2005)

Arnove, A. (ed.), *Iraq Under Siege: The Deadly Impact of Sanctions and War* (South End Press, 2000)

Atkinson, Rick, *In the Company of Soldiers* (Little, Brown, 2004)

al-Azmeh, Aziz, *Islams and Modernities* (Verso, 1995)

Barakat, Sultan, *After the Conflict – Reconstructions and Redevelopment in the Aftermath of War* (I.B.Tauris, 2005)

Batatu, Hanna, *The Old Social Classes and the Revolutionary Movements of Iraq* (Princeton University Press, 1978)

Batatu, Hanna, *Iraq's Underground Shia Movements: Characters, Causes and Prospects* (MERIP Reports: Islam and Politics no. 102, January 1982)

Bell, Gertrude, *The Letters of Gertrude Bell* (Penguin, 1987)

Bilal A. Wahab, 'How Iraqi oil smuggling greases violence', *Middle East Quarterly* xiii/4 (Fall 2006)

Budge, Ernest Wallace, *By Nile and Tigris, A Narrative of Journeys in Egypt and Mesopotamia on Behalf of the British Museum Between the Years 1886 and 1913* (AMS Press, 1975)

Bulloch, John and Morris, Harvey, *Saddam's War* (Faber and Faber, 1991)

Catherwood, Christopher, *Winston's Folly, Imperialism and the Creation of Modern Iraq* (Constable & Robinson, 2004)

Chatterjee, Pratap, *Iraq, Inc. A Profitable Occupation* (Seven Stories Press, 2004)

Chehab, Zaki, *Iraq Ablaze – Inside the Insurgency* (I.B.Tauris, 2005)

Chestnot, Christian et Malbrunot, Georges, *L'Irak de Saddam Hussein, Portrait Total* (Editions 1, 2003)

Cockburn, Andrew and Cockburn, Patrick, *Out of the Ashes* (HarperCollins, 1999)

Cole, Juan, *Sacred Space: Holy War, The Politics, Culture and History of Shi'ite Islam* (I.B.Tauris, 2002)

Cole, Juan, 'The United States and Shi'ite religious factions in post-Ba'athist Iraq', *Middle East Journal* lvii/4 (Autumn 2003)

Cole, Juan and Keddie, Nikki (eds), *Shi'ism and Social Protest* (Yale University Press, 1986)

Cordesman, Anthony and Obaid, Nawaf, *Saudi Militants in Iraq: Assessment and Kingdom's Response* (Center for Strategic and International Studies (CSIS), 19 September 2005)

Dabrowska, Karen, *Iraq, The Bradt Travel Guide* (Bradt, 2002)

Dizard, John, 'How Ahmed Chalabi conned the neocons', *Salon* (May 2004)

Dodge, Toby, *Inventing Iraq: The Failure of Nation Building and a History Denied* (Columbia University Press and Hurst & Co., 2003)

Dodge, Toby, *Iraq's Future: The Aftermath of Regime Change* (Routledge, 2005)

Emirates Center for Strategic Studies & Research, *Iraq – Reconstruction and Future Role* (I.B.Tauris, 2004)

Ende, W. and Brunner, R. (eds), *Twelver Shi'ism in Modern Times* (Brill, 2000)

Ferguson, Niall, *Empire* (Allen Lane, 2003)

Fernea Robert A. and Louis, Wm. Roger, *The Iraqi Revolution of 1958, The Old Social Classes Revisited* (I.B.Tauris, 1991)

Galbraith, Peter, 'Iraq: Bush's Islamic republic', *New York Review of Books* (August 2005)

Gemzell, Martin (ed.), *Focus Iraq* (Stockholm, 2002). Available at: http://www. swedishtrade.se/irak/docfile/6951_Iraq_Report.pdf

Hadad, Sama, *The Development of Shi'i Islamic Political Theory* (2005, provided by the author)

Hallaq, Wael W.B., 'Was the gate of Ijtihad closed?', *International Journal of Middle Eastern Studies* xvi/1 (1984)

Hamzeh, Ahmad Nizar, *In the Path of Hizbollah* (Syracuse University Press, 2004)

Hefner, Robert W. (ed.), *Remaking Muslim Politics: Pluralism, Contestation, Democratization* (Princeton University Press, 2005)

Hiro, Dilip, *Neighbours Not Friends: Iraq and Iran after the Gulf Wars* (Routledge, 2001)

Hitti, Philip, *History of the Arabs* (Macmillan Education Ltd, 1970)

International Crisis Group Middle East Briefings and Reports

    Iraq Backgrounder: What Lies Beneath, No. 6, 1 October 2002

    Voices from the Iraqi Street, No. 3, 4 December 2002

    Radical Islam in Iraqi Kurdistan: The Mouse That Roared? No. 4, 7 February 2003

    Iraq Policy Briefing: Is There an Alternative to War? No. 9, 24 February 2003

    War in Iraq: What's Next for the Kurds? No. 10, 19 March 2003

    War in Iraq: Political Challenges after the Conflict, No. 11, 25 March 2003

    War in Iraq: Managing Humanitarian Relief, No. 12, 27 March 2003

    Baghdad: A Race against the Clock, No. 6, 11 June 2003

    Governing Iraq, No. 17, 25 August 2003

    Iraq's Shiites under Occupation, No. 8, 9 September 2003

    Iraq's Constitutional Challenge, No. 19, 13 November 2003

    Iraq: Building a New Security Structure, No. 20, 23 December 2003

    Iraq's Kurds: Toward an Historic Compromise? No. 26, 8 April 2004

    Iraq's Transition: On a Knife Edge, No. 27, 27 April 2004

    Reconstructing Iraq, No. 30, 2 September 2004

    Iraq: Can Local Governance Save Central Government? No. 33, 27 October 2004

    What Can the US Do in Iraq? No. 34, 22 December 2004

    Iraq: Allaying Turkey's Fears Over Kurdish Ambitions, No. 35, 26 January 2005

    Understanding Islamism, No. 37, 2 March 2005

    Iran in Iraq: How Much Influence, No. 38, 21 March 2005

Bahrain's Sectarian Challenge, No. 40, 6 May 2005

The Next Iraqi War? Sectarianism and Civil Conflict, No. 52, 27 February 2006

After Baker-Hamilton: What to Do in Iraq, No. 60, 19 December 2006

Keiko Sakai, 'Modernity and tradition in the Islamic movements in Iraq: continuity and discontinuity in the role of the "Ulama"', *Arab Studies Quarterly* xxiii/1 (Winter 2001)

Kienle, Eberhard, *Ba'ath Versus Ba'ath – The Conflict Between Syria and Iraq* (I.B.Tauris, 1990)

Lewis, Bernard, *The Assassins, A Radical Sect in Islam* (Weidenfeld & Nicolson, 1996)

Longrigg, Stephen H., *Iraq, 1900 to 1950: A Political, Social and Economic History* (Oxford University Press, 1953)

Lyon, Wallace, *Kurds, Arabs and Britons – The Memoir of Col. W.A. Lyon in Kurdistan, 1918–1945* (I.B.Tauris, 2001)

Makdisi, G., 'Muslim institutions of learning in eleventh-century Baghdad', *Bulletin of the School of Oriental and African Studies* xxiv (1961)

Makiya, Kanan, *Republic of Fear: The Politics of Modern Iraq* (University of California Press, 1998)

Makiya, Kanan, *The Monument – Art and Vulgarity in Saddam Hussein's Iraq* (I.B.Tauris, 2003)

Mallat, Chibli, *The Renewal of Islamic Law: Muhammad Baqer as-Sadr, Najaf and the Shi'i International* (Cambridge University Press, 1993)

Mallat, Chibli, 'From Islamic to Middle Eastern law – a restatement of the field', *American Journal of Comparative Law* 52/1 pp. 209–286 (Winter 2004)

Matar, Fuad, *Saddam Hussein, The Man, The Cause and The Future* (Third World Centre, 1981)

Mufti, Malik, *Sovereign Creations, Pan-Arabism and Political Order in Syria and Iraq* (Cornell University Press, 1996)

al-Musawi, Muhsin, *Reading Iraq – Culture and Power in Conflict* (I.B.Tauris, 2006)

Nakash, Yitzhak, *The Shi'is of Iraq* (Princeton University Press, 1994)

Nakash, Yitzhak, 'The Shi'ites and the future of Iraq', *Foreign Affairs* 82/4 (August 2003)

Philips, Sarah, *Cracks in the Yemeni System* (Middle East Report, July 2005)

Polk, William, *Understanding Iraq* (I.B.Tauris, 2005)

Randall, Jonathan, *After Such Knowledge, What Forgiveness: My Encounters with Kurdistan* (Westview Press, 1999)

Ra'uf, 'Adil, *Muhammad Sadiq al-Sadr: marja'iyat al-maydan: mashru'a althaghayyiri wa-waqa'i' al-ightiyal* [*Muhammad Sadiq al-Sadr: The Religious Leadership of the Arena: His Transformational Plan and the Facts of the Assassination*] (Damascus: Markaz al-'Iraqi li'l-I'lam wa-al-Dirasat, 1999)

Ritter, Scott and Hersh, Seymour, *Iraq Confidential – The Untold Story of America's Intelligence Conspiracy* (I.B.Tauris, 2005)

Rodenbeck, Max, *Cairo – The City Victorious* (Picador, 1980)

Roy, Arundhati, *The Ordinary Person's Guide to Empire* (Flamingo, 2004)

Ruthven, Malise, *Freya Stark in Iraq and Kuwait* (Garnet Publishing, 1994)

Schulze, Kirsten (ed.), *Nationalism, Minorities and Diaspora: Identities and Rights in the Middle East* (I.B.Tauris, 1996)

Shanahan, Rodger, 'The Islamic Da'wa party: past development and future prospects', *Middle East Review of International Affairs* viii/2 (June 2004)

Sluglett, Marion and Sluglett, Peter, *Iraq Since 1958 – From Revolution to Dictatorship* (I.B.Tauris, 2001)

Storrs, Ronald, *Orientations* (Ivor Nicholson & Watson, 1937)

Tarbush, Mohammad A., *The Role of the Army in Politics: A Case Study of Iraq to 1941* (Kegan Paul International, 1982)

Tripp, Charles, *A History of Iraq* (Cambridge University Press, 2000)

Van Bruinessen, Martin, *Agha, Sheikh and State* (Zed Books, 1992)

Walker, David, Comptroller General of the United States, *Stabilising Iraq: An Assessment of the Security Situation in Iraq* (US Government Accountability Office, September 2006)

Wallach, Janet, *Desert Queen, The Extraordinary Life of Gertrude Bell* (Weidenfeld & Nicolson, 1996)

Wiley, Joyce N., *The Islamic Movement of Iraqi Shi'ites* (Boulder, CO: Lynne Rienner, 1992)

Notes

INTRODUCTION AND ACKNOWLEDGEMENTS

1 Both Sunnis and Shia believe in the centrality of the Qur'an as the word of God, his final Prophet, Mohammed, and with some variation the Sayings of Sunna, or Tradition, attributed to him. Mainstream Sunnis and Shia share the basic prescriptions on the consumption of pork, wine, and the necessity of fasting, praying, pilgrimage and alms-giving.

2 Philip Hitti, *History of the Arabs* (Macmillan Education Ltd, 1970), pp.470–1.

3 Only the infamous aberration of Nizar al-Aziz's blue-eyed son, Hakim, tarnishes the Fatimid record of communal harmony. Born to a Russian Melkite mother, he demolished the Holy Sepulchre in Jerusalem and forced Christians to dangle crosses from their necks, and Jews bells. In a fit of self-delusion, he declared himself God incarnate, in the process triggering the birth of the Druze.

4 Hitti: *The Arabs*, pp.444–5.

5 Max Rodenbeck, *Cairo – The City Victorious* (Picador, 1980), p.135.

6 The Assassins began as a school of Ismailis, an offshoot of Shiism, who built a string of mountain fortresses running from Almut near Tehran to the Anti-Lebanon. Acolytes recruited as erstwhile suicide-bombers were reputedly doped with hash, prompting their Christian and Sunni detractors to dub them hashashiyin, or assassins.

7 The Shia practice of *ijtihad*'s tendency to self-sustaining intellectual vitality was consolidated by the outcome of the Shia controversy in the seventeenth and eighteenth centuries, in which the Usuli school, championing *ijtihad*, defeated the literalist and anti-rationalist Akhbari school.

8 Hitti: *The Arabs*, p.488.

9 Quoted, Malise Ruthven, *Freya Stark in Iraq and Kuwait* (Garnet Publishing, 1994), p.48.

10 Like Twelver Shias, the Alawites believe in the 12 Imams. After the twelfth Imam disappeared, Abu Shu'ayb Muhammad ibn Nusayr (d.874) claimed his mantle, thus giving birth to the movement, otherwise known as Nusayris. The Imams are seen as pre-existent heavenly spirits around God's throne who later descended to earth in physical bodies to lead humans in praise back to God. Unlike normative Islam, Alawites believe in reincarnation. From the first, they sought alliances with the Shia against Sunni persecution. Ravaged by Saladin for allying with the Crusaders, they found brief respite under the Mongol conquest of Aleppo, only to be ravaged again when the city was regained by the Mamluk Sultan Baybars, who forced them to replace their castles with mosques. The Persian Nawruz, or New Year, and the Mihrajan are also celebrated by the Alawis, revealing strong Persian influences.

CHAPTER 1

11 Denis Halliday's resignation speech, 30 September 1998.
12 Interview, Baghdad, February 2003.
13 Interview, Baghdad, November, 2003. Nadhmi attributed his unusual margin of independence to an act of charity he performed as a student at Cairo University in 1959. Nadhmi, then a Baath party member, offered his bed to a 21-year-old Saddam, who had fled Iraq after a botched attempt on the life of Iraq's first president, Abdel Karim al-Qassim. The two men went on to study law together at Cairo University. Ever since, he had straddled the thin line between being Saddam's most artful apologist and most subtle critic.
14 International Crisis Group, *Voices from the Iraqi Street*, December 2002. 'With surprising candour,' she wrote, 'a significant number of those Iraqis interviewed expressed their view that, if such a change required an American-led attack, they would support it.'
15 Interview, Baghdad, February 2003.
16 Interview, Baghdad, February 2003.
17 Interview, Baghdad, March 2003.
18 Omar was the second caliph (*khalifa*) in Sunni Islam. He, along with his predecessor Abu Bakr and successor Othman, are considered usurpers by Shiites.

CHAPTER 2

19 Iraqi state television, March 2003. Hussein Sadr subsequently became the Americans' favourite cleric, almost alone amongst Ayatollahs publicly meeting with US officials, including US Secretary of State, Colin Powell.

20 The Iraqi authorities claimed to have uncovered a telegram allegedly sent by Ayatollah Khomeini to al-Sadr naming him as 'responsible for the Islamic Revolution in Iraq'.

21 Until 1965, the leaders of the Arab Socialist Ba'th Party were Shias, most notably Fuad al-Rikabi.

22 In the mid-1970s, civilians received a subsidy of 2,500 Iraqi dinars [$7,500] per wife, military personnel 4,000 ID [$12,000].

23 Interview, Baghdad, February 2003.

24 See the interview with a Mahdi Army commander, *AFP*, 30 November 2006. Sadr's followers were prepared, he said, for 'revolution against the rulers, had it not been for the conspiracy which killed Muhammad Sadiq al-Sadr in 1999'.

25 Interview, Baghdad, March 2003.

26 Interview, Baghdad, March 2003.

CHAPTER 3

27 Interview, Amman, March 2003.

28 Mudhar Shawqat, a Canadian-based businessman, and Sherif Ali bin Hussein, a Hashemite scion who aspired to revive the monarchy.

29 Under the Iraqi monarchy, the Chalabis owned Iraq's largest bank, the Rafidain, and Ahmed's uncle, Abdel Hadi al-Chalabi, was speaker of parliament. When Iraq's monarchy was toppled and 42 royals slaughtered, the Chalabis fled the country with much of the monarchy's assets.

30 Robert Dreyfus, 'Tinker, Tailor, Neo-Con, Spy', *The American Prospect*, 18 November 2002.

31 Interview, Amman, May 2003.

32 Interview with the driver, Baghdad, April 2003.

33 Only on one occasion, following the defection of one of the most senior members of Saddam's inner circle to Jordan, did King Hussein break ranks. In a speech welcoming Saddam Hussein's son-in-law, Kamal Hussein, he publicly linked his own family's history to that of Iraq's majority sect:

    'As for us, the tombs of our martyrs are studding the land of Iraq.... This has been our history since the days of Ali bin Abu Talib [the Prophet's son-in-law venerated by Shias], his sons, Hassan and Hussein... and finally in the era of King Faisal II and his family, whose precious blood flowed in Karbala. I have no ambitions other than to see soon Iraq emerge from the total darkness and its long night of suffering to see the dawn of its freedom and liberation from all the causes of suffering.'

34 Interview, Amman, May 2003.

35 The stock-markets in Gulf states marked all-time highs in anticipation of the spoils of a US-led war. At a time of global economic downturn, Kuwait's index in 2003 rose 22 per cent on the previous year. In Dubai, an investment manager launched a $50 million Iraq Fund two months ahead of war to acquire prime real estate in Baghdad, whose prices were expected to soar after a US takeover.

36 *The Economist*, 11 July 2002.

37 Interview, Jordanian security official, Amman, March 2003.

CHAPTER 4

38 Hadi al-Amiri, secretary-general of the Iraqi Badr organisation, quoted in *Sharq al-Awsat*, 25 April 2005.

39 Interview, Amman, March 2003.

40 Interview, Baghdad, April 2003.

41 Judith Miller, 'Clerics seek factories', *The New York Times*, 14 April 2003.

42 Interview, Baghdad, June 2003.

43 The paramilitary force was one of the few to actively defend southern Baghdad against US troops, who responded by dropping yellow packets of cluster bombs.

44 According to the registrar, the bodies were gunned down in March 1991 in the aftermath of the Shia uprising. A survivor said the Republican Guard had arrived at dawn with megaphones and summoned all adult males to assemble without delay on the main Baghdad to Karbala road. Following a roll call, 17 had been randomly shot, and the remainder herded into 40 buses parked at the side of the road. When those were full to capacity, soldiers had flagged down empty juggernauts to transport the rest. Further up the road, the freight was blindfolded, machine-gunned, and buried by bulldozer.

45 Interview, CPA religious affairs advisor, Said Hakki, Baghdad, October 2003.

46 Charles Clover, 'Abdelmajid al-Khoi returns to Najaf', *Financial Times*, 7 April 2003.

47 Interview, March 2003.

CHAPTER 5

48 The Badr Brigades took their name from the battle in 624, when the Prophet Mohammed led a force of 300 followers to victory against a far larger army of pagans from Mecca.

49 In return for generous state scholarships, Iran expected its novices to submit to its religious authority. Shia opposition groups across the Arab world found

their funding depended on recognition of the Velayat Motlagheh, Farsi, for the supreme cleric's absolute and unchallenged rule.

50 Not all the returning Shias were Iranian sympathisers. Jawad al-Khalisi returned from Britain to Baghdad in May 2003 to reopen a college the Baath closed in the early 1980s. His anti-coalition message won widespread support.

51 Interview, Karbala, May 2003.

52 The force was located in the Kurdish north as the remnant of an international force monitoring the ceasefire of Turkey's Kurdish separatists. The Anglo-American component had withdrawn after six years of ceasefire, leaving Turkey's 'liaison force' to continue alone.

53 Interview, July 2003.

54 He echoed a speech made by Abdullah's father, King Hussein, in 1996 in which he emphasised his 'ancestral responsibilities' towards Iraq: 'I was [King Faisal II's] deputy and heir to the Presidency of the Arab Union that brought the two countries together.'

55 The attack was launched by a particularly bombastic British secretary of state for war. 'I do not understand this squeamishness about the use of gas. I am strongly in favour of using poisoned gas against uncivilised tribes [to] spread a lively terror,' wrote Winston Churchill in a 1919 memorandum. Christopher Catherwood, *Winston's Folly* (Avalon Publishing Group, 2004), pp.186–7.

56 Interview, September 2003.

57 Interview, November 2003.

58 When Iraq's cash-strapped treasury protested, Jordan replied they were being held to cover Iraq's debts to Jordanian companies, minus a 33 per cent commission to the state. A rush of inflated claims – and withdrawals – quickly followed.

59 Interview, March 2003.

60 UN Iraq Office, Security Update, 20 September 2003.

61 Presidential statement, 11 November 2003.

CHAPTER 6

62 American wars for democracy were not new, and were rooted in part in America's own revolution. The British embassy in Washington recorded a conversation between US President Woodrow Wilson and the British Foreign Secretary Sir Edward Grey in 1914 regarding a military coup in Mexico that had much displeased Washington:

'Suppose you have to intervene, what then?'

'Make 'em vote and live by their decisions.'

'But suppose they will not so live?'

'We'll go in and make 'em vote again.'

'And keep this up for 200 years?' asked he.

'Yes,' said I. 'The United States will be here for 200 years and it can continue to shoot 'em for that little space till they learn to vote and to rule themselves.'

63 Nicole Winfield, 'US, Iraqis seek to form government', *Associated Press*, 15 April 2003.

64 Senior staff suggested that relations between the military and their civilian subordinates were so dire that Garner's team was deliberately starved of proper communications. Timothy Garner, a former ambassador to Sudan who ran Iraq's Industry Ministry under Garner, blamed 'the military communications staff where, with one or two notable exceptions, the lack of vision was exceeded only by the lack of competence... and cell-phone contractor MCI, who did not produce a functioning telephone during the entire six weeks of Garner's tenure, crippling our mission. A few phones finally appeared on June 3.' Timothy Carney, 'We're getting in our way', *The Washington Post*, 22 June 2003.

65 Testimony to US Senate Committee hearing, April 2003.

66 Interview, Baghdad, May 2003.

67 Bremer, 'The advice Clinton should have followed, Op-ed', *Wall Street Journal*, 5 August 1996.

68 Interview, Dead Sea, Jordan, July 2003.

69 Interview, Baghdad, August 2003.

70 *Newsnight*, BBC2, 19 March 2004.

71 For instance, he told the US Congress: 'I firmly believe that haste [to establish an Iraqi government] would be a mistake. Iraq has spent a quarter century under a dictatorship as absolute and abusive as that of Nazi Germany.' Testimony to US Congressional Committee, September 2003.

72 In time, Bremer came to recognise the error of his one-conquest-fits-all policy. 'In a psychological way, the [German] people understood they'd gone into total war and been defeated ... The difference here is, what was defeated was a regime, and the Iraqi people have quite understandably a distaste for the occupation.' Michael Hirsch, *Newsweek*, January 2004.

73 UNICEF's Geoffrey Keele said that he 'hope[d] to have the remainder 52 million ready by the end of November [2003].' Interview, September 2003.

74 Even America's coalition partners protested that the decision aggravated the chaos. 'A year was lost in creating a capable Iraqi security sector,' snapped Bremer's British counterpart, Jeremy Greenstock, on his return to Britain. *The Economist*, 6 May 2004.

75 *The New Yorker*, 24 November 2003.

76 Interview, Baghdad, October 2003.

77 Richard Sale, 'Anti-Baath edicts criticised for fuelling insurgency', *UPI*, 21 November 2003.

78 Interview, Najaf, May 2003.

79 William Booth, 'US halts elections throughout Iraq', *The Washington Post*, 28 June 2003.

80 Interview, Basra, June 2003.

81 Interview, Basra, June 2003.

82 A full text of the speech can be found at http://www.guardian.co.uk/politics/2003/may/29/iraq.iraq1

83 Ethnically, the Council also aspired to be representative: 68 per cent were Arabs and 24 per cent were Kurds, the remaining 8 per cent reflecting one Assyrian and one Turkoman.

84 Interview, Baghdad, August 2003.

85 While three Americans manned the education ministry, 58 ran his media operations. Many were card-carrying Republicans. His official spokesman, Dan Senor, had previously worked with the Carlyle Group, an investment firm with Bush family ties, and as former press secretary to Republican senator, Spencer Abraham, who became Bush's Energy Secretary.

86 CPA Public Affairs Office List, 28 May 2004.

87 Multinational Forces Public Affairs release, 20 January 2005.

88 Soldiers would also post pictures of mutilated corpses to such websites as Nowthatsfucked.com accompanied by such captions as 'What all Iraqis should look like' in exchange for access to web porn. See Chris Thompson, 'The War pornographers', *eastbayexpress.com*, 21 September 2005.

89 Christopher Varhola, 'Letters from the front, American challenges in post-conflict Iraq', *AmericanDiplomacy.org*, 27 March 2004.

90 Pentagon press briefing, 28 September 2003.

91 Gertrude Bell, quoted by Robert Fisk, 'Iraq, 1917', *Independent*, 17 June 2004.

CHAPTER 7

92 Speech by Bremer, attended by the author, Dead Sea, 23 June 2003.

93 Presentation attended by the author, Baghdad, 21 September 2003.

94 Presentation attended by the author, Baghdad, 21 September 2003.

95 *Newsnight*, BBC2, 19 March 2004.

96 Interview, Baghdad, September 2003.

97 In real terms, the Congressional supplemental amounted to about a sixth of the Marshall Plan's value. It was intended to pay for a spending plan, which included the construction of 8,000 prison cells at the cost of $50,000 each.

98 UN efforts to hold the Coalition to account for its oil expenditures proved even less exacting than under the oil-for-food programme. It established an

International Advisory and Monitoring Board, mandated by the UN Resolution 1483 to scrutinise expenditures, but this was largely dismissed by the coalition. 'If we have to deal with 2000 UN auditors,' griped David Oliver, the burly Pentagon accountant drafting the CPA budget, 'we will have no money or time left for Iraq.' Interview, Baghdad, September 2003.

99 Occasional protests went unheeded. After the CPA awarded a $283 million contract for a power station – the largest single civilian project approved by the CPA – to a little-known Texan company, Southeast Texas Industrial Services Inc., without public tender, the UK representative [Chris Segar] suggested that 'projects funded by the DFI [the Development Fund for Iraq, where oil revenues were deposited] should normally be open to international tender.' Minutes of the Program Review Board, 15 February 2004.

100 Quarterly Report of the Office of the Inspector General, CPA, 30 October 2004.

101 Testimony by CPA senior aviation official to Congress, 14 February 2005.

102 Order 37 lowered corporate tax rate from 40 per cent to a flat 15 per cent. Order 40 granted access to Iraq for foreign banks with the rights to repatriate all profits untaxed. And, most radical of all, Order 39 abolished restrictions on foreign investment.

103 On 22 May 2003, President Bush issued an executive order 13303, 'Protecting the Development Fund for Iraq and Certain Other Property in Which Iraq Has An Interest.' It stated that 'any attachment, judgment... or other judicial process is prohibited, and shall be deemed null and void, with respect to the following: (a) the Development Fund for Iraq, and (b) all Iraqi petroleum and petroleum products.'

104 The list of contractors contained many of the leading contributors to US political party funds: Bechtel, a construction company based in San Francisco, assumed effective responsibility for the Ministry of Public Works; Stevedoring Services of America administered Iraq's only Gulf port, Um Qasr. Washington Group won a $110 million contract to start to revamp the electricity sector. BearingPoint, the sister business consultancy of the CPA's auditors KPMG, won the $80 million contract to plan the privatisation of the public sector. US bankers JP Morgan Chase headed the consortium managing the Trade Bank to procure government purchases. USAID hived out the task of Health ministry planning to Boston-based Abt Associates and local government to Research Triangle Institute International (RTI) of North Carolina. Some had close ties to the US administration involved in the tendering, particularly the office of Douglas Feith, the Under Secretary of Defence for Policy, who oversaw reconstruction. Feith's deputy at the Pentagon, Christopher Ryan Henry, had been SAIC's vice-president six weeks prior to the invasion. Frank Dall, the director of CAII, was a former head of USAID's Middle East programme. The

vice-president of Abt Associates, which won a $40 million USAID contract for reform of the health ministry, had been USAID's mission head in Russia.

105 Charles Clover, 'Education minister hits at USAID over textbook policy', *Financial Times*, 24 November 2003.

106 Open-ended and infinitely expandable, KBR's commissions ranged from cleaning the portaloos to building military supermarkets in Kuwait the size of aircraft hangers and hiring the Iraq Survey Group to hunt for Iraq's missing weapons of mass destruction. Known as the Logistics Civil Augmentation Program, or Logcap, the contract was the brainchild of Richard Cheney, who as Bush senior's defence secretary, had awarded his future company the first contract after the 1991 Kuwait war.

107 In addition, KBR could reap far more in such overheads as insurance and travel. According to an analysis in the *Winston-Salem Journal*, KBR could charge commissions of $850,000 on a single liaison officer costing an annual $350,000.

108 Interview, Baghdad, October 2003. Some US officers, however, suspected that the contractors had other motives. General Janis Karpinski, who ran Iraq's prisons, complained that 'sub-contracting work is the weakest part of the system. Why should other [non-Iraqi] nationalities care if things go wrong if they are here for only two years? Iraqis care because they see work as a way of getting the country on its feet.' She knew of 'no single security incident' involving Iraqi contractors. She was dismissed following exposure of the Abu Ghraib torture scandal, perpetrated in part by US contractors.

109 Interview, Baghdad, October 2003.

110 Interview, Basra, June 2003.

111 Interview, Amman, November 2004.

112 KBR was fined a fraction of 1 per cent of its $8 billion earnings from Iraq for excessively hiking the price of its oil imports.

113 A senior Iraqi finance official seeking to monitor the trade estimated that a third of Iraq's fuel imports were being recycled. Interview, Amman, November 2004.

114 'The high price of gasoline for Iraq', *NBC News*, 5 November 2003.

115 Donald Rumsfeld, 'Help Iraq to Help Itself', *Wall Street Journal*, 29 September 2003.

116 KBR benefited from the throwaway culture, since under its contract it earned a commission for buying replacements. When a convoy commander, David Wilson, protested at the wanton dumping of $85,000 Mercedes trucks to his KBR seniors, he was fired. Testimony submitted to Congressional Committee on Government Reform, 22 July 2004. See http://www.corpwatch.org/article.php?id=11373

CHAPTER 8

117 Interview with Ali Rubai, secretary to one of Najaf's four Grand Ayatollahs, Sheikh Fayadh, Najaf, May 2003.

118 Statement, 18 April 2003, issued by his London office.

119 Interview with Michael Samanov, deputy commander of the Marine battalion in Karbala, May 2003.

120 Interview, Najaf, May 2003.

121 Interview, Said Hakki, Kuwait, January 2004.

122 His furious Kurdish faction leader, Massoud Barzani, promptly recalled him to the Kurdish capital, Irbil, and banned him from public engagements, fearing that in elections a Shia majority would stymie their aspirations for self-rule. Interview, Abd al-Rahman, Baghdad, September 2003.

123 Quoted in an interview with *The Washington Post*, 'Occupation Forces Halt Elections Throughout Iraq', 28 June 2003.

124 Interview, Basra, January 2006. So servile had Whitehall grown to the White House, however, that as soon as the Financial Times published the interview, D'Angelo was forced to retract his statement. The governor, John Bourne of Dhi Qar province, was removed.

125 Interview, Karbala, March 2004.

126 Interview, Karbala, March 2004.

127 Interview, Sheikh Majid Shabib, February 2004.

128 Berry found limited support from the local branch of the Research Triangle Institute (RTI), which had a USAID contract to assist local governance. 'Mr Berry opposed local elections because he saw too much meddling from religious leaders,' said its regional office director. 'People are born to be free, including from religious clerics who want to control people's lives.' Interview, Karbala, March 2004.

CHAPTER 9

129 Interview, Ahmed Chalabi, Baghdad, November 2003.

130 'The Americans played a big role in this new sectarianism,' said Ismael Zayer, the editor of the daily *al-Sabah al-Jedid*. 'They characterise the Iraqi people by their sect. They will ask you: "Are you a Sunni or a Shiite?" Why are they asking this question? Now it has become a trend.' Quoted *After Baker-Hamilton: What to Do in Iraq*, International Crisis Group Middle East Report No. 60, 19 December 2006.

131 Under the monarchy Iraq's first 11 prime ministers and all but only one of its top 60 officers were Sunni. The republic continued the tradition: two Sunni

governorates, Tikrit and Anbar, alone spawned four presidents, a host of prime ministers, and thousands of senior security personnel.

132 After Badran's defection as an Iraqi diplomat in Moscow, Allawi had made him a seventh member of the party's politburo.

133 Lest anyone accuse him of sectarianism, however, he chose a Sunni restaurateur, Kamal al-Gailani, as finance minister, and installed a bodyguard to keep watch as his secretary.

134 In the provinces, nepotism was even more prevalent. The US-appointed governor of Babel was reported to have advanced 21 relations into local government, a total only bettered by the British-administered governor of Meysan.

135 Interview, Governing Council spokesman, Hamid Kifai, Baghdad, April 2004: q.v. Pamela Constable, 'New flag meets with Iraqi disapproval', *Washington Post*, 26 April 2004.

136 Interview, member of the Governing Council's Finance Committee, January 2004.

137 The central licence covering Baghdad went to Orascom, owned by Egyptian magnate Naguib Sawiris in alliance with Nadhmi Auchi, an Iraqi dubbed Saddam's banker in the western press and the 11th richest man in Britain: q.v. Nicolas Pelham, 'How the contest for Iraq s mobile telephone contracts sank into disarray', *Financial Times*, 26 November 2003.

138 Interview, Louay Mirza, Amman, December 2004. Mirza, a confidante of Uday's, had fled Baghdad after a drunken night at a Baghdad night-club degenerated into a shoot-out between Uday's followers and those of his uncle, Watban.

139 Interviews, Oil Ministry officials and Chalabi advisors, Baghdad, London and Amman, 2004. After the war, Mortaza posed as a well-endowed middleman for London-based broker, Projector, and by November 2003 he wielded such influence over Chalabi's men that according to a senior Iraqi oil official, he had secured the dismissal of the head of the State Oil Marketing Organisation, Mohammed Jibbouri, with whom he had quarrelled over the terms of a pre-war oil shipment for a European oil company.

140 Interviews, Badran, Lakhani, security contractors and US Treasury Department, December 2004 and January 2005. The 20-tonne cargo of cash was smuggled by plane to Lebanon, with the help of Custerbattles LLC, a US security company contracted to protect Baghdad Airport, only to be impounded by the Lebanese authorities. After Badran's own intervention, the Lebanese were persuaded to return the money, and the advance to Lakhani reissued. Lakhani was subsequently blacklisted by the Pentagon for submitting an invoice for $157,000 for constructing a helicopter pad for coalition forces in Mosul that he never built.

141 Interview, former business associates, December 2004.

142 Interview, senior Iraqi finance official, Amman, December 2004.

143 RAG won further contracts from the Interior Ministry, then headed by Sabah's brother-in-law, Badran. Another of Sabah's business partners was Sudhir Jaya, a Singaporean merchant, who built his wealth trading with pre-war Iraq, and other such savoury regimes as Myanmar. After forming a company, the two men used their political and economic ties to win payment for lapsed oil-for-food deals and for lifting oil at discretionary rates. 'You know someone who draws a salary of $100 or $200 a month at SOMO [the State Oil Marketing Organisation] can see the benefit,' said Jaya's office manager, Ramesh Kudva. 'It comes down to price.' Interviews, Sabah Allawi, Kudya, and RAG employees, December 2004 and January 2005.

144 Interview, Baghdad, May 2004.

145 Interview, Chalabi advisor, September 2003. He returned to London in 2004.

146 Interview, editor Iraqi Media Network, April 2004.

147 Interview, Baghdad, September 2003.

148 Interview, Entifadh Qanbar, Baghdad, September 2003.

149 Bremer's deputy, Ambassador Richard Jones, had disclosed in Kuwait in January 2004 that four foreign banks had won licences to operate in Baghdad, but days later only three were announced.

150 The Governing Council commissioned KPMG to conduct the first of a series of investigations, though they proved less cooperative when the same firm began delving into Iraq's post-war financial affairs.

151 Interview, Baghdad, December 2003.

152 They included parliament speaker Saadoun Hammadi, information minister Mohammed Said al-Sahhaf, deputy president Taha Mohieddin Maarouf, presidential advisor on weapons of mass destruction General Amer al-Saadi, and the post-1991 prime minister Muhammad Hamza Zubaydi.

153 Moreover, by nominating the Badr commander Abdel Aziz al-Hakim as one of the Governing Council's nine presidents, Bremer ensured that from the first the Badr Brigades were inside his new state.

154 In the words of Abdel Aziz Hakim, Hakim's brother: 'The occupation force is primarily responsible for the pure blood that was spilt.' Hakim combined the two roles of Governing Council representative and Badr Brigade commander. Interview, Baghdad, August 2003.

155 Interview, local Baath party leader, Najaf, August 2003.

156 Interview, Najaf, August 2003.

157 Interview, Baghdad, October 2003.

158 Interview, Saadoun, December 2003. Within six months the company had upped the value of its contract from $40 million to over $100 million.

159 Interview, Baghdad, December 2003.

160 Interview, Baghdad, July 2004.

161 Interview, al-Jaber, Amman, December 2004.

162 Interview, Sumaidy, January 2004. With western Iraq slipping evermore into insurgent hands, other council members spoke in favour of restricting polling to the more stable north and south – in effect a temporary disenfranchisement of the Sunni Arab west, where the Council's support was most negligible.

163 Interview, Rubaie, January 2004. He continued: 'We have international recognition. We have set up committees. We pass legislation. Why should we disband ourselves? It does not make sense.'

164 Such favouritism was not exclusively Shia. The payroll of the irrigation ministry, a preserve of the Patriotic Union of Kurdistan, reportedly mushroomed from 25,000 to 200,000. Interview, irrigation ministry official, Baghdad, December 2003.

165 Interview, Kubaysi, October 2003. Shias responded that the Saddam regime had built the mosques as Salafi outposts to humiliate Shias in their holy city. Under new masters, the mosques were quickly renamed Fatima Zohra, after the Prophet's daughter who is revered by Shias, instead of Omar, a Sunni Caliph whom Shias revile.

166 'Bremer realises they [the Iraqis] have to have good relations with all their neighbours,' said a senior US official. Interview, Baghdad, December 2003.

167 If Tehran could recognise other Arab states led by American clients, argued Iran's Supreme Leader Ali Khamanei, it could recognise the Governing Council.

168 Interview, Baghdad, November 2003.

CHAPTER 10

169 Friday sermon by Sheikh Ahmad Abdel Ghafur al-Samarrai, April 2004.

170 Interview with al-Samarrai, April 2004.

171 Interview, Baghdad, March 2004.

172 Initially, the regime had resisted the influx. Mohammed Madhloum, an Iraqi Airforce pilot from Ramadi, who had emerged as a Salafi leader in the 1990s, was captured and killed, and a subsequent uprising by his tribe, Dulaim, suppressed.

173 Interview, Baghdad, June 2004.

174 Interview with Lieutenant Colonel Barry Johnson charged with Detainee Operations at Abu Ghraib prison, Baghdad, June 2004. Subsequently, however, limits were placed on free speech in the prison, and the megaphone withdrawn. 'Its unauthorised use to foment discontent caused him to lose this privilege,' apologised Johnson subsequently, but he noted that the megaphone could still be used to hail mealtimes 'and other sanctioned activities'.

175 Interview with PUK officials and Ansar al-Islam supporters, London, December 2001.

176 After one of its more celebrated sons blew himself up in Tel Aviv's Dolphinarium Disco in the summer of 2001, Islamist groups in the town held a memorial.

177 Interview with Afghan veteran and Bin Laden associate, London, May 2004.

178 Interview with Jordanian Islamists, Amman, April 2004.

179 Interview with Jordanian prime minister Ali Abu al-Ragheb, January 2003.

180 Interview with coach Andy Hill, Sheffield, November 2003.

181 A year later in Ramadi, US marines found another 25-year-old Briton, who claimed to be pursuing 'peace work' but whose hands were coated with explosives. Pleased to find an enemy who understood English, US marines taunted him with threats he would be gang-raped in Abu Ghraib. 'When deadly force bumps into hearts and minds', *The Economist*, 29 December 2004.

182 Interview with Arab Afghan veteran, London, November 2003.

183 Interview, London, November 2003.

184 Lisa Myers, 'Judge caught on tape encouraging Saudis to fight in Iraq', *NBC News*, 26 April 2005.

185 Mustfa al-Ansari, 'Asma'a al-Muqatleen al-Saudieen fi al-Iraq' (the Names of Saudi Fighters in Iraq), *Al-Osb'iah*, Issue 40, 13 June 2005.

186 *Al-Thoura*, mouthpiece of the Syrian Baath party, February 2004.

187 For instance, Iyad al-Samarrai, spokesman for Prime Minister Ibrahim al-Jaafari, claimed that 'suicide bombings are not at all part of the Iraqi people's culture and heritage. There are no schools that produce suicide terrorists inside Iraq at all.'

188 UN security officers also had intelligence that Saddam had obtained 120 explosive vests made from TNT imported from Eastern Europe before the war. Interview, Baghdad, September 2003.

189 Anthony H. Cordesman and Nawaf Obaid, Saudi Militants in Iraq: Assessment and Kingdom's Response, *Center for Strategic and International Studies* (CSIS), 19 September 2005.

190 Zarkawi's readiness to accommodate Saddam loyalists reached its acme with video-recording from his movement wishing an incarcerated Saddam happy birthday.

191 For instance, in January 2006, al-Qaeda in Iraq posted a statement on a website saying that it had joined five other insurgent groups in Iraq to form the Mujahideen Shura Council, or the Consultative Council of Holy Warriors.

192 USAID Mission Iraq SAFE Report, 9 February 2004.

193 Interview, Baghdad, December 2003.

194 The context was comparable: Ibn Taymiya was preaching in the face of the Mongol conquest of Baghdad, which had forced his family to flee to Damascus, and in which Shias were alleged to have been complicit.

195 Interview, Baghdad, June 2004.

CHAPTER 11

196 Interview, Baghdad, April 2004.

197 Interview, Baghdad, April 2004.

198 Interview, Baghdad, April 2004. Policy wags in Washington had advised the Coalition to do likewise and engage with Sufis, on the grounds that it represents 'a traditionalist form of Islamic mysticism that represents an open, intellectual interpretation of Islam'. Cheryl Benard, 'Five pillars of democracy', *RAND Review*, Spring 2004, Vol. 28 No. 1. 'Civil democratic Islam: partners, resources, and strategies'. The article includes a helpful picture of whirling Turks. This may have struck a cord with some in government. According to an article on the US Government's Muslim world outreach strategies, 'One solution being pushed' by the Administration is 'offering backdoor US support to reformers tied to Sufism, a tolerant branch of Islam'. 'Hearts Minds and Dollars', *US News and World Report*, 25 April 2005.

199 Interview with Barakat Saadoun, Falluja, April 2004.

200 Interview, Falluja, April 2004.

201 On the eve of Bremer's handover to an Iraqi government in June 2004, rebels launched simultaneous morning car-bombings and attacks across five cities, killing 72 Iraqis and three American soldiers.

202 Interview, Samarra, May 2004.

203 Interview, Ramada, June 2004.

204 Other ex-regime nobility included Tariq Aziz's wife, Victoria, and their son Ziad, who arrived in Amman aboard a US Hercules-30 military jet together with a senior former regime security official.

205 The Jordanian intelligence department, which handled the kingdom's Iraq file, registered an average of 18 new house purchases by Iraqis a day, and required that Iraqis seeking residence deposit $100,000 in a Jordanian bank.

CHAPTER 12

206 In local folklore, Kufa was also the site where Noah had been cursed by doubters when building his ark and the revered fourth Caliph and founding father of Shia Islam Imam Ali had been murdered.

207 Interview, Najaf, May 2003.

208 The Houses of Hakim and Sadr had long vied for Shia leadership. Both were Arab and together had dominated Iraqi Shia politics for almost a century. As a youth Hakim's father, Mohsen al-Hakim, had raised the battle-cry for Jihad, against Britain's invasion of Iraq during the First World War, and later became Najaf's Grand Ayatollah. After his death in 1970, his sons had fled the Baath

regime. The eldest, Mehdi, was killed in Khartoum in 1988, but Muhammad found refuge in Iran where he bowed to Khomeini's authority, earning the opprobrium of many Iraqi Shias, including exiles in the Iranian shrine city of Qom, who pelted Hakim during a visit with shoes.

209 One of the rare occasions when Hakim's father, Grand Ayatollah Mohsen Hakim, intervened in politics was following the 1958 Revolution when he declared communism heresy, and land reform and the sequestration of private property contrary to the Sharia.

210 In volatile sermons, Sadr II had decried the Iraqi rush to American pop and clothing long before American armies invaded Iraq. He was once reputed to have chided a couple who had dressed their toddler in dungarees – 'Why do you imitate western ways, when they try to subject you to their monopoly? Think, Analyze.' Cited by John Cole, 'The US and Shiite religious factions in Iraq', *Middle East Journal*, Autumn 2003.

211 Interview, Khazraji, Baghdad, May 2003. Khazraji was held for over a year at Camp Bucca near Basra.

212 Interview, Karbala, November 2003.

213 Quoted in Iraq Study Group report, December 2006.

214 Interview, Baghdad, April 2004.

215 Al-Arabiya TV, Dubai, 8 May 2004.

216 Interview, Diwaniya, April 2004.

217 The call was made by Sadri preacher Sheikh Qais al-Khazali, in a sermon broadcast through a hastily erected sound-system in front of the Green Zone.

218 Press conference, Baghdad, 4 April 2004.

219 Interview, Baghdad, April 2004.

220 'When the judge summons you, you must obey the law. If Muqtada does not present himself, military intervention is the only option,' said Ali al-Ghurafi, Najaf-based secretary to turbanned Governing Council member Mohammed Bahr al-Uloum. Interview, Najaf, April 2004.

221 Press conference, Baghdad, 11 May 2004.

222 In Basra, the British successfully negotiated the withdrawal of Sadr's militiamen and their rocket launchers from positions atop the roof of the city's governorate building.

223 In August 2006, the Mahdi Army chased Polish forces out of Diwaniya, prompting the Badr Forces to counter-attack in clashes that left 81 people dead. Fighting only abated after a US warplane dropped a 500-pound bomb on a Mahdi army position in support of the local SCIRI government. *CNN*, 28 August 2006. US support for SCIRI was further highlighted the following December when President Bush received Hakim in Washington.

CHAPTER 13

224 The fourth broke during the transfer.

225 Baker–Hamilton report, December 2006.

226 Amongst the two dozen journalists the New York-based Committee for the Protection of Journalists reported killed by US action were two Iraqi journalists with the CPA's own television network, shot dead outside a US base in Samarra. Yasser Salihee, a *Knight Ridder* journalist who had reported from inside Falluja and Mosul, and was shot with cruel irony on his day off by US snipers returning from his local grocers in June 2005.

227 The Baghdad mobile operator, Iraqna, threatened to suspend operations because US forces were blocking its frequencies, both to prevent their use for detonating bombs and to thwart communication between insurgents. Americans and rebels alike raided Iraqna's premises and seized its databases in the hope of tracing informers.

228 'When deadly force bumps into hearts and minds', *The Economist*, 29 December 2004.

229 Even when awards were made, the bureaucracy often proved too painfully convoluted to apply them. By April 2004, US forces had paid out a total of $4 million to 6,000 claimants. Interview with US review board official, Baghdad, April 2004.

230 Interview, Red Cross personnel, Basra, May 2003.

231 Interview with Bechtel official, Baghdad, April 2004.

232 Officially 10 per cent of the $18 billion of US reconstruction funds were assigned to security, although security consultants estimated that western security companies consumed over 25 per cent. For the UK, a historic centre for mercenaries, private security was by far its biggest export to Iraq. Fourteen months into the invasion, David Claridge, managing director of London-based Janusien, assessed post-war revenues of UK-based military companies such as his, worth up to £1 billion. Interview, August 2004.

233 Unlike members of the US armed forces, no charges for instance were brought against two foreign contractors, Steven Stephanowicz of CACI International and John B. Israel of the Titan Corp. of San Diego, cited in a Pentagon report as assisting in abuse of the Abu Ghraib detainees.

234 Asked by a reporter whether torture had taken place in Iraq, Defence Secretary Donald Rumsfeld replied: 'My impression is that what has been charged thus far is abuse, which I believe technically is different from torture.' The subsequent trials focussed on court-martialling those at the bottom of the chain of command, not at the top.

235 Jones handpicked a mediation team comprised of Iraqis who favoured a revival of Sunni or Baathist power under US patronage: Hajm al-Hassani, then

deputy leader of the Iraqi wing of the Sunni Muslim Brotherhood, the Iraqi Islamic Party; Ibrahim Jannabi, a former Iraqi intelligence officer; and Iyad Allawi.

236 In press statements, Brahimi wooed old-regime Sunnis with celebrations of Sunni Arab nationalism, denunciations of Israel, and attacks on Shia-backed deBaathification. 'It is difficult to understand that thousands upon thousands of teachers, university professors, [and] medical doctors ... who are sorely needed, have been dismissed,' Brahimi had told me in February 2006. Brahimi's ties to Sunni Arab leaders were underscored by the marriage of his daughter, Reem, a pre-war CNN correspondent in Baghdad, to a Jordanian Hashemite prince in 2004.

237 Interview, Baghdad, May 2004.

238 In an attempt to rein in Brahimi, the Governing Council's Finance Committee, again chaired by Chalabi, launched an investigation into the misappropriation of Iraqi funds by the son of his boss, Kofi Annan.

239 More than a dozen Chalabi associates were issued arrest warrants, including his intelligence chief, Aras Karim, accused of providing Iran with classified information and counterfeiting Iraqi dinars, and his nephew, Salim Chalabi, accused of plotting the murder of a finance ministry official while acting as administrator of Saddam's tribunal. Suspicions that Chalabi was himself funnelling secrets to Iran reportedly prompted the Bush administration to sever his monthly stipend of $340,000. 'I think Chalabi's group is permeated with Iranian influence,' said former CIA counter-terrorism chief Vince Cannistraro. Quoted Richard Sale, Iraqi CPA Fires 28,000, *United Press International*, 21 November 2003.

240 Interview, Baghdad, November 2003.

241 Haifa al-Azawi, 'US Iraq appointee a fraud and a danger', *al-Arab*, 12 February 2004.

242 After abandoning Baathism as an Iraqi diplomat in Paris, Adel Abdel Mahdi flirted briefly with Maoism. He discovered political Islam amongst Palestinians in Beirut, joining SCIRI in the 1980s. After the assassination of Mohammed Baqir al-Hakim in August 2003, he became SCIRI's deputy leader. Interviews with Abdel Mahdi, Baghdad, July 2004.

243 Iraqi historians have debated whether the 1963 Baath coup was engineered by US intelligence nervous of Qassim's leftist tendencies. King Hussein amongst others claimed the CIA supplied the names and addresses of the 1,500 leftist leaders killed in the ensuing bloodbath.

244 Jon Lee Anderson, 'A man of the shadows', *The New Yorker*, 24 January 2005.

245 Interview with Dagham al-Qathim, London, November 2004.

246 Jon Lee Anderson, 'A man of the shadows', *The New Yorker*, 24 January 2005.

247 Quoted in Robert Dreyfuss, *The American Prospect*, 18 November 2002.

248 Fresh from Clifford Chance, Chalabi's nephew Salim Chalabi launched a Baghdad-based law firm – the Iraqi International Law Group – with Mark Zell, a Jerusalem-based spokesman for Israeli settlers. Their website claimed their clients 'number amongst the largest corporations and institutions on the planet', which given that Zell's former partner was Douglas Feith, the Pentagon's architect of Iraq's post-war planning, was not just hyperbole. After the relationship was exposed, Chalabi cut ties with Zell and expelled a senior INC member for visiting Israel.

249 Interviews, INA politburo member Saleem al-Iman and Yemeni oil engineer, Abdullah Jaashan, London and Amman, December 2004. In the late 1980s, Allawi led a team of Chevron officials to South Yemen in pursuit of exploration rights in Bloc 3 near Shabwah. Jaashan claimed Allawi short-changed him of his commission.

250 Allawi persuaded both Washington and Massoud Barzani's Kurdish Democratic Party to abandon Chalabi's aborted uprising in March 1995, and the following October was implicated in a massive bombing of the INC's headquarters in Salahudin; the CIA investigated, but did not release the results. Following a series of car-bombs that ripped through Baghdad, including one outside a cinema, Allawi sought US backing for his 'zipless coup' scheduled for June 1996; the coup was aborted after Baghdad executed 120 senior military personnel, all of them Sunnis, including the three sons of Allawi's intelligence chief, Mohammed Shahwani. Thereafter, the INC and the INA switched from coup-plotting to competing to supply Anglo-American intelligence with evidence of weapons of mass destruction. It was Allawi (not Chalabi) who supplied MI6 with the claim, on which Blair strongly relied for his case for war, that Saddam could deploy chemical and biological warheads within 45 minutes.

251 The deal provoked an outcry from Ahmed Chalabi on the grounds that the $40,000 per recruit would have been better spent in Iraq than Jordan. Interview, Baghdad, May 2004.

252 The only exception was SCIRI deputy Abdel Mahdi, Allawi's fellow Baathist conspirator at Baghdad University, who was appointed finance minister.

253 They included oil minister Thamer Ghadhban (Imperial College, London), trade minister Mohammed Jibouri (Glasgow), science and technology minister Rashad Mandan Omar (London), and Adnan al-Jannabi (Loughborough University). The five Kurds in his cabinet all had British degrees.

254 Al-Naqeeb had been a childhood friend of Saddam's sons, Uday and Qusay, when his father, as ambassador of Madrid, had hosted Saddam's family on his summer holidays.

255 Interview, Baghdad, June 2004.

256 Interview, Baghdad, August 2004.

257 Interview with Jannabi, Baghdad, July 2004: 'In a difficult security situation, we need to fight the terrorists by all means, and one of the main means is the media. We need them all to cooperate. It's for national security.'

258 Infiltration was rife. Iraq's chief of staff, General Amer al-Hashimi, was removed from his post after a relative he lived with was caught planting a roadside bomb. Several of the insurgents killed in the November 2004 storming of Falluja bore the insignia of the new Army's military academy, and less than a month later an Iraqi soldier billeted at base in Mosul exploded himself in a mess tent, killing 18 American soldiers.

259 Early US attempts to investigate violations of human rights met with protestations that America was infringing Iraq's sovereignty. 'The Interior Ministry will not tolerate any pressure from anyone in its continued work to arrest criminal gangs,' protested its spokesman, Qathim Sabah, after US military police raided an interior ministry outhouse where police were alleged to be torturing detainees with leather straps. Interview, Baghdad, August 2004.

260 Interview, Baghdad, July 2004.

261 Interview, Baghdad, August 2004.

CHAPTER 14

262 The complaints echoed those of King Faisal, who had griped to his British advisors that while his forces had 15,000 rifles, his opponents had 150,000.

263 DynCorp operated its lucrative Police Training Academy contract from Jordan, but months after its launch failed to achieve its monthly target of 1,500 graduates, despite press-ganging ice-cream sellers into enrolling, according to western diplomats interviewed in Jordan. Of those that did make the passing-out parade, about half had either deserted or been killed within six months.

264 Interviews with coalition advisors, Baghdad, August 2004. They insisted Allawi honour a $259 million contract the CPA had signed, appointing a US company, Anham Joint Venture, to be Iraq's sole supplier of arms and body armour for two years under which the import of heavy weapons, even a silencer for a pistol, was proscribed.

265 For background on Spicer and the activities of his company, Sandline, see Pratap Chatterjee, 'Commando wins Iraq contract', *CorpWatch*, 9 June 2004, and Simon Sheppard, 'Foot soldiers of the New World Order: the rise of the corporate military', *New Left Review*, March 1998.

266 Interview, former Spicer associate, July 2006.

267 For instance, Egyptians could not try British nationals in Egypt, 1882–1922. American immunity from prosecution formed a key grievance under the Shah of Iran.

268 Official Saudi estimates were even higher. A Saudi source estimated there were 77,000 Sunni insurgents, of whom some 17,000 were affiliated to Jihadi groups, of whom 5,000 were foreigners. The remaining 60,000 were former Iraqi army cadres, whose officer corps had command and control facilities in Syria. Sharon Behn, 'Saudis report Shi'ite "state" inside of Iraq', *The Washington Times*, 18 December 2006.

269 Conventional mine detectors often failed to work because of the plethora of soft drink cans which Iraqis as well as Coalition personnel chucked out of car windows.

270 Interview, November 2006.

271 Interview, Amman, December 2006.

272 Michael Hirsh, 'Racing the Clock in Iraq', *Newsweek*, 9 February 2004.

273 Samarrai was the only minister charged with corruption to be convicted in an Iraqi court. Sentenced to two years in prison in October 2006, he reportedly escaped two months later by travelling on a Chinese passport and a false identity from Baghdad Airport. Prior to his arrest, Samarrai, who himself owned an Illinois-based engineering company, KCI, had spent much time in Amman soliciting contracts for projects to build generators and was in the words of Iraq's Commission of Public Integrity one of the largest 'squanderers of public funds'. Interviews, Baghdad and Amman, December 2004.

274 Interview, London, October 2004.

275 Interview with Trade Minister Mohammed Jabouri, Amman, December 2006. Jabouri had overseen the distribution of oil coupons at the Oil Ministry under Saddam.

276 According to the Commission of Public Integrity, the Housing Ministry charged jobseekers $200 for employment as guardsmen. The headmaster of the Iraqi school in Paris, Rashid al-Tikriti, was alleged to have rented out the school hall for social functions. Interview with Judge Radhi, Baghdad, July 2004.

277 Quoted Hannah Allam, 'Audit: Iraq fraud drained $1 billion', *Knight Ridder Newspapers*, 11 August 2005.

278 Interview, Amman, December 2004.

279 Interview, Amman, December 2004.

280 Interview, Baghdad, July 2004.

281 See note 244. Amongst the worst offenders was the Transport Ministry, where, the Commission reported, nine committee members, 14 director-generals and the minister were investigated for misdemeanours ranging from adding fictitious names to the payroll to overcharging fourfold for the purchase of a second-hand Boeing. After leaving government Allawi accused the commission of political bias, accusing it – unfairly – of singling out Sunnis. Although Samarrai was Sunni, many cited, including Allawi's Transport Minister, were Shia.

282 Interview, December 2004.

283 'By decreeing that Baathists are not allowed to stand for election they are ousting most of the pre-war internal intelligentsia from the franchise,' said Faleh al-Khayat, a senior Shia technocrat forced out of the Oil Ministry in the purge of Baathists. Interviews, Baghdad, December 2004.

284 Interview Wamidh Nadhmi, Baghdad, December 2004.

285 Statement released on http://www.islah300.org, 23 January 2005.

286 *Al-Dustour*, January 2005.

287 The election fell short of international standards. The UN failed to assemble its much-trumpeted protection force ensuring most of the 100 international observers remained cloistered either in the Green Zone, or Amman. In southern Iraq, leaflets threatened voters who did not vote for the Shia list, and in vast swathes of the Sunni Arab north-west and the contested Turkomen and Arab constituencies surrounding Kirkuk, ballot sheets failed to arrive. In addition, many candidates had to run anonymously for security reasons, giving voters little idea for whom they were casting their ballot.

288 Of 275 parliamentary seats, the Shia List won 140 (51 per cent), and Shia groups close to Sadr 14 more, securing the Shia bloc an absolute majority. Thanks to the Sunni Arab boycott, Kurds secured 75 seats or 27 per cent of the vote, far more than the 20 per cent of the population they comprised.

289 Of the 38 government posts, 18 were assigned to Shias (including one Kurd and one Turkoman), 19 to Sunnis (ten Kurds, nine Arabs and one Turkoman) and a single Assyrian Christian.

290 Jibouri, a powerful Sunni tribal leader and businessman, was the first prominent politician to be tried for corruption after the invasion, raising accusations of sectarian bias. Jim Muir, 'Iraq moves to tackle corruption', *BBC News*, 8 October 2006.

CHAPTER 15

291 Interview, Amman, December 2004. Others cited the historical precedent of the precipitous Kurdish elections soon after the 1991 Gulf War, which had plunged the Kurdish enclave into fratricidal war. Interview, Mahmoud Othman, Baghdad, August 2004.

292 'What the public wants', available at www.worldpublicopinion.org, 2–5 January 2006.

293 *The Washington Post*, 17 April 2005.

294 In the December 2005 elections 45 per cent of votes cast by members of the security forces were for the Kurdish list, against 30 per cent for the Shia list and only 7 per cent for the three Sunni Arab lists. Richard Oppel, 'Iraqi vote shows lack of Sunnis in army', *The New York Times*, 27 December 2005. There were

also some overwhelmingly Shia units, such as the first brigade of the sixth division deployed in counter-insurgency operations. Tom Lasseter, 'Sectarian sentiment extends to Iraq's army, undermining security', *Knight Ridder Newspapers*, 12 October 2005.

295 *The New York Times*, 15 May 2005.

296 Edward Wong and John F. Burns, 'Iraqi rift grows after discovery of prison', *The New York Times*, 17 November 2005. In a raid on 8 December 2005, US forces found 625 (mostly Sunni Arab) detainees, some bearing signs of torture, crammed into a prison run by the Interior Ministry's Wolf Brigade. See John F. Burns, 'To halt abuses, US will inspect jails run by Iraq', *The New York Times*, 14 December 2005.

297 The Fadhila was founded in 2003 by the Najaf-based cleric Muhammad al-Ya'qubi, a disciple of Muqtada's father, whose popular base is concentrated in the far south.

298 Iraq Study Group report, December 2006: 'the government sometimes provides services on a sectarian basis. For example, in one Sunni neighbourhood of Shia-governed Baghdad, there is less than two hours of electricity each day and trash piles are waist-high. One American official told us that Baghdad is run like a "Shia dictatorship" because Sunnis boycotted provincial elections in 2005.'

299 Quoted by Dahr Jamail and Ali Al-Fadhily, *Electronic Iraq*, 27 December 2006.

300 Like Jaafari, many ministers had spent years in Iranian exile. President Jalal Talabani's PUK had also relied on Iranian support, earning them the Baathist sobriquet 'agents of Iran' (*'umala Iran*).

301 Quoted in 'Iran in Iraq: How much influence?', *International Crisis Group*, 21 March 2005.

302 *The New York Times*, 13 July 2005.

303 Khalilzad was the only prominent survivor of Wohlstetter's circle.

304 US policy could, however, be deeply confused. In May 2005, Coalition troops stormed the Baghdad home of Iraqi Islamic Party leader and former Governing Council president Mohsen Abdul Hamid, who despite his boycott of the elections was a key Sunni interlocutor. In a dawn raid, troops blindfolded him, his sons and his guests, and led them away for interrogation. In an ironical twist, Jaffari intervened to obtain his release, securing an embarrassed note from US forces 'regretting any inconvenience'. *The New York Times*, 30 May 2005.

305 According to an observer of the constitutional process, 'meetings of the Kurdish/Shia Leadership Council or, as it was known more informally, "the kitchen" (*matbakh*) took place at irregular intervals in private residences and compounds in the International Zone. Sunni Arab negotiators had no seat at the table, and were presented later in August with a fait accompli constitution in which they had played no significant drafting or negotiating role.' Jonathan

Morrow, 'Draft constitution gained, but an important opportunity was lost', United States Institute of Peace (USIP) Briefing, October 2005, available at www.usip.org.

306 See for instance a report from Falluja in *al-Watan*, a government-backed newspaper of 28 April 2006: 'Reliable sources from the city told *al-Watan* that American military patrols were roaming Falluja's streets late on Wednesday while calling [on loud speakers]: "Honourable people of Falluja... Beware of Iranian elements that have infiltrated the city and are planning to liquidate prominent social figures... You must notify the US forces or the local police about them".'

307 More US soldiers were killed in November 2006 – a month when the military conducted no major operations – than November 2004 when 137 died and marines conducted their assault on the city of Falluja, or in April 2004 when US forces had fought rebels on two flanks – in pitched battles in Anbar and a Shia revolt in the south.

308 Estimate provided by Anthony H. Cordesman of the Center for International and Strategic Studies, November 2006.

309 Dr Gilbert Burnham of the Johns Hopkins Bloomberg School of Public Heath, Baltimore, published in *The Lancet*, October 2006. Estimates from the Iraq Body Count, which derives its figures from the media, ranged between 44,000 and 49,000 civilian deaths for the same period. The wide discrepancies were a reflection of Coalition policy of either failing or choosing not to release any official tally to the public.

310 According to some estimates, over 40 per cent of Iraq's professionals had fled the country by 2006. See Sami Zubaida, 'The Missing Middle Class', in *International Herald Tribune*, 21 April 2006.

311 Steve Negus, 'Shia shrine attack blamed for refugee exodus', *Financial Times*, 3 May 2006.

312 When Diwaniya fell to Sadr forces in August 2006, the USA restricted action to aerial bombardment, rather than ground attacks as in Najaf in 2004.

313 'Rumsfeld's memo of options for Iraq war', *The New York Times*, 3 December 2006.

314 Amit R. Paley, 'Looters ransack base after British depart', *Washington Post*, 26 August 2006.

315 *Daily Mail*, 13 October 2006. Official leaks forecasting an imminent downsizing may have designed more to mollify an impatient domestic public than an expression of intent to withdraw. In the summer of 2005, the British press reported that London and Washington planned to pull back forces from 14 of Iraq's 18 provinces into four secure bases, and cut total troop numbers from 176,000 to 66,000 by early 2006. British forces, said the article, would be cut from 8,500 to 3,000 by early 2006, concentrated in a single base around Basra.

However, in January 2007, the US still had 140,000 troops in Iraq, and Britain 7,500. 'We don't really have an exit strategy,' said Rumsfeld in Baghdad. 'We have a victory strategy.' 12 April 2005.

316 Senior Marine Intelligence officer in al-Anbar, Colonel Peter Devlin, in a memo reported by the *Washington Post*, 28 November 2006.

317 Baker–Hamilton report, December 2006. Simon Walters, 'Secret plan to quit Iraq', *Mail on Sunday*, 10 July 2005.

318 *After Baker-Hamilton: What to Do in Iraq*, No. 60, 19 December 2006.

319 For instance, during the battle for Diwaniya between Sadr and SCIRI, a huge blast ripped through the pipeline in the town's industrial zone killing 27 people, including some siphoning its oil. *Associated Press*, 28 August 2006.

320 A day after Sistani called for restraint in September 2005, Ayatollah Mohammed Yaqoubi issued a religious edict calling on Shias 'to kill terrorists before they kill you'.

321 For a transcript of the testament written seven weeks before the execution see http://news.bbc.co.uk/2/hi/middle_east/6213119.stm

322 Each community interpreted the killing according to its own experience. Hamas, for instance, saw it as a parable for the fate of regimes which did not bow to US will. 'We consider the execution of President Saddam Hussein on this day by the American administration as a representation of the killing of the Arab regime which does not say "No" to the American administration.' Statement by Hamas spokesman, Ismail Radwan, 30 December 2006. Given that its patron, Iran, supported the execution, Hamas' comments compared to other Sunni Arab groups were surprisingly mild.

323 The US helped further preserve his memory by flying his body ostentatiously to his final resting place in Awja, alongside his two sons. Unlike Zarkawi, who was buried anonymously within the Green Zone, his grave was given all the trappings of a Sunni pilgrimage site.

324 Hakim calls for federal south, *Reuters*, 11 August 2005.

325 Article 109 of the constitution confers management of oil and gas in 'current fields' on the federal government, encouraging both Kurds and Shias to claim that new fields would be the property of the region rather than the centre. Under the formula, southern provinces would secure the largest reserves located in the Majnoun islands in Amara close to the Iranian border and Basra, and Sunnis those around the Mosul. Ironically, the Kurds fare worse with only 6 per cent of the country's oil reserves, even assuming their control of Kirkuk. Advocates compared it to the Canadian model, in which the provinces controlled mineral reserves. Detractors envisaged the emergence of local dictators-cum-oil-tycoons ruling over individual fields.

326 Article 134 (1) of the constitution reads: 'The High Commission for de-Baathification shall continue its functions as an independent commission,

acting in coordination with the judiciary and executive branches within the framework of the laws regulating its functions.'

327 Ellen Knickmeyer and Jonathan Finer, 'Iraqi vote draws big turnout of Sunnis', *The Washington Post*, 16 December 2005. The Islamic Army in Iraq declared in an internet posting three days before the elections that 'orders have been issued to avoid polling stations to preserve the blood of innocent people'. *Daily Star*, 14 December 2005.

328 Stephen Negus, Call for Sunni state in Iraq, *Financial Times*, 15 October 2006 and Sunni Fighters Claim Ramadi, *al-Jazeera*, 21 October 2005.

329 A host of flashpoints abound in the provinces, of which the most prominent are the Sunni towns of Muhammadiya, Yusufiya and Iskandiriya intersecting the roads between Baghdad and the Shia shrine cities to the south; Samarra – another Shia shrine city – in the heart of predominantly Sunni territory; and Diyala province – a mixed blend of Kurds, Turkomen and Sunni and Shia Arabs between Baghdad and the Iranian border.

CHAPTER 16

330 Olivier Roy, *The Failure of Political Islam* (I.B.Tauris, 1994).

331 The difference between Shias and Sunnis after the Twelfth Imam's Occultation can be summarised in the Qur'anic verse: 'O ye who believe! Obey God, and obey the apostle, and those charged with authority among you [*wali al-amr minkum*]' (Qur'an Sura 4:59). For Sunnis, the *wali* was the temporal ruler, to whom unquestioning obedience was due even if he was sunk in sin. For Shias, the *wali* was the guardian of the Imam's tradition, the *Curia*.

332 Mohammed Baqir Al-Sadr, *Lamha fiqhiya*, p.20. See Sama Hadad, *The Development of Shi'i Islamic Political Theory* (October 2005).

333 For instance, despite his personal distaste for a federal Iraq, Sistani was quoted by Ibrahim Jaafari as saying the clerics would bow to the people's choice.

334 In February 2004, 400 Iranian public figures reportedly petitioned Sistani to overrule a decision by the Guardian Council to disqualify 2,500 candidates from parliamentary elections. 'Your Excellency is insisting that the first and last word in the matter of choosing rulers and representatives belongs to the Iraqi people. How wonderful it would be if your Excellency would express your opinion regarding the farce that some in your native land of Iran are attempting to impose on its people, who are wide awake, under the rubric of "elections".' Sistani politely sidestepped the appeal. Ali Nourizadeh in *al-Sharq al-Awsat*, 5 February 2004.

335 Khamenei replied by condemning Iraq's clerics as US agents. 'The USA wants to make Najaf a centre for clergy who are willing to make compromise with

them,' he chided. In a move with echoes of Saddamism, Iran's leadership nationalised Sistani's foundation for alms collection.

336 Lebanese connections with Najaf were long-standing. Its leading Shia luminaries – Hassan Nasrallah, Mohammed Hassanein Fadlallah, and the acting president of the Higher Shia Council Abdelemir Qabalan – had all studied there. But, following Saddam's crackdown in the 1970s, the traffic headed the other way. Clerics fled to Lebanon, joining forces with exiled Iraqi bankers, such as the Chalabis, to preserve Najaf's flame. Hazim Chalabi, Ahmed's brother, became the dean of an Islamic University in Beirut that the Chalabis funded. The Chalabis also became bankers to a Lebanese offshoot of Dawa, *Harakat al-Mahrumin*, the Movement of the Dispossessed, launched in 1974, which aimed to promote Shia rights as the largest but poorest of Lebanon's 17 sects.

337 Hizbollah first competed in elections in 1992. By 2004 it controlled 60 per cent of Shia municipalities. Its decision to enter national government, however, only followed Sistani's campaign in Iraq.

338 Bahrain's Shias were traditionally Akhbari, following clerics in neither Najaf nor Qom (see note 7). However, the mainstream Usuli school of both Iraq and Iran had made considerable inroads on the island.

339 Quoted Agence France Presse, 4 January 2005.

340 Despite a small radical group who followed Khomeini, the bulk of the Eastern province followed two elderly traditionalist clerics, Ayatollahs Mirza al-Tabrizi and Sistani, who were both students of the quietist, Khoi. Further south, in Hasa, there was a large community of Sheikhia, an even more quietist school whose spiritual leadership resided in Basra. The mountains of the far south-west harboured an isolated and hounded community of Ismailis.

341 Despite the ban on political parties, many independent candidates signalled their political allegiances. The Islamic Movement, a liberal reformist group of Najaf-trained clerics, won seven of ten Shia council seats. The Dawa party was favoured by the Shia elite.

342 www.rasid.com.

343 Tewfiq al-Saif, a Shii activist who had led protests in the mid-1990s, for instance became a regular columnist in the Saudi press. 'The government tends not to recognise rights officially, preferring to turn a blind eye. But there's a very wide change in official behaviour and the language of the media,' he said. Interview, London, July 2005.

344 One of Ahmedinajad's mentors was said to be Ayatollah Mesbah Yezdi, who opposed the 1988 ceasefire in the Iran–Iraq war on the grounds it would delay the advent of the Mahdi. His apocalyptic vision chimed with his claim that he communicated with the Hidden Imam, challenging the Ayatollahs represented by Khamenei.

345 The Zaydis take their name from Zayd Ben Ali, the grandson of Hussein the son of Ali; Zaydi doctrine holds that, following its first three imams (Ali; Hassan and Hussein), the imamate was open to whichever descendant of the prophet could best prove his claim. The Zaydis established two states, one in Iran in the ninth century, the other the Yemeni Imamate dating back to 893 CE.

346 Though themselves Shia, the Free Officers who led the coup extinguishing the Imamate had the support of Sunni Arab republics such as Egypt.

347 Wadai had fled Saudi Arabia, charged with inspiring the Salafi capture of Mecca precinct in 1979.

348 Amongst the tens of thousands of Muslims estimated to have passed through his retreat was John Walker Lindh, the American Taliban subsequently captured in Afghanistan. The centre was also a refuge for veterans of the Afghan Jihad, an estimated 40,000 of whom travelled to Yemen in the mid-1990s to fight with President Saleh against the former Communist rulers of South Yemen.

349 Shia demands for a system of one person, one vote had been denounced by Maronites as well as Sunnis as a ploy to subvert their 1,600-year struggle to preserve Christianity in the Arab Muslim heartland.

350 Interview, Beirut, November 2005.

351 Quoted in *Crisis Group*, 'Israel/ Palestine/ Lebanon: Climbing out of the Abyss', 25 July 2006.

352 *Gulf Times*, 30 July 2006.

353 Video recording released by *al-Jazeera*, 27 July 2006. In an exchange of correspondence with Zarkawi from 2004 to 2005, Zawahiri had questioned the timing of targeting of Shia, though not the *takfiri* principle that they had been excommunicated from Islam, and were thus heretics. His position on the Shia did, however, appear to soften with time.

354 Wahhabi–Shia cooperation was not without precedent. In the 1960s, the Saudi National Guard, a force of tribal Salafis, sided with Yemen's Shia Imamate (as well as the Shah of Iran and the British) against what they perceived as godless Nasserists sweeping the old order aside.

355 Jim Krane, 'Arabs urged to eject US from bases', *Associated Press*, 6 December 2006.

356 This principle was rooted in a second tenet that radical Islamists shared with Shia theology: the practice of *Ijtihad*. While the three main law schools of Sunni Islam had formally closed the gate of *ijtihad* by the thirteenth century, the smallest Sunni school – that of the Hanbalis, to which Salafis and many Jihadi groups subscribe – had insisted on keeping it open to ensure the revelation remained a living, evolving and eternally relevant corpus independent of state authority.

357 Dubai TV, 23 August 2006.

358 The triumvirate of Sunnis who oversaw Lebanon's economy was dissolved: former chief of staff Hikmet Shihabi was exiled to Los Angeles (where Hariri brought him a villa); vice-president Abdul Halim Khaddam lost the Lebanon file and then defected; the third member, Rafiq Hariri, was killed; a fourth powerbroker, Ghazi Kanaan, Syria's ruthless viceroy in Lebanon for 15 years, officially committed suicide in October 2005.

359 Soon after Bashar's father Hafez al-Assad seized power in November 1970, Imam Moussa Sadr, a Shia leader in Beirut, ruled that Alawites were Shia Muslims.

CHAPTER 17

360 In August 2005, a Jihadi group based in Iraq fired a salvo of rockets at Aqaba and Eilat, narrowly missing a US vessel.

361 Simultaneously, he also reined in Salafi militants, arresting 800 Jihadis and purging 2,000 of the kingdom's 100,000 Wahhabi clerics. In a public awareness campaign on state television, Jihadis were castigated as *Khariji* deviants unsettling the stability of the Muslim community. See Juan Cole, 'What Michael Moore (and the neocons) don't know about Saudi Arabia', *Salon.Com*, 5 August 2005.

362 *Washington Post*, 8 December 2004. In an interview ahead of Iraq's January 2005 elections, he warned that Iran had sent more than a million of its people across the 910-mile border into Iraq to vote in the January 2005 elections: 'I'm sure there's a lot of people, a lot of Iranians in there that will be used to influence the outcome. It is in Iran's vested interest... to achieve a government that is very pro-Iran.' With Shiism at the gates of his kingdom, Abdullah may also have had his eye on the largesse Saddam had secured from Gulf states when he served as a buffer against the forward march of the Ayatollahs.

363 *Al-Arabiya*, 8 April 2006.

364 Foreign Minister Sheikh Mohammed al-Sabah, quoted in 'Gulf states fear Shiite victory in Iraq', *Daily Jang*, 4 January 2005.

365 Bahrain state newspaper, *Akhbar al-Khalij*, 18 February 2005.

366 The population movement was huge. By 2006, Shias fleeing both Iraq and Lebanon had increased Syria's Shia population from 70,000 in 1990 to 1 million.

367 Egypt imprisoned Muhammad Al-Darini, a Shia convert who established a Shia society, the Higher Council for the Protection of Ahl Al-Bayt. Darini claimed that Egypt was home to over 1 million Shi'ites, hiding behind 76 Sufi

orders. In a speech to the Egyptian Journalists' Union in Cairo, Muslim Brotherhood leader Qaradawi warned that while he welcomed the rapprochement with Hizbollah, if Shias tried to proselytise amongst Sunnis, 'what has happened in Iraq between Shi'ite and Sunnis will [repeat itself] in all other countries'. Quoted in the Egyptian newspaper *al-Masri al-Yawm*, 2 September 2006.

368   Faiza Saleh Ambah, 'Discord accompanies Bahrain vote', *The Washington Post*, 25 November 2006.

369   In a Sunni constituency, 400 votes was enough to secure a place in parliament; an MP in a Shia constituency, by contrast, required 13,000 votes. The authorities also erected a polling booth along the causeway connecting Bahrain to Saudi Arabia to encourage naturalised Saudis to vote.

370   Nawaf Obeid, 'Saudi Arabia will protect Sunnis if the US leaves', *Washington Post*, 29 November 2006. Obeid was managing director of the Saudi National Security Assessment Project in Riyadh. Shortly after publication of the article cited, Obeid was dismissed and the Saudi ambassador to Washington, Turki al-Faisal, resigned. See Sharon Behn, 'Saudis report Shiite "state" inside of Iraq', *The Washington Times*, 18 December 2006.

371   Vali Nasr, 'Role reversal in the Middle East', *theglobalist.com*, 27 September 2006.

372   A former Jordanian information minister, Saleh Qallab, wrote in the daily state-controlled newspaper *al-Rai*, 18 October 2006: 'I wish Allawi would stage a military coup. Gathering together the shattered pieces of Iraq requires an iron fist.'

373   Interview, Beirut, March 2005. His warnings were reiterated by Joseph Samaha, a prominent columnist with *al-Safir* newspaper. 'We are really in a dangerous situation with lots of factors leading to civil war,' he said. 'We have two different mobilisations, with no national consensus over Lebanon's future. How can we remain one country?' Interview, Beirut, March 2005.

374   Samir Al-Saadi, 'Nasrallah accused of "Adventurism" for plunging Lebanon into costly war', *Arab News*, 29 August 2006. Israeli officials claimed they enjoyed Saudi backing. Interviews, Jerusalem, July 2006.

375   Interview, Beirut, 2006.

376   Interview, Ghassan Tueni, publisher of *al-Nahar* newspaper, Beirut, April 2006: 'The Shias look at the state as something they have to grab. They are so voracious.'

377   *Associated Press*, 3 January 2006.

378   Interview, Beirut, March 2005.

379   Elaine Shannon, 'Iran and Syria helping Hezballah rearm', *Time Magazine*, 24 November 2006.

380   *BBC News online*, 8 December 2006.

Index